T0279801

Praise for *Wild Chorus*

"Wild Chorus *is a heart-song of lyric writing, deep tenderness, and more-than-human wisdom. Through her extraordinary and transformative encounters with animals from wolves to whales, animal-adept Brenda Peterson affirms the vital and vivid connections between us and the rest of creation, connections that keep the world alive. This book is beautiful, brave, and important.*"

—SY MONTGOMERY, AUTHOR OF *THE SOUL OF AN OCTOPUS*

"*In a period of time in which so many people feel alienated from nature, Brenda Peterson seamlessly draws us into the fascinating worlds of a wide variety of non-human animal beings so that we can experience what life is like for them.* Wild Chorus *explores how, when we open up our senses and hearts to what animals are saying to one another and to us, we can rewild ourselves and feel at one with the magnificent animals with whom we share our awe-inspiring planet.*"

—MARC BEKOFF, PhD, AUTHOR OF *REWILDING OUR HEARTS* AND *THE EMOTIONAL LIVES OF ANIMALS*

"*In* Wild Chorus, *Brenda Peterson demonstrates her ability to understand animals and her talent in writing about their personalities and individual traits. Her stories about wolves perfectly parallel my studies of wild wolves in Yellowstone National Park. Highly recommended!*"

—RICK MCINTYRE, AUTHOR OF *THE ALPHA FEMALE WOLF*

"*This is a book for animal and nature lovers like no other.* Wild Chorus *invites readers to discover the ways of being that wild animals can teach us all. Peterson explores how wild animals can become our guides and fellow travelers, teaching us how to find joy while adapting to a changing world.*"

—MARY GETTEN, AUTHOR OF *COMMUNICATING WITH ORCAS*

"*Nature writing at its finest: elegant, revelatory and absolutely finely crafted. A deep-sea diver, her territory is the immense psyche of the American dream.*"

—JOY HARJO, FORMER US POET LAUREATE AND AUTHOR OF *WEAVING SUNDOWN IN A SCARLET LIGHT*

Praise for Brenda Peterson

"Peterson's nature writing conveys the power of the vanishing wild and explores new possibilities for animal and human bonds."

—BLOOMSBURY REVIEW

"Peterson writes of nature with an intimacy that tugs at the reader's deep memory."

—ORION MAGAZINE

"Gives voice to the animal in us all."

—BOOKLIST

"Brenda Peterson is amazing, a soulful and profound observer of nature, from whales to humans, in all their glory and distress."

—DIANE ACKERMAN, AUTHOR OF *THE HUMAN AGE*

"Peterson has a mystical appreciation for the natural world that is evident in her prose whether she is writing about animals as brothers and sisters, watching for whales in winter, or swimming with dolphins."

—SPIRITUALITY & PRACTICE

"A prolific author of books on wildlife . . . Peterson developed an intimate understanding of predators, prey, and ecosystems."

—THE WALL STREET JOURNAL

"A lifelong love of animals combined with a jeweler's eye for multifaceted philosophical meanings provide Peterson with a wealth of fascinating anecdotes."

—PUBLISHERS WEEKLY

Wild Chorus

*Finding Harmony with
Whales, Wolves, and
Other Animals*

BRENDA PETERSON

MOUNTAINEERS
BOOKS

MOUNTAINEERS BOOKS is dedicated to the exploration, preservation, and enjoyment of outdoor and wilderness areas.

1001 SW Klickitat Way, Suite 201, Seattle, WA 98134
800-553-4453, www.mountaineersbooks.org

Printed in Canada
Distributed in the United Kingdom by Cordee, www.cordee.co.uk
27 26 25 24   1 2 3 4 5

Design and layout: Melissa McFeeters
Cover and interior illustrations: Levi Hastings

An earlier version of "Growing Up Game" appeared in *Seattle Weekly*. Portions of "Girls in Woods, Women on Waves" appeared in *O, the Oprah Magazine*. "Beluga Baby" is reimagined and revised from an essay in *Edge Walking on the Western Rim*. "Wolf Music" is excerpted from *Wolf Nation*. "Animal Allies" originally appeared in *Orion* magazine. "The Dog Who Didn't Love Me" was first published in *Medium*. Portions of "Great Blue" first appeared in *Singing to the Sound*. Peggy Shumaker's poem "Caribou" is reprinted from "Scent of Snow" with permission of the author.

Library of Congress Cataloging-in-Publication Data is on file for this title at https://lccn.loc.gov/2023034517. LC ebook record available at https://lccn.loc.gov/2023034518.

Mountaineers Books titles may be purchased for corporate, educational, or other promotional sales, and our authors are available for a wide range of events. For information on special discounts or booking an author, contact our customer service at 800-553-4453 or mbooks@mountaineersbooks.org.

 Printed on 100% recycled, FSC-certified materials

ISBN (hardcover): 978-1-68051-664-7
ISBN (ebook): 978-1-68051-665-4

An independent nonprofit publisher since 1960

For all the animals—in gratitude.

"To perceive the world through others' senses is to find splendor in familiarity and the sacred in the mundane."

—ED YONG, *AN IMMENSE WORLD: HOW ANIMAL SENSES REVEAL THE HIDDEN REALMS AROUND US*

"Attention is the rarest and purest form of generosity."

—SIMONE WEIL, *GRAVITY AND GRACE*

"The whole universe is humming. Every star, every planet, every continent, every building, every person is vibrating along to the slow cosmic beat . . . humming in tune with the entire universe."

—ADAM FRANK, "SCIENTISTS FOUND RIPPLES IN SPACE AND TIME," *THE ATLANTIC*

"Love the earth and sun and the animals."

—WALT WHITMAN, *LEAVES OF GRASS*

Contents

Introduction
ANIMAL APPRENTICE

I WAS RAISED as a wild animal. In my early years living in a remote Forest Service lookout cabin in the High Sierra, we were surrounded by many more animals than people.

Imprinting on animals, I fully expected to grow up to show off the most luxurious velvet antlers, to howl harmoniously as a wolf, to steal unseen like a fox through the seemingly endless old-growth forest. On the Plumas National Forest bordering California and Oregon, wild animals were my first kin: sisters and brothers, playmates, storytellers, teachers. The drama of their daily lives was equal to, and influenced my own. Animals knew about the world in ways different from the few humans around me. Bobcats coached me to run for my life and escape wildfires; eagles perched on tree thrones taught the stillness of a raptor's attention; coyotes played and prowled nearby in a yip-yip language that made just as much sense as the strange sounds people barked. The solemn deer heads stationed above my crib watched over me more mindfully than any human, their amazed, unblinking eyes devoted to my every chat or screech.

My father told me that he once discovered me climbing the wooden slats of my crib, reaching for the dark, glossy nose of his favorite deer trophy in an instinctive mimicry of the Michelangelo human hand longing and reaching for God. Before any religion or education or human notion of dominance got to me, wild animals *were* my gods.

Some part of me has never left this first forest or the wild animals who were my partners and mentors. My lifelong relationship with other animals is equally as dramatic, intimate, and revelatory as any of my bonds with humans. I see animals and humans as equal characters in an interdependent story—co-creators. Nature is not just a backdrop for our human dramas—often it is the main event.

Even in urban ecosystems, animals are our neighbors, our teachers, our fellow survivors. Animals must live in the moment. And because their presence is so instinctive, their observations so perceptive, their sensory skills so extraordinary, and their alliances so sensible, they model for us lessons offering a radically different knowledge. Animals give us unique, enlightening guidance for adapting to a drastically changing world. From animals, we can learn compassion, bonding, and family values; play, rest, and communication; the symbiosis of living *with* nature and how to live *within* nature. I call this apprenticing with animals, because with nature, we are the novices, the animals the experts. Animals have so much to teach us about ourselves.

The Covid-19 pandemic revealed that the earth—and other animals—*without* us will survive and firmly reclaim their natural territories. While we stayed inside, many animals played outside and thrived. It is we who are now as endangered as many of the species we've destroyed. Animals are our allies as we all face extinction. This book is a survival guide and love story—a celebration of the wonder and wisdom of other animals.

CONNECTION

Listening to Animals

WHY ARE SOME of us as devoted and connected to other animals as we are to our own kind? It's not simply compensatory, or because our own species has neglected, disappointed, or failed us. This embrace of those who are the Other, especially other species, is rather a widening of our humanity. It is an evolution of what it means to be human—to belong to more than just our own, rather recent, *Homo sapiens* lineage. In his seminal essay, "Why Look at Animals," John Berger believes that animals offer people another kind of relationship. "Different because it is a companionship offered the loneliness of man as a species."

What can we learn from animals that we may not learn from humans? Exploring the extraordinary sensory worlds, culture, and survival strategies of other animals reveals different ways of knowing our natural world. Like whales and wolves, my primary sense is auditory, and I've learned astonishing lessons on how to harmonize with other animals and my own kind. For example, howling for wolves is a form of "social glue," like humans singing around a campfire on nights that may be long and dangerous. Humpback whales' haunting lullabies echo across a thousand miles of ocean and are memorized by new generations.

When I encounter wild animals, listening is as vital as observing. I navigate the world with my ears more than my eyes. Perhaps that's why I've apprenticed myself especially to acoustic creatures who dwell in the sea, dolphins, seals, and whales; while on land, animals who engage me most are the great singers of the natural world—wolves and birds. Sound is not just background music for our visually driven lives. It can be the main accompaniment melody. Hearing is our first sense and the last to leave us when we die.

The original creation song we hear—a mother's heartbeat—thrums in steady, reassuring rhythms. Our womb is a noisy cavern, as we float and somersault in the shush of amniotic waves. Blind before birth, we simply listen for nine long months: heart and blood pulsing, voices familiar, but not yet embodied, muffled music rocking us in the darkness. Then the whoosh of an undertow drags us out of our warm hideaway into the shock of breathing air and blinding light. We wail, we protest—a suddenly single self, solo. The solace is our own heart's pit-a-pat that beats a percussive, lifelong soundtrack.

Research has recently shown that dolphin calves listen to their mother's signature whistle in the womb. When they are born, the family pod will go quiet while the new calf learns to echolocate or "see with sound" and discover a signature whistle all her own to identify herself. New technologies are eavesdropping on what many of us have been listening to for years—animal conversations. In "Talk to Me," Elizabeth Kolbert echoes Melville in *Moby Dick* wondering, "What has the whale to say?" By attaching suction cups to deep-diving sperm whales, researchers are using computers to study the whale's sophisticated, percussive "codas" that sound like "someone pecking out a memo on a manual typewriter." These clicking codas are collected in a database in the Caribbean listening stations of CETI (Cetacean Translation Initiative.) By looking for patterns, scientists believe these whale dialogues "must be fundamentally important to why we're here."

Science is finally proving that many other species have "the capacity for vocal learning" and language—a cultural skill and heritage that we once assumed belonged only to humans. In a *New York Times* article "The Animals Are Talking. What Does It Mean?" Sonia Shah documents that mice, birds, seals, chimpanzees, baboons, turtles, octopus, bats, even insects, are talking. Gorillas are already using sign language and bottlenose dolphins are using underwater keypads to choose their toys "like a kind of vending machine" that is "strikingly similar to the early stages of language acquisition in children." Now that we are recognizing and listening to other voices than our own, "We have emerged into a remade world, abuzz with the conversations of fellow thinking beings, however inscrutable."

What will happen when we decipher, using all our senses, other animals talking? What more will we discover about ourselves and animals? Harmonizing with the other—even those with four legs, fur, wings, antennae, claws, tails, and fins—requires humility, imagination, and curiosity. Most of all, it reminds us we are not here alone—lonely. We never have been and never will be.

GROWING UP GAME

THE DIZZYING SOLITUDE of our cabin, high on the Forest Service fire lookout station in the Pacific Northwest mountains, was encircled by a massive forest whose trees had clouds for foreheads. Those dense woods sheltered other animals as wild and hidden as we two-leggeds. As a tiny girl at night in my cabin crib, I listened to the scurry of red fox, the low hoot of night owls, and elk bugling deep in the woods.

Every morning, my father and other foresters marched off into the wilderness, leaving their womanly tribe behind, to bear and tend to the few children. At night, when I fretted with colic, my father lay me on his belly, a muscular, grounding plateau that breathed beneath me. His skin was fragrant with the scent of sweat and something else I recognized when I made my first forays into the forest and smelled my father there in the sharp, green aura of cut timber. My father was a walking giant conifer, I believed then, crawling behind him on the forest floor, my second skin.

One of my earliest memories is of scooting across the vast continent of crinkled linoleum in our cabin kitchen, down the splintered back steps to the wildflowers growing wheat high. Here I was eye-level with grasshoppers, who scolded me on my solo trip outside. I made it to the shed, a cool and comfortingly square space that held phantasmagoric metal parts, deep whiffs of dirt and grease.

I played a long time before a maternal shriek made me lift on my haunches to heed those urgent, possessive sounds that were my name. My head bumped into something hanging in the dark. Gleaming white, it twisted mid-air, cold against my cheek, emitting a musty odor, not unlike the slabs of my grandmother's great arms after her cool, evening bath. Feeling the sleek body of the doe, I marveled at her skin and elegant sinew. Instinctively, I felt both awe and kinship as the deer swung gently back and forth, hanging from the rafters, her dangling hooves bumping my face. The doe was like a white-barked birch, but upside down.

When my father found me in the shed, he let me watch him strip away the fur, flensing a length of the doe from flank to shoulder.

"We'll make some little moccasins for you. It's a perfect, smooth skin," my father patted my head. "One bullet hole." His long knife sliced through the doe's belly, and bloody bowels tumbled out in a slop of ropey guts.

I'd never seen the inside of an animal. It fascinated me.

"Some people eat the innards *and* the meat," my father explained. "But you don't like liver, do you?"

He'd learned to love the weirdly tough texture of the hearts, kidneys, and liver of wild game on his family farm in the Ozarks. As a child, my father was so anemic that he ate liver three times a day for the iron. On the national forest, we mostly ate venison and elk meat; also rainbow trout, rabbit, geese galore, and even rattlesnake, which tastes just like chicken but has many fragile bones to carefully slither your way through. I was four before I ever had a beef hamburger, and I remember being disappointed by its fatty taste and the way it fell apart at the seams whenever my teeth sank into it.

In the shed, my father patiently continued stripping away the last of the deer skin. He took up in his familiar, teasing tone. "Sorry, little girl. This time . . . I was just a tad faster."

At first, I thought he was talking to me, because he used the same fond voice when he told his favorite bedtime stories or the hunting tales that accompanied our suppers. But then I realized: he was chatting with this dead deer he'd downed with one magnificent shot straight and true through the heart.

On an earlier hunting trip, the deer had heard him coming. She'd stood with magnificent eyes tuned, dark, and attentive to the dawn light as my father crept on his belly over the ridge. Father said she scented him first before she met his eyes. As he raised his gun, squinting for aim, she was poised as if she had all the time in the world.

"It was a perfect shot," my father always said. "But that doe didn't drop. She just up and disappeared. Maybe she flew away," he concluded, as if he half-believed himself.

"Maybe she changed into something else you couldn't see," I told my own story.

After glancing at me for a long moment, my father decided not to correct me. I could see that small click in his hooded eyes that signaled, *She's just a little girl. Let it go.* But when we left the forest, my father and I would endlessly debate wildlife politics and climate change. He once told an Alaska wolf summit audience that I was "his worst critic."

No matter where we lived as I was growing up, my father continued hunting and bringing home wild game. He hunted in Alaska and Montana, in Virginia and Oregon, disappearing for weeks and returning to us with bloody coolers filled with wild game. By that time, we had huge gardens and my mother added to our meals fried okra, collard greens, corn fritters, wilted lettuce (our favorite because of the rare, blackened bacon), new potatoes and peas, stewed tomatoes, barbecued butter beans. She was a splendid and inventive cook, creating her own recipes for sweet-and-sour moose meatballs, elk burgers, and venison stew that had the subtle spice of a gumbo.

When I went off to college, my father gave, or provisioned, me with fifty pounds of moose meat. Well, in 1969, eating moose at the University of California was a contradiction in terms. Hippies didn't hunt. I lived in a rambling Victorian house that boasted sweeping circular staircases, built-in lofts, and a landlady who dreamed of opening her own health food restaurant. I told my vegetarian housemates that my moose meat, in its nondescript white butcher paper, was from a side of beef my father had bought. They would have recoiled if I'd told them the truth; though the carnivores in the house gratefully helped me finish off the game.

I was twenty-one, living in New York City, before I ever tasted lamb, cooked by famed food expert Judith Jones, my first editor and also editor to Julia Child. She'd fixed Child's roast leg of lamb recipe on a cast-iron stove that took up half her Manhattan apartment's kitchen. I approached the tender meat with a certain guilty self-consciousness, as if I had unfairly stalked those sweet-tempered, shaggy creatures myself. But how would I explain my squeamishness to urban foodies, that I was shy with farmed lamb because I had been bred on wild things?

Part of it, I suspect, had to do with the belief I'd also been raised on—we become the spirit and body of animals we eat. Eating venison as a child, I liked to think I too was agile and lovely, just like the deer. I would never be caught grazing while someone crept up and conked me over the head. If someone wanted to hunt me, he must be wily and outwitting. He must earn me.

My father had also taught his children that animals were our brothers and sisters under their skin. They died so that we might live, and for this sacrifice we must be thankful. "God make us grateful for what we are about to receive," took on new meaning when we imagined the animal's surrender to our own appetites. We also used all the parts of an animal. An elk became steaks, salami, and sausage—his antlered head went on the wall to watch us earnestly. Every Christmas Eve, as we made our deerskin moccasins, we munched on sausage cookies made from moose meat or venison.

"*Think* about what you're eating," my father reminded us.

We thought of ourselves as intricately linked to the food chain. We knew, for example, that a forest fire meant, at the end of the line, we'd suffer, too. We'd have buck stew instead of venison steak; the meat would be stringy and withered-tasting.

Once, in my early teens, I rode along on a hunting trip as the "main cook and bottle-washer," though I don't remember any bottles—none of the hunters drank alcohol. There was something else coursing through their veins as they rose long before dawn and disappeared, returning to camp with trout or a doe or pheasant or rabbit. We ate innumerable cornmeal-fried fish and had rabbit stew seasoned only with blood and black pepper.

That trip was the first time I remember eating game more mindfully. My father and Buddy Earl had shot a big doe, and she lay with me in the back of the tarp-draped pickup truck all the way home. It was not the smell I minded—it was the glazed, great eyes and the way her head flopped around crazily on what I knew was once a graceful neck. I found myself petting her, murmuring all those graces we'd been taught as kids. *Thank you for the sacrifice, thank you for letting us be like you so that we can grow up strong as a wild animal.* But I felt ill at ease as I bounced along in the back of the pickup with the deer.

What was uneasy is still uneasy—perhaps it always will be. It's not easy when you really start thinking about the eating-game food chain, the sacrifice of one for the other. The necessary compassion and gratitude of the carnivore. It's never easy when you begin to think deeply about the most basic actions, like eating.

Why do some people consider eating meat purchased at a butcher shop somehow more righteous than eating something wild? Perhaps it has to do with our collective unconscious that sees the animal bred for slaughter as doomed. But that wild doe or moose might live on without the hunter. Perhaps on this primitive level of archetype and intuitive knowing, we even believe that what is wild, will live on.

My father often told this story around a hunting campfire: His own father, who raised cattle during the Great Depression, once fell on such hard times that he had to butcher the family's pet lamb for supper. My father, born and bred on wild game, took one look at the family pet on that meat platter and pushed his supper away. His siblings followed suit. To hear my grandfather tell it, this was the funniest thing he'd ever seen.

"They just couldn't eat Bo-Peep," Grandfather said. When my father told the story years later at our dining table, it was funny, but I noticed for the first time his sadness. Eating had become a conscious act for him that day when Bo-Peep offered herself up.

My parents are both in their mid-nineties. My father no longer gets dropped off by small planes on the Alaska tundra to hunt caribou or elk. My mother no longer cooks; but she proudly displays her favorite soul food cookbook that I gave her for her birthday, with its luscious pictures of smothered potatoes and sausage, fried catfish, and barbecued ribs.

I eat bison delivered weekly in a sustainable Imperfect Foods box, still preferring the sweetness of bison for my burgers or sloppy joes. When my father asked what I'd want for my birthday, I asked him to send me something he rarely gives: several of his deer and elk skins. One soft leather swatch sits on the arms of my rocking chair, to keep my laptop from sliding off. And to remind me of my animal skin.

Recently he sent me, like a precious heirloom, a pair of his huge moccasins. There will be a struggle over which of his children inherits his majestic rack of moose antlers and deer trophies. In our family, we all still eat wild game. When someone offers me game, I eat it with all the qualms and memories and reverence with which I grew up eating it. I will always have this feeling of awe and kinship, and something else—deep knowledge of what I do, of how I've become what I eat, lean and lovely and mortal.

FIRE AND FLOOD,
FOREST TO SEA

DURING THOSE FORMATIVE years in the vast Plumas National Forest, our daily lives were dwarfed by the diversity of other animals and powerful trees my father called "The Standing People"—Douglas-firs, ponderosa pines, all old growth yet to be clearcut.

In the woods, I'd often overheard the squirrels discussing us whenever my father or I called out with pleasure over discovering some treasured pinecone or shed antler. There was moss and lichen for my knees to slide along, gummy resin of pine needles to prick my palms, and the moist sweetness of leaf-rot against my cheeks. Everything vegetable in me loved this scent, and I rooted in it on all fours with hands and face pressed into the forest bottom. Trees were never still, but talking, wet mists whispering through quaking aspen and blue spruce.

"Every tree makes its own song when the wind blows through branches," my father taught me. "Every animal knows to listen for the first crackle of far-off wildfires. That's when they run or find rivers to protect them from flames."

Like all the other animals, I was rooted in this remote forest and never expected to leave it for any flat land or city I'd read about in stories, where people lived on narrow streets lined by skyscrapers instead of trees.

"Will we ever live in cities?" I asked my father.

"Doubt it, honey," he'd laugh. "I work for the forest, and way up here, they forget about us. So we just work for the bears and squirrels and the trees themselves."

When I was school age, he was promoted out of the field and moved my mother, baby sister, and me down to sea level and away from the wild forest. I was unimpressed by San Diego's spindly palm trees and the scrubby coastal sagebrush; but I'd delightedly lean way out of the car window to sniff the honey-mint scent of eucalyptus stands with their ragged, rainbow bark. En route to San Diego, my forester father introduced us to the Giant Sequoia National Monument. Those trees were living giants, like in fairy tales or creation myths.

Awestruck, I easily fit into a narrow crack in one massive trunk and disappeared. My father didn't call me from hiding out of my wooden womb. He knew I would follow him as he hiked along through these ancients, their girth as wide as other worlds of red bark and conifer canopies.

"Timeless, these trees," he breathed. "Some over three thousand years old. Largest trees in the whole, wide world. Logged in the late 1880s, before we came to our senses." He stopped at a short pine stump. "You know, honey, tree rings tell the age of a tree." He traced the round center of the stump with a reverent finger. "You start in the middle at the first dark circle and count outward. Each ring is a year. You can see burns and weather written in tree rings."

My father placed my palms on the craggy bark. "Fire tells the tree's story."

I wondered if I would hear the deep thud of a heartbeat in the General Noble Tree.

"Trees and fire are related," my father continued as we walked deeper into the park's Converse Basin Grove. "Trees need to be tempered by wildfires to survive and stay healthy. Fires thin the underbrush or duff . . . that just acts as tinder to fuel the most terrible fires. But fire also adds minerals to the soil. Burnt pinecones pop open to release new seeds to make new trees." He paused to pick up a cone and hand it to me as a keepsake. "Trees need fire to thrive."

It was hard for me to understand that something as terrible as fire— furious flaming fingers stripping and snapping branches with the ripping sound of thunder—could be good for the forest.

"And what about the wildfires you can't stop?" I asked. I had witnessed my father coming home from fighting them, his face covered in soot and his uniform darkened with smoke.

"They're . . . terrible," he admitted. Then, he sighed, as if breathing in the green perfume of the forest—fragrant pine and pungent musk. Sweet and sharp.

Several young sequoias stood silhouetted, tall and black as night. Bare branches, broken limbs. I'd come upon animal corpses in my first forest, but not that many smoke-blasted trees.

"What do the animals do in a wildfire?" I asked my father.

"They run," he said simply. "Or climb a tree. Sometimes they retreat to rivers that can halt big flames. After the fire has passed, the burn is brand new habitat for small mammals."

"New?" I asked, remembering a forest we'd once visited that had been ravaged by hungry fires.

"Yes, honey, dead and downed trees make way for new green growth so deer and elk can graze. Forest animals, trees, and wildfires have existed together for thousands of years. Learn from trees. Be strong, root deep. When fire comes for you . . . stand your ground."

Raised on fear of forest fires, schooled by Smokey the Bear's dictums: "Only You," and the horrific scene of Disney's Bambi fleeing flames, I didn't understand then what seemed like a counterintuitive lecture on the evolutionary bond between fire and forests. But I did understand that, like all other animals, I must also learn the survival skill of adapting. It would serve me well in the decades to come when my father's work with the US Forest Service would move us every year and a half between West and East Coast forests, with a stint in Montana. We wandered along with him as nomads, region to region. Until he would one day climb to the highest lookout, way above timberline—as chief of the Forest Service.

"Trees and animals adapt to changes in their landscape . . . so can you," my father always said. "When you can't adapt, you don't survive."

I had trouble adapting when my father briefly settled us in suburban San Diego. Instead of sheltering ponderosa pine and cedar, there were tidy rows of little houses on a hot, paved street. I could no longer run around barefoot on a soft, forest floor. I imprinted one tiny hand in wet concrete on our driveway, as if to assure myself that I was still real. How would I know I existed without the company of trees and all the wild animals? I missed the whispering coolness of our forest, how the Standing People had fiercely protected and even hid us from anything outside our look-out station. Endless sunlight, without shade, now exposed us. Birdsong was the only natural music I could hear. No snuffling beavers in rivers or yipping coyotes at our windows. Just the insistent sounds of more people than I'd ever seen. They were so loud, busy, and unpredictable.

As if to orient me in this human landscape, my mother said, "Let's all go to the beach!"

Raised a Midwestern girl, my landlocked mother's dream was always to live by water. A champion diver in college, she'd been an aquatic dare-devil. Living now within a quick drive of the Pacific Ocean was her respite from the tedium of domestic life and raising three daughters. One beach picnic, my parents were happily distracted. I took this opportunity to run shouting, arms wide, straight into the turbulent surf, where a wave slapped me down. Caught in a churning undertow, I spun until all my air was gone. As if in another womb, I instinctively opened my mouth like a guppy, breathing in the dark, nutrient-rich liquid.

There was no panic, no struggle. I tucked myself in tiny somersaults and suckled seawater. No up or down, no sea bottom or sunlight, just the swirling embrace of warm saltwater. The ocean had its own light and many creatures visited me: bright blowfish and bioluminescent bacteria shone through the water like constellations. There were pink coral and purple sea anemones, sea cucumbers slithered past as my fingers sought their velvety, speckled backs. Blazing orange sea stars inched past snaggle-toothed, slinking eels—and just when I closed my eyes to rest from such undersea splendor, I heard the far-off moaning lullaby of a humpback shushing me to sleep.

I would have gratefully slept forever right there on the sea floor. But the ocean had another fate for me. She hurled me back up onto the beach like flotsam. My father, rather rudely, woke me. Desperately cranking my arms like an old-fashioned Model T and thumping my chest, he then sucked seaweed from my mouth in artificial respiration. I was reluctant to open my eyes, which stung with sand and salt. There were lots of people around, a crowd skittering like sandpipers. Mother was screaming my name as if I didn't know who I was. What I remember most is my dismay at being brought back on land—and the dawning, disloyal conviction that my real home might be this mighty ocean, she who had chosen to take me back to my primal birthright.

"You could have drowned!" My mother was beside herself.

"You *did* drown," my father said grimly.

"It's not scary," I assured them. "Drowning. I wasn't alone."

Then I tried to explain about the jellyfish who made their own light, and an underwater world that was as alive and vital as my first-seen forest. But I didn't yet have the right names for all these wonders. I tried to imitate the sounds of creatures I'd met and heard chanting to me: the cackling shrimp, the sonorous baritone blue whale, maybe the sashay and menacing hum of a shark. Most of all, the high-pitched chatter of dolphins circling me as I sank. And what was that pulse and sway of green, underwater plants?

Later, my first-grade teacher, a surfer, seemed to understand my fascination with oceans and the astonishing marine life.

"Marine creatures are kin to us," he said. "We are *all* mammals."

Of course, having felt so at home underwater, I already knew that. My long life would never be dust-to-dust, but water-to-water.

Since that long-ago drowning, I've often returned to the embracing undertow and underwater worlds when dreaming. My near-death encounter, like my birth forest, was accompanied by more animals than people. It's perhaps why those who know me best often tease that I'm only half-human. Drowning has determined my afterlife and lifelong ocean activism, writing about the sea and marine mammals. The sea inhabits and inspires my imagination more than my land life. In novels, like *The Drowning World*, I've created underwater civilizations; in nonfiction, for adults and kids, I've encountered many cetaceans. For decades, I have lived by water.

Many nights, I still find myself sleeping on the sea floor. I recognize, almost casually, that I'm not human, but aquatic, with all manner of gills, fins, antennae, exoskeletons, moon shells. In one of my favorite dreams, I am an octopus with red suction cups, jetting through the water and squirting ink in my elegantly elusive wake. A dream I only tell children is of living inside the belly of a blue whale, like Jonah. I'm only so much silly krill, slipped through the whale's mouth. Children, knowing the power of being small, don't mind imagining themselves as tiny, shrimplike crustaceans. The innards of a great whale is no stranger a residence than being a water baby in the womb.

When my father's Forest Service fellowship to Harvard moved us across the country to Revere Beach, Massachusetts, I was seven. We lived in a rundown beach apartment right across the street from the Atlantic Ocean. I didn't have to wait for my busy parents to take me to the ocean. All my sisters and I had to do was cross the quiet street and spend all day exploring tide pools, building driftwood forts, and spying on couples who'd come to roll around on the sand as if they were drowning together on land. The Atlantic on the Massachusetts shore was colder than the Pacific in Southern California, but the surf, when illuminated by summer sun or marine mists, was welcoming. We splashed and floated for hours, adorned ourselves with handmade seashell necklaces, and our pigtails were never free from sand. My father was lost in the Harvard library that year and had no time for hunting. So, we lived on lobster from the fish factory behind our apartment. It was less expensive than hamburger, so we had no idea it was a delicacy.

Walking to school, we often got distracted by the dilapidated amusement park where we spent our meager allowances on cotton candy and peanuts. Once, I saw someone fall off the roller coaster; it didn't seem real, more like a cartoon dive. A policeman hurried me on, but I was still late for my third-grade class. There were only eight kids in my class, and only one other girl. Mrs. Mivstovki, our young and devoted teacher, with her elegant French twist and handmade, tailored clothes, introduced us to a kid's version of Ovid's *Metamorphoses*. With its myths of couples who effortlessly turn into trees and lovers who fling themselves off cliffs only to change into seagulls midair, the book was more enthralling than any Grimms' fairy tales. Ovid was all about transformation from human to animal—and back again. A metamorphosis and spiritual path that I fervently believed in, having been changed by the sea.

"Living here so close to the ocean, we can easily imagine sea goddesses and water nymphs," Mrs. Mivstovki smiled, looking very much like Venus rising from the sea herself. She spread her arms toward the bank of open windows where the reassuring surf music accompanied our lessons. "Poseidon is the Greek god of the sea and all waters. Also called Neptune, he rules the underworld. Sailors prayed to Poseidon to spare them storms that might sink and drown them." Mrs. Mivstovi paused. "He was not the most sweet-tempered god and could raise the waves to destroy even those on land."

I took copious notes in my red, jumbo-lined journal, and painted sea nymphs with girl faces. Mrs. Mivstovi went on to describe how the whole world was once flooded; not just by a god as mighty as Poseidon, but because floods, like wildfires in a forest, both destroyed, reshaped, and nourished the shore. She called these "deluge myths." I well recognized these sea and flood stories from my Sunday School of the Biblical Noah's ark. That Old Testament prophet had been wise enough to conserve every animal species, but just a few human beings. Noah, like Poseidon, was my favorite myth.

I often privately prayed to Noah or Poseidon, instead of some God who wasn't even here on earth but way up in heaven—*above it all*. I preferred my gods in the sea or on a sturdy ark full of every other animal on earth—from blubbery hippo to stealthy tiger or tiny mice and rat-tailed squirrels. When I imagined a long-ago flooded world, sailing in Noah's well-built ark, crowded with many animals and just one human family, it was like returning to the correct ratio found at the small, wooden cabin of my birth forest—the balance of many more animals than people.

Only now, in my child's imagination, there were whales and dolphins, all the marine creatures who still populated my drowning dreams and beachcombing days. Noah's ark was my creation story. It embodied a world in balance; humans were again in the minority, and all animals thriving, ready to create a new world. Whether it was in a remote cabin in the wilderness or an ancient ark, animals were the most important species to survive the end of the world by flood. They were the real prophets because they knew how to create a world all over again. The reason Noah saved all animals and just a few people was because animals were much more valuable; they had skills and cultures and knowledge. They knew things we had forgotten, or had never bothered to learn.

Animals had been my gods, teachers, and allies since that first forest; why wouldn't I include their teachings and wisdom in my developing spiritual traditions? They had been present at my birth and they'd surrounded me in my near-death drowning. Animals would become my lifelong companions and, I hoped, would be with me when I died, and beyond.

I began to ponder and ask these life-and-death questions as a child who spent every hour that I was not in school on the Atlantic shore. Whenever I saw a beached jellyfish, a seal pup napping in driftwood, or once, the sad, stranded body of an Atlantic white-sided dolphin, I'd wonder where the animals went when they died, or drowned. Would I follow them into the next, new world? And here on earth, did animals commit sins, as the Bible was always warning about? Did animals know what was right and wrong? Did they also try to live a good, kind life?

I began even as a child a lifelong search for other traditions that compassionately included other animals. Beginning in my teens I studied Indigenous beliefs, Buddhism, "nature mysticism" (as espoused by deep ecologist and Buddhist teacher, Joanna Macy), and animism. Eventually I settled on Taoism—a simple but ancient Asian philosophy of dualism, a reunion of opposites, an embrace of the Other—like land and sea. Taoism is rooted in nature and living in harmony with the Tao, often known as The Water Way. As Lao Tzu writes in the classic *Tao Te Ching*'s "Water and Stone":

> *What's softest in the world*
> *rushes and runs*
> *over what's hardest in the world.*

It was during that time living on the Atlantic and watching whales and so many dolphins right offshore that I began to believe that perhaps it wasn't just the undertow that had tossed me back onto my afterlife of land dwellers. Mrs. Mivstovski taught us about the Greek singer, Arion, who was thrown overboard to drown but a dolphin carried him back to shore. I reasoned that maybe I was also denied the serenity of drowning thanks to the curiosity and compassion of wild dolphins who believed I had something I needed to do—perhaps for them. So, they beached me. Maybe that was why, after that drowning, I'd always had imaginary friends who were dolphins—most altruistic of mammals who have, since antiquity, rescued the drowning. Arion was a singer, so I would become a storyteller. Under Mrs. Mivstovski's devoted eye, and with the abiding companionship of the Atlantic, I diligently began writing sea stories, creating my own ark for the animals.

Mrs. Mivstovski's deluge tales were never frightening, only familiar. I fully expected that one day the whole world, like me, would again be drowned, renewed. When my father began his meteoric rise in the Forest Service, moving us like nomads to Montana, to Virginia, back to Northern California, and then to Georgia, he always commuted into his city office, while finding us homes near rivers, bays, forests, and creeks. Wherever I moved as an adult, even in New York City or Boulder, Colorado, I'd find some ramshackle waterfront apartment—on Manhattan's Hudson River, or in the Rocky Mountains—and continue my apprenticeship to forest and sea. I was a student of all the animals who inhabited those green or blue realms. The one time I was landlocked, as writer-in-residence at Arizona State University, I almost died from the desert's dehydration and a weird lung fungus called "valley fever." And the only time I lived without the daily companionship of animals, I landed in the hospital with the diagnosis "failure to thrive."

In 1981, I finally found my beloved home in Seattle. For decades, I've lived on the Salish Sea, so close that I can listen to the surf all night, a soundtrack to my undertow dreams. My daily walks are often in the moss-strung madronas and wise pines of Schmitz Park, the last stand of old-growth trees left in the city. Whenever I walk these nearby trails, I pray for higher wisdom and for guardians of our air, water, land, to be present. I petition for humans to rise to our highest responsibilities, compassion, and generosity—to our next generations, and to all animals and the natural world that we share.

Every day I can move between forest and sea and can easily drive to the Olympic Mountains or Cascades Range. Floating in marine mists, Seattle seems like an entire city underwater with its "celestial rivers" of rain. The deluge myths of my childhood seem ever nearer as climate change is sinking cities, flooding sea-level countries worldwide.

But it is not just coastal lands that face rising seas. Now, our Pacific Northwest record rainfalls flow inland, creating flooding as far as Montana and Wyoming. In the spring of 2022, our atmospheric rivers shockingly created torrential rains as far away as Yellowstone National Park. So much hard, unrelenting rain falling on snow melted hills and cliffs triggered massive mudslides. For the first time in a century, Yellowstone was closed. This "one-thousand-year event," with four times as much rain as in an average year, collapsed bridges. Rivers overran roads, and ten thousand park visitors were evacuated. Wooden cabins slid and sailed off into previously dry, now suddenly turbulent, creeks.

Such an inland deluge had long been predicted by scientists, just not so soon. These days, even seemingly landlocked regions like Yellowstone must plan for a flooded future, to "embrace the unexpected," as a National Wildlife Federation chief scientist told *National Geographic*. Climate change planners "had focused on the features that draw visitors to Yellowstone—like bison and wolves. Roads, bridges, and houses getting washed away were not on their radar." Like Yellowstone, other national parks as far north as Denali in Alaska, are facing future flooding from melting permafrost.

The future *is* flooded. Even as the West Coast is stricken with historic droughts and unprecedented wildfires, global warming also increases the risk of ravaging month-long "megastorms" in California and record rainfall in the Pacific Northwest. Fire, droughts, and floods—not just on our coasts but worldwide.

All of my family still lives on the East Coast. Several siblings are in Florida, where fish sometimes swim down main streets in Miami, and a sister has built her beach cottage on pilings. My elderly parents perch on the unstable shores of North Carolina's aptly named Cape Fear coast, where each hurricane season threatens their home. My family was once so worried about my little waterfront apartment, so intimate with the Salish Sea, that they voted me, "Most Likely to Drown in My Own Home." Now, they must also reckon with their own rising seas.

As we all face a future deluge, why not remember the Great Flood myths etched in our geologic record and retold in our stories? Why not tell our children stories of how to survive the next Great Wave?

Here in the Pacific Northwest, we are reminded of our historic deluge tales by our many earthquake and tsunami drills on Oregon and Washington Coasts. For eons, high tides and tsunamis have sculpted and often collapsed this rugged coastline. In 1750, the Makah village of Ozette was buried in a giant mudslide that collapsed a cliff. A "sea of mud" swallowed cedar longhouses, snuffing out oxygen, entombing people like "the Pompeii of the West" as archaeologists call this rich cultural site. Ozette disappeared, kept alive only in the deluge stories told by elders, until over four centuries later when another huge wave and storm unearthed it. The village was rediscovered, its ancient timbers revealing "buried homes . . . household items, tools, weapons, and walls elaborately carved and inlaid with seal and sea otter teeth."

Ozette is "a place of fault lines, geological, historical, and human," wrote Linda Hogan in the National Geographic book on gray whales we penned together. When the Makah village was rediscovered, it "held the saved pieces of a broken world, which might now be mended." In the ruins were alder tree branches still green and spring pollen found entire in this "world held still" by mudslide.

Coastal tribes still live in what they call the "tsunami hazard zone." This high-risk tsunami zone runs from northern California to southern British Columbia. Coastal dwellers and especially local communities, often perched on the very edge of the sea, are at risk. According to the

US Geological Survey, "The zone has produced earthquakes measuring M8.0 and above at least seven times in the past 3,500 years. The intervals between quakes vary: from as little as 140 years to as much as 1,000." The last massive quake that trigged a devastating tsunami was three hundred years ago. Geologists predict that this coastal region is due for another big quake and flood—anytime now.

Anyone doubting the geologic truth of these deluge myths has only to visit the Makah reservation or tune into YouTube's myriad sneaker waves videos. My favorite shows people casually perched on Oregon's Cannon Beach—when out of nowhere, a wave rises. In a minute, the shore dwellers are swept into the mini-tsunami, tumble around, and disappear. The video doesn't reveal if they survived. Our Pacific Coast is also at risk from tsunamis that arise in distant countries.

Water is a world-changer. Living by water, with the daily company of great blue herons, sunning seals, migrating gray whales, and harbor porpoises, I've never felt lonely. Sometimes at night, listening to the siren voice of a south wind singing off the Salish Sea, when my bed rocks from high tide waves off the break wall, I close my eyes and again return to the very bottom of the ocean. My luminous tail flukes are anchor and ballast in the welcome undertow. Graceful tentacles of kelp and sponge's spiky tendrils wave in reunion. Resting, I gaze up at the shy shadows of an octopus, the white belly of a beluga whale, the darting cloud of a million minnows.

Far above is the sun, its warmth shining down like memory; below, pulled by the moon, the water glows a calm, blue green. Everywhere in surrounding sea caverns are other changelings. They're dreaming of a world far above where they sometimes visit. Maybe fathoms deep in the sea is where all the old and new souls are dreaming and shapeshifting—reborn.

GIRLS IN WOODS,
WOMEN ON WAVES

BECAUSE I WAS born on a vast forest and drowned in the sea, apprenticed to both land and sea animals, I always assumed that girls belonged in the woods and the waves. My childhood was a series of forests or beaches we explored as our own private wilderness. Our mother declared every morning as we ventured off to our tree houses or driftwood forts, "Come home at twilight."

Even the years I spent as a young woman in New York City, working as an editorial indentured servant at the *New Yorker* magazine, I lived in a shabby waterfront apartment at the very top of that stony island of skyscrapers and asphalt. Alongside the Hudson River's often ice-gripped waters bordering Inwood Hill Park, I ran with my Siberian husky pup before descending into the earthen bowels for an hour-long subway ride to midtown.

The largest old-growth forest in Manhattan, Inwood Hill Park's trees include century-old black willow, eastern cottonwoods, white pines, weeping cherry trees, drought-resistant *Ginkgo biloba*, citrus-scented orange osage, tall tulip poplars, and, the tree the city's forest managers call Socrates (the "oldest and wisest tree"), western hemlock. Unlike the dutifully manicured trees of Central Park, this neighboring Inwood forest is full of decomposing, fallen trees—nurse logs and fertile stumps teeming with fragrant rot and burrowing insects. Here in the shade and shelter of mature trees, among the oldest tree species planted on the continent, I could gratefully take root, even in a city thronged with millions of people. Spending my long days in a dingy twentieth-floor editorial office, I could plant a miniature window garden of tiny corn, spindly tomatoes, and scented herbs that bravely grew, covered in soot. In winter, when other New Yorkers flew south to Florida, I spent my holidays freezing in what was then just a small fishing village, Kennebunkport, Maine, living off cheap meals of fresh lobster rolls and shrimp chowder.

After five years enduring the human wilderness of Manhattan, I moved to a run-down animal farm in rural Colorado that my mother had inherited from my late great aunt and uncle. They had no children, so had taken in every stray dog, cat, or abandoned animal; they raised exotic chickens and my uncle had invented a self-service worm dispenser for the fishermen who came to the nearby lake. In the shadow of the Rockies, I planted blue corn on acres I irrigated, mostly at night, to escape the hot blare of sunshine. Our acres bordered the communal ditch, and I fought with developers for several years in fierce water wars over these precious rights. It was these two water shares that I sold to support my move to Seattle in 1981.

In Washington, I finally found the right balance of forest and sea that I believed was my birthright, my true home. I now live a continent away from my family, all of whom have settled in the South. As the only "Left Coaster," I often try to coax them to visit. Finally, in 2005, when I was researching gray whales for a National Geographic book, my parents happily agreed to accompany me to a remote birthing lagoon in Baja, Mexico. My folks were in their late seventies. My father had retired as chief emeritus of the US Forest Service in 1987 and was then the executive vice president of IWA, the International Association of Fish and Wildlife Agencies. My siblings worried my parents were too old for encounters with such a gigantic, wild animal. But my parents have always been adventurous outdoors. I often tease them that our childhood was "camp or die." The prospect of flying in by four-seater plane to land on a dirt strip five hundred miles from the nearest town, and camping in canvas tents on an isolated Mexican lagoon, with curious coyotes strolling by the outhouse and no electricity, was an invitation they happily accepted.

My favorite memory of my elderly parents was watching them trundle together, holding hands, over the slippery, white sands down to the twenty-foot-long small Mexican skiffs called pangas. In their red and blue slickers, hip boots, and floppy rain hats, they were ready to dare the rough waves and sea spray that was akin to going through a car wash while sitting on the hood of a car.

In these birthing lagoons, humans are so small, the minority, a very young species compared to the ancient gray whales who have migrated here for thousands of years to give birth. Imagine turquoise lagoons inset like jewels in salt flats where every spring up to twenty thousand gray whales journey in the longest mammal migration on earth. This whale nursery is off the shore of a tiny village, San Ignacio. In 1998, San Ignacio was chosen as a United Nations World Heritage and Whale Sanctuary. (Despite objections from marine mammal biologists, in 1994 the gray whale had been taken off the endangered species list.) We camped in two-person canvas tents and gathered in the mess tent at sunset with the eighteen other whale watchers and researchers to tell stories of our day's encounters with what scientists call "Friendly Whales."

For thirty years, scientists have tried to fathom why wild gray whales approach humans, seeking physical contact.

"Whale watching takes on a whole new meaning when the whale is also watching you," says renowned oceanographer Sylvia Earle.

Modern physics teaches us that in the act of observing, we change what we see. Those of us who study animals, who spend our days in the field watching, noting, and trying to understand their societies, are aware of this law of physics and humbly admit that just as we are observing, we are also keenly—with senses often far beyond ours—observed. And doesn't this then mean that we are changed in the act, as well?

All night, we heard them breathing—sonorous sighs from the mother whales accompanied the short exhalations of their newborn calves. It was an otherworldly, but intimate, symphony. Where else in the world could we listen to wild animals sleeping so close to and trusting a human camp? It was as if we all belonged together here under the brilliant burden of stars.

In the mornings, our wooden panga skimmed across warm waters. Eight of us in the boat raised our binoculars; a grandmother on board sang sea shanties to attract the mother-calf pairs. This was my fifth research trip to the nursery lagoons; but for many others on this journey, including my parents, it was their first time claiming a connection to nature that is everyone's inheritance.

"It's so big out here!" exulted Alexa, a teenage girl with a diamond in her nose and pink hair. "No more malls!"

This was Alexa's second expedition to Baja's birthing lagoons, and her high school science project. She had taken a course in marine biology at the Hatfield Science Center on the Oregon Coast and hoped to become a cetacean scientist. At a time when most girls her age were falling into the confusing feminine dilemma of self-doubt and shrinking aspirations to fit into high school society, Alexa was reaching out to a vastly diverse natural world. The wild would hold and mirror her biggest dreams. Natural rhythms of tide and wind could center her and soothe her adolescent fear that she was out of place. Alexa was discovering a sense of belonging—in an unexpected lagoon oasis in the middle of what might seem a forbidding desert. In a nursery teeming with new life and hope for the future. Alexa's parents said that while researching and planning this Baja adventure, her self-esteem and grades had greatly improved.

Alexa was the first to sight a nearby blow. "Whales at three o'clock!" she informed us.

We heard the grays before we sighted them: gray whales sound like the ring of Chinese gongs as a mammoth body surfaced from these shallow waters. We cut our motor and very gently drifted alongside the whale. I smiled, watching Alexa's mother grip her daughter's yellow life preserver as her daughter leaned far out of the skiff, ecstatic to touch the whale's long snout with its white brush of baleen.

I recognized Alexa's happiness from my own childhood devotion to wild animals. The High Sierra and the Pacific and Atlantic Oceans were bigger than any rules or traditional roles afforded to many girls. Those of us fortunate enough to know nature as children may have been the last generation of girls to declare woods, waves, beaches, and deserts our natural habitat. We were pirates and wild horses. We were shape shifters and young naturalists. We knew how to build fires, recognize poisonous plants, and paddle our own dinghies.

Today it can be too dangerous for girls to run through the forest alone, kayak solo, or sail free. Girls are often limited to the "natural" habitat of strip malls, play dates, gyms, and two-dimensional screens of social media. No virtual reality or metaverse will ever replace or compare with the natural world. What do we give up that is vital to our independence and intuition when we are denied or afraid to claim nature and other animals as our extended family?

Exploring nature and bonding with other animals can be an essential survival strategy for young people, especially girls. A recent Centers for Disease Control and Prevention study discovered that teenage girls after several years of living through the pandemic are enduring the "worst mental crisis in a decade, with nearly a third reporting they've seriously considered taking their own lives." Girls are also twice as likely as boys to experience "sexual assault and persistent feelings of sadness or hopelessness." The isolation of the pandemic, online misinformation, the stress of school, and peer group pressures intensified by social media all have taken a terrible toll, particularly on teenage girls. One way to balance this stress is simply for young girls to get outside and claim their territories in the woods and on the waves. To apprentice themselves to other animals besides human beings.

Women know in our bodies, our souls, and our histories what it means to be domesticated, managed, and tamed. Yet recent medical research has revealed that our bodies work on an innate circadian clock that changes with the seasons. Unlike men, women experience shifts in melatonin (a hormone produced by the pineal gland that regulates sleep) with the ebb and flow of sunlight and seasons. So even if we live in cities, our bodies are still physically synchronized with the greater body of earth.

"Must be spring," my father used to tease me as he picked twigs and leaves out of my unruly hair. "You're running wild again!"

I understood Alexa's wildness now, as our boat seemed to fly across shallow waves toward a gray whale mother's blow.

"Kids are whale magnets," Renaldo, our boatman, grinned. He and his family had been guardians of the whale nursery for generations. "The whales, they always choose boats with kids. Maybe we are *their* float toys?"

Perhaps that helps explain these "Friendlies"—the unique contact between grays and humans that was first documented in the 1970s, three decades after the US banned the commercial hunting of gray whales in 1946. That a young mother was calling out the old whaler's alert—"Thar she bloooows!"—that we reached out hands instead of harpoons, was a small redemption of human history.

Our boat tipped with the swell of a gigantic body, as a barnacled 45-ton gray mother, the length of a semi-truck, glided straight toward us. Slowly, she surfaced. Her blow was a prismatic rainbow, her huge snout rising, baleen-striped mouth dazzling.

Eager hands scratched and stroked the supple gray skin, which feels as smooth and cool as melon. That eye held ours, gazing at us as if from the bottom of the ocean. These grays are the elders of all whales, their fossil record dated at over 60 million years old. To touch such a living ancestor is like being called backward in time to a sea teeming with marine life—mammals like us, who nurse their young and breathe air.

The calf surfaced, curious but shy. He was brand new, no more than a few days old, with baby whiskers and no barnacles. Only 15 feet long, he was nursing on milk so rich he would gain one hundred pounds a day. When the calves are two to three months old, they will embark on the perilous 12,500-mile journey between Baja and the Arctic, an obstacle course of orca attacks, supertanker boat propellers, commercial and subsistence hunters, and other hazards. Thirty percent of the calves will not survive.

Another of our naturalists and boatwomen was 21-year-old Lupita, Renaldo's niece and a native of San Ignacio village. She has inherited the lagoon's conservation legacy from her family as Keepers of the Whales. In her salt-encrusted slicker and sun hat, her hair in thick braids, Lupita was a seasoned guide. "My grandfather taught me everything that I know about taking care of the lagoon and the grays," she said proudly.

A mother-calf pair approached our boat, and everyone leaned out, splashing and calling to the newborn whale, who pirouetted in curiosity and then lifted a glossy snout to see us better with those gentle, brown, unblinking eyes, the size of softballs.

"Why does the mother let her baby come to people?" one of the whale watchers asked as he leaned far out, laughing, and vigorously rubbing the smooth, baby whale skin. It feels like silk and rubber. There were not yet as many barnacles or sea lice embedded in this newborn calf's skin as on the mother's mottled back. The spray from the newborn's double blowhole was sweet, like a surprising shower over us. A rainbow of water and prismatic light.

"Why do they trust us?" a woman asked, tears streaming down her face.

Lupita replied with a faint smile, "Grays are a mystery whale. Why do they breach? Why let us touch them? For only scratching? No, I don't think so. I think the whales also want to have fun."

Lupita was quiet, maneuvering the boat expertly and cutting the motor so we were drifting, almost tilting sideways with the weight of eight people on one side, leaning out to touch the gray whale mother and her playful calf.

"Gray whales teach us about second chances," Lupita said thoughtfully. "That's why they're called 'Comeback Whales.'"

Gray whales have come back from the brink of extinction twice in the last century—a living example of the resilience of nature, when humans can learn to get out of the way. Researchers have discovered from fossil remains that a gray whale can live up to 150 years.

"We are taking care of the whales." Lupita guided the boat gracefully alongside them. "They are also taking care of us. Whales are our neighbors. They are born here, like we are born here. They return to the lagoon, just like we do. We are related by this lagoon."

Humans and animals are also related by a changing ecosystem. These most watched of all whales had rebounded to twenty-six thousand in the 2000 census. Their return has been seen as a success story of restoration. But like all happy endings, the future is still full of doubt and danger; Russia continues its commercial hunting, while Japan and Norway are fiercely lobbying to resume. In Washington State, the Makah tribe is again lobbying the feds to resume hunting gray whales; and they may be successful in their petition, as they were in the controversial harpoon hunt of what researchers believed was a "friendly whale."

There was a significant downturn from 2017 to 2019, with a dramatic drop in calves counted and a rise in gray whale strandings all along the coast. CNN recently reported that "since 2019, the number of gray whales strandings has reached 500 in all, a fraction of the many thousands that likely died and sank to the ocean floor." This die-off is eleven times the average yearly stranding of fifteen whales, prompting the National Oceanic and Atmospheric Administration (NOAA) to declare an Unusual Mortality Event (UME) amid concerns that retreating ice in the Arctic and warming waters have affected the whales' ecosystem, "another piece of Earth's biome rewritten by climate change." The grays depend upon lipid-rich small crustaceans in their northern feeding grounds. Bottom-feeders, gray whales use their baleen to filter the sea floor and cycle nutrients, working like natural ploughs to keep the ocean healthy.

In late winter 2018 and early spring 2019, San Ignacio Lagoon counted just 37 calves, as opposed to 104 the season before. Using drone photography, researchers could identify individual whales and track their return to the lagoons. The lagoon researchers also noticed a "25% jump in skinny whales and a giant reduction in cow-calf pairs." A healthy, robust gray whale has a fatty hump behind the blowholes. But drone photos revealed emaciated grays with a dip at the skull, showing starvation. In the spring of 2022, this UME of skinny whales and decrease in calves continues. "If you don't have the energy or health to bring offspring to term and take care of them . . . you'll abort and preserve yourself at least so you'll continue to live," noted Steven Swartz, of the Laguna San Ignacio Ecosystem Science Program.

What we were fortunate enough to encounter in Baja were the healthy, hearty gray whales we dearly hoped would continue to thrive. On our last day in the lagoon, a mother whale did something I'd not witnessed in the five years I'd been visiting San Ignacio. She turned belly-up under our small boat, touching the boat to float us all very gently on her belly. Her blowhole underwater and closed, the mother whale held her breath. Her huge, pectoral fin lifted her baby up to our amazed, outstretched hands.

Eye-to-eye with a newborn calf, we hushed. Were we the first humans this calf had ever seen? Would we be the last? Would he remember us? The calf lifted a long snout out of the waves and twirled in a slow twirl called a "spyhop." His fins reached out like awkward wings. Inside each pectoral were the skeletal remains of a hand, reminder that these grays once walked on land. Rolling on his back, the newborn calf offered a gleaming white-pink belly to scratch. The navel cord was still attached.

I will always remember this newborn's trust and tenderness, as he turned to let us scratch smooth, new skin. The mother whale turned on her side to float nearby our boat, and we were shocked to see the white slash of a harpoon scar.

We all gasped. "Oh, no," someone breathed, tracing the mother's scar with an outstretched hand.

Time stopped. We floated in silence, a reverie, with only the cries of cormorants and pelicans, the lapping of mild waves against our boat. Sixteen hands rested tenderly on the mother whale and her calf. The baby's breath misted over us, smelling fresh and salty. Our baptism by this baby blow was strangely sweet and surprisingly warm.

Renaldo said softly, "Up until the 1930s, there was Yankee whaling in our nursery lagoons. Whales live long . . . so some of these very same whales you see were also once hunted here."

Here was the biggest mystery: Why do gray whales trust humans again, and why do they lift their newborn calves for us to touch? Is it for self-preservation, this contact with a predator? Why do they ever come close again to our shores? What should we give them in return?

As if reading our thoughts, Lupita said, "Every time a whale comes to us with her baby, she looks up into our eyes and says . . . she forgives us." Lupita looked across this turquoise lagoon, the pale pink salt flats, the three small mountains in the distance and concluded, "*Las ballenas*, the whales, and God . . . they are one. They both say, even when we are hurt, to forgive."

Animals can teach us compassion, I realize, as I rest my hand on the calf's smooth dome of a head. With *pati* (Latin for passion), to suffer with—that's the root meaning of compassion. Were these elder gray whales approaching us with what we usually only allow ourselves: humanity, loving kindness, abiding together in this beautiful, broken-hearted, and dangerous world?

Suddenly the calf twirled in the water, inhaled another quick breath, and dove back down to roll atop her mother's wide belly to nurse. With a rising wave of her tail fluke, the mother signaled a deep dive, her calf in tow; but not before giving us one last gaze with that ancient hundred-year-old eye. We called out, singing, and just for a moment the mother-calf pair lingered alongside our boat, listening, their blows percussive bubble blasts and underwater moans a counterpoint—harmony.

Would they remember us if we met this pair again in California, or Oregon, off Vancouver Island, or even far north in frigid Alaskan waters? We, who follow them along their 10,000-mile migration, will always be haunted by this question.

As the whales drew a deep breath and at last dived, Alexa chanted to the calf, "'Safe journey, little one. Safe journey. Until we meet again."

On the summer solstice of a new century in a land of long light and midnight sun, I was reminded of Alexa's prayer for the gray whale calf as we followed their migration along the West Coast far north to Alaska's Kodiak Island. This island is also called the "Northwesternmost Hawaiian Island," or the "Emerald Island." Kodiak had seen an unprecedented die-off of gray whales in that summer of 2000, and the beached grays showed signs of starvation.

Were the deaths caused by food scarcity because gray whales fed farther away from increasing coastal development? Was it because, as some NOAA researchers theorized, gray whales had rebounded so well that their food supply had reached its "carrying capacity?" This idea did not consider the huge pre-hunting populations of grays that had once thrived in these waters. More likely the gray whale deaths signaled and warned us about the dismal state of our oceans.

In her oceanside Kodiak home, we met Stacy Studebaker, a long-time island resident who teaches biology at the local high school. It was the summer solstice of a new century, and we were concerned about the die-off of gray whales off the West Coast that had begun in 1999 (and would continue until 2021).

"It's a strange year for marine mammals," Studebaker told me. "Four gray whales have washed up on our Kodiak beaches. Some gray whales may not make the long migration between Baja nursery lagoons and the

Arctic. There are gray whales here year-round, especially around Ugak Bay, with its rich food sources of amphipods and other crustaceans."

Studebaker tugged her baseball cap over her dark blonde hair as she surveyed the activity of a handful of volunteers outside taking measurements of a gray whale carcass from Pasagshak Beach. I asked her how she came to take on this enormous task.

"I was grading student papers at a cabin on Pasagshak Beach when I looked up and saw gray whales in twos and threes lolling very close to shore," she said. "They were rolling and churning in the chilly, shallow surf, maybe scratching their barnacles, or feeding."

Excitedly, Studebaker and her husband, a high school English teacher, walked down to the shore and marveled at the whales within a hundred feet of them in the surf.

"I think they were playing. One of them made eye contact with us." Her voice fell. "But that day we didn't only see healthy whales. Out in the bay, we saw a dead whale floating offshore. We fetched our kayaks and paddled out to the gigantic body. What in the world could we do?" As the day progressed, Studebaker watched the dead whale float across the bay and eventually wash up on the sandy beach. Still fresh and intact, it was a perfect specimen.

Like a forensic detective, Studebaker wondered why this whale had died. "He wasn't emaciated" she said, "so we could probably rule out starvation. Maybe he died of old age. Or he died after the military sonar tests around Kodiak that many are protesting. There were no signs that he collided with a ship." There is also the trawling fishery of the sea bottom where these whales feed, sifting muddy sediment through their baleen. "Bottom trawling disrupts and destroys a lot of marine life." Finally, the whale might have succumbed to toxic algae blooms or coastal pollution, because these whales hug the shore near cities and are more susceptible to runoff. Studebaker paused and shook her head. "Imagine what these whales must swim through along their migration route." A partial necropsy was done but it was inconclusive.

Whatever had killed this whale, his story had just begun. The great gray lay beached, his forlorn body rising like a gentle mountain, huge mouth opened to reveal the pale brush slats of baleen; those wide pectoral fins still teeming with barnacles and sea lice. The tides and waves had simply washed the whale up on the beach, his dusky body one with the dark sand.

"My science brain and imagination went into hyperdrive," Studebaker said. "As far as I knew, no one has ever tried to preserve a complete whale skeleton in Alaska by burying the carcass and then reassembling it for future display. This could be a giant science experiment."

"In my research into the historic illustrations from whaling centuries, I couldn't find one single drawing of a complete gray whale skeleton," Studebaker continued. "I found every other whale, but not a gray. We needed a template for rearticulating the skeleton. Maybe we could turn a tragedy into a wonderful project for our community and someday find a local artist to make an accurate drawing of the skeleton."

It *would* take a village to prepare a grave big enough for a gray whale. The plan was to bury the whale in a huge pit so that the flesh would decompose but bears and other large scavengers wouldn't disturb the body and scatter the bones. It took four days for Studebaker to get the proper permissions and assemble an expert group of volunteers to figure out how to preserve the whale for possible future rearticulation. A local contractor, Mike Anderson, used his track hoe to dig an eight-foot deep, forty-foot-long burial pit. He wrapped a heavy chain around the whale's tail and with his trusty track hoe towed the whale's body up the beach to the trench that was now as big as a ravine. Volunteers carefully lined the pit with blue porous landscaping fabric so they could find the body later. The whale was then rolled into the trench and covered with more soil and sand.

Witnessing such communal devotion on this beach was deeply moving. Here were people engaged not only in conservation, but also respectfully honoring a neighbor or mammal cousin who deserved to be remembered.

Of special concern was the preservation of the tiny digits inside the whale's flippers," Studebaker explained. "So, we wrapped the whale's flippers in fabric and duct tape to make mittens. In many museum whale skeletons these finger bones are often lost. We wanted to preserve a complete skeleton."

It was a huge experiment with many unknowns: The biggest question was how long would it take a 36-foot whale's flesh to decompose underground in cold Alaskan soil? Three or four years? Ten? *Some said never.* Was there enough bacteria and small scavengers in the sand for total decomposition?

At the burial, volunteers sprinkled cowpies from a nearby cattle ranch into the pit to add more bacteria to help with the decomposition. Three years after burial, as the gray whale lay deep underground, the Kodiak National Wildlife Refuge asked Studebaker if her buried gray whale might become part of a permanent display in the new visitor center they were planning for downtown Kodiak. "I was overjoyed at this idea! Someday, the whale would have a permanent home!"

"By 2004, I was really getting anxious," Studebaker told me in recent follow-up interviews. "I'd have dreams of what might be happening underground to our gray whale. I'd go visit the burial site where the ground was sinking above the whale, which was an indication that something must be going on down there."

In May 2004, the Kodiak Fish and Wildlife Service teamed up with Studebaker's volunteers to dig a test pit to determine the state of the bones. "We dug down through the sand and hit bare bones," she said delightedly. "So, we planned to excavate the entire skeleton that following August."

Mike Anderson returned, using the track hoe to carefully scrape away the sand down to the skeleton, creating a wide terraced pit. Then by hand, volunteers excavated the whale bones one by one, using large, industrial, stainless-steel spoons to scrape off the excess sand and tissue. It took three days to get the whale bones out—all of the ribs, vertebrae, the long jawbones, the huge skull, and the pectoral fins with all finger bones still beautifully intact.

Studebaker sent me many photos of the laborious process of resurrecting the whale. They included portraits of three little girls proudly hoisting one of the whale's heavy, knobby vertebrae, of a mother and her young daughter in their turquoise and pink scrub gloves cleaning a rib bone, and of townspeople deep inside the trench in white forensics suits, flensing the last flesh off the long-buried skeleton.

"It was really stinky work since the blubber and organs had turned into a gelatinous soup," Studebaker laughed. "But still we had an overwhelming amount of people who bravely volunteered to come in shifts."

"We transported all the bones to town where we washed them first, then let them sit outside at a nearby NOAA facility for nine months, so the bones could drip fat. It was important to make sure all of the fat was out of those bones so that it would not later discolor the bones or drip on the floor beneath the skeleton displayed in a heated room," Studebaker said.

Since she lacked the knowledge for preserving and rearticulating the skeleton, she recruited Lee Post, an expert on whale bone skeletons in nearby Homer. He coached Studebaker and her volunteers through the entire process, and he created a rearticulation design for the whale so that it would fit into the new Kodiak Refuge Visitor Center. Holes were drilled in the vertebrae and strung onto a steel pipe to form the main structure of the whale. Vertebrae were strung in order and locked in place, with clear silicon caulking replacing cartilage. Other bones were pinned together with steel rods. Custom metal pieces had to be fabricated by a local welder. All of the bone work was done at a nearby fisheries facility and stored there, awaiting the completion of the visitor center. In October 2007, all assembled parts of the whale skeleton were moved in five big pieces into the new visitor center on Kodiak Island.

"We worked for three long days up to Halloween night. Curious trick-or-treaters were knocking on our windows, looking at the whale, like it was some kind of monster," Studebaker concluded. "When the skeleton was finally in place, we cracked a bottle of champagne and toasted the whale."

To have this seven-year project finally complete, surrounded by the people who helped, was an emotional moment for Studebaker. The whale was magnificent, elegantly suspended from the ceiling in a large dark ocean blue room under dramatic lighting.

"When visitors come now to see the gray whale at the visitor center, read our photo essay, and hear about the volunteers who honored this whale, they are mostly interested in the human story behind the whale skeleton."

Today the gray whale skeleton is much cherished in Kodiak, not just by all the islanders who helped make this elegant rearticulation possible, but also by the visitors, including many cruise ship tourists, who all marvel at the impressive skeleton. The whale still seems to float, dangling from the ceiling. It hangs eye level to viewers from the second floor above the entrance to the visitor center. You can view the whale from all sides.

"Many visitors are in awe of the gray whale," Studebaker told me. "Some people even say prayers to the whale. Most whale skeletons in older museums look so static and uninteresting," Studebaker explains. "But Lee Post's design for our whale's backbone is in a beautiful, more lifelike S-curve, sloping down, with its flippers out to the side as if steering. It looks like the whale is still swimming through the waves. It is a masterful piece of artful engineering."

So many gray whales wash up on our beaches that never receive this kind of reverence. But this one lives on, his bones a reminder of the fellow creatures who share our seas. Our human story has always included other animals. The stories these gray whales are telling now is a preview of our future. Climate change has continued to drastically change the gray whale's underwater world—and so our own. In 2019, Van Daele, a tribal biologist for the Sun-Aq tribe, recalled camping out on Kodiak's Pasagchak Point. Where once the elders had seen "smokestacks of water, thick with gray whales and humpbacks . . . that summer there was only silence."

If we simply pay close attention, listen to what animals are revealing to us about our shared waters, we may change our survival strategies. It will come as we acknowledge and remember them, keep the memory of lost animals, alongside memorials of our own. Telling stories that embrace animals using the respect and delight we employ for our own species' tales is vital to developing our own sense of compassion. A kinship not just for humans, but for all living and sentient beings.

It is especially vital that women, like Lupita, Alex, or Stacy Studebaker, study and reclaim nature. Our nurturing skills are essential to preserving our own, and other, species. Women are actively helping to define this new century of the living wild, with our survival skills of cooperation and preservation, instead of conquest and exploitation. We seek not only adventure but also intimacy, connection, and a healthy habitat for children. In this time of dwindling wilderness and massive species extinction, girls belong in the woods and on the waves. A woman's place, more than ever, is in the wild.

BELUGA BABY

SOMETIMES ANIMALS CALL on us to expand our own beliefs and assumptions about life—and death. Connecting with a pregnant beluga whale, Mauyak, modeled both grief and hope for me. In 1992, when I was first invited by Alan, one of the young beluga's keepers, to meet Mauyak at Point Defiance Zoo in Tacoma, Washington, I was startled by the beluga's openness.

"Mauyak's got some good moves," Alan laughed as Mauyak spurted me with water, then swam backward. "Especially for a whale who's thirteen months pregnant!"

That affectionate play was on display even in the limited circumference of the zoo tank as Shikku, a younger female beluga; Inuk, a male beluga; and Mauyak all frolicked with a tiny harbor porpoise aptly named Magic.

Mauyak at ten years old *was* huge, gleaming a ghostly white as she twirled in the pool. She was 11 feet long and 1,500 pounds—as long as an SUV and as much as a VW Beetle. Underwater, Magic darted between the three belugas. The juvenile porpoise was all mischief as he stroked Mauyak's belly with his snout and snapped at Inuk over a float toy. And then, in a twirling ballet, Magic shot straight up out of the water, dived down deep again, at last nipping at Shikku's open mouth in a series of small kisses. The air echoed with squeaks and high-pitched shrills as the whales and dolphin carried on their own conversations.

Mauyak means "soft snow" in Inuit, referencing their home Arctic waters. She was born in 1982 and captured in Canada's Hudson Bay on July 9, 1984. Pregnant for the first time, Mauyak lived up to the "sea canary" reputation of all belugas, with complex calls: bird-like chirping, ultrasonic chirrups, urgent tweets, creaks and farts, rapid-fire whistle bursts, some hilarious *harumphing* like chimpanzees, and an eerie space-age ricochet like a sci-fi soundtrack. Belugas make more sounds than any

other species, except us. Sometimes belugas even sound like humans
researchers in British Columbia's Vancouver Aquarium claim that their
captive belugas vocalize their own names, having spent so many years
around people. Many researchers, like my friend Jim Nollman, author of
The Beluga Café, believe that "of all animals, belugas are the most likely to
possess a true language."

Jim spent three years recording and listening to belugas in frigid
waters with a team from the Russian Academy of Science. (YouTube has
many audio clips of Jim playing music with other animals, from cetaceans
to birds.) In the wild, belugas will live twenty-five to thirty years. Jim and
his colleagues were trying to test their theory that belugas have a language. He notes, "How ironic that the most likely candidate for ET living
right here in the oceans of planet Earth now exists on the edge of extinction." Long hunted, belugas are understandably shy around humans. But
among their own pods, belugas are some of the most sociable and gregar-
ious of all whales. Mauyak's sociable generosity embraced me she swam
over to greet us.

"Offer her your hand," Alan smiled and instructed me. "It's her way of
sensing you with her sophisticated sonar."

On the dock, I knelt before Mauyak as she trilled and lifted her gleaming head to my hand. In response to her lively vocalizations, I sang a little
snippet of an upbeat Broadway tune, which Mauyak picked up and eerily
mimicked. In perfect rhythm to my staccato beat, Mauyak harmonized
with her clicks, pops, and a long whistle like a one-whale band accompanying me.

I placed my palm on her shining head and felt it expand to sound me.
Mauyak's round forehead throbbed as she also sang out a blast of beluga
calls through her blowhole. I could feel the vibrations of her voice, like
touching a snare drum as it shimmers and trembles against the palms.
Whale skin is seven times more sensitive than human skin. Astonishingly
cool and elastic, Mauyak's forehead felt like the silken skin of honeydew
melon. The elegant buoyancy, the vibrations under your hand, is hard to
explain. She uses her huge, oil-filled melon for echolocation, its sonar
pulse under my palm like a gigantic heartbeat.

Otherworldly, I thought as I watched that white dome swell and retreat like a wave rippling atop her head. Like meeting an alien mind that moves alongside mine, but so unfathomably. I could only rest my hand on such a mind as it worked, scanned, recorded, and responded with whale music. All I knew was that the physical sensation of Mauyak's sonar was a blissful communion, a knowing and sensory conversation between species.

Even though my palm was flat on this huge creature's tongue, I did not feel an iota of fear. With one flick of her mighty flukes, she could have damaged my hand and dragged me underwater, her massive bulk easily drowning me. But a beluga has never in documented history harmed a human. They treat us with the mothering kindness of a gentle giant toward a young species still struggling to understand. It is as if they wish to do no harm.

I softly crooned some jazzy riffs, and Mauyak harmonized with whistles, grunts, moos, and groans. All the cetaceans in the tank joined in. My scat-singing was not as spectacularly high as Magic's ultrasonic dolphin bleeps when he accompanied me with his manic counterpoint. Nor as rhythmically sophisticated as Mauyak's staccato trills and Shikku's bass notes that sounded like a rusty door's hinge.

As I sang, Mauyak rolled on her side to loll and look up at me with her unblinking dark eye. Eye contact, like sound, is a primary way of communicating with cetaceans. They have excellent eyesight, both underwater and above. To be truly seen by a wild animal feels astonishing. As Mauyak raised herself up higher on the dock to get a better look at this singing human, she held me in her steady regard.

Exchanging this intimate gaze with an animal was not at all like looking in a mirror, like the way it feels with a domestic cat or dog. Scientists have now documented cetaceans are self-aware; that means when they look in a mirror, they recognize themselves, not just some unknown image. What is it they see?

"We know so damn little about belugas," Alan said, nodding and humming along companionably as Mauyak turned her head to include him in her scrutiny, "especially about their birthing."

The zoo staff was nervous about Mauyak's impending birth. It was only a month away. The statistics are grim. Fifty percent of firstborn belugas die, even in the wild.

"Of the eight belugas born in captivity so far, only two have survived," Alan continued, trying to keep any worry from his voice.

Mauyak, like most cetaceans, was extremely sensitive to human emotions. That's why Alan had approved my singing to her such silly and complicated songs—to engage her big brain and ease some of the discomfort from her pregnancy. Even after twenty years of researching and working with dolphins and whales, we only know a quarter of what we should about cetaceans.

"The limits, you know, are not in the whales," Alan noted. "They are in us."

He told me about an experiment he'd conducted, in which he placed eye cups on dolphins and asked them to recognize certain symbols using their echolocation. "It took me months to design that experiment," Alan said, laughing. "And those dolphins learned the symbols in five minutes."

So, he had to create a more difficult problem. But each time they kept quickly figuring it out until he no longer had the technology to test their abilities. The last, most sophisticated test Alan could design asked them to discern, while blindfolded, a symbol through their sonar that was only one-thousandth of an inch square.

"They aced that, too!" Alan concluded. "While the dolphins were at it, they also identified different carbon densities in metal rods and differentiated colors."

Recently, human technology has come up with our own sophisticated sonar. According to John Sutphen, a medical doctor who is also involved with cetaceans, human ultrasound can already hear "the flow of blood through the microscopic capillaries of the fingers . . . as a veritable roar." Cetacean sonar is far beyond what we've yet devised. Whales use their echolocation to hear one another's bodies and therefore read each other's emotional states. Their echolocation can bounce off the inside cavities of the body, listening and gauging the echoes sounding from the brain, the heart, the kidneys, liver, even the ovaries.

In *Mind in the Waters*, Sutphen writes that "cetaceans are aware of each other's health and general well-being. Cancers and tumors must be self-evident. Strokes and heart attacks are as obvious as moles on our skins." Along with scanning the physiological state, cetaceans can recognize emotional fluctuations such as "sexual arousal, fear, depression, and excitement."

I was reluctant to say goodbye to Mauyak, keenly aware that her imminent labor in such a small pool, even though she had the best of veterinary care, was risky. I wondered, as I rested my hand one last time on her forehead, *Would she be able to safely deliver her first calf?*

"I'll be thinking of you, Mauyak," I called out as I took my leave. She spun and circled the pool, chirping. "Good luck with the birth."

I eagerly awaited word from Alan about the birth of Mauyak's calf. But when he called, I already had heard the news on the radio. During the birth, the young female beluga, Shikku, was in the pool with Mauyak in the hope that, as in the wild, she might assist with the birth. Often a family member of the pod will act as a midwife, lifting the newborn to the surface for the first breath. Researchers have noted that some newborn calves have teeth marks on their dorsal fins where auntie midwives have pulled them out of the womb—the way humans use our hands. Of course, Shikku was too young to know how to help Mauyak. Neither whale had any training from a family pod, as they would in the wild.

For hours, Mauyak corkscrewed and twisted painfully in the small pool. She couldn't travel far and spin through the waves to ease and encourage her long labor. Mauyak kept rolling over the zoo's scuba divers in a slow-motion embrace, as if trying to ease her labor pain. Finally, a bloody slate-gray newborn calf struggled out, flukes first, and floated to the surface.

"Everyone started cheering and clapping," Alan told me on the phone. "But the 150-lb. calf just floated too quietly, then started sinking. His little black eyes on each side of his head were darting back and forth—so we knew he was alive. But the baby seemed to be struggling for air." Alan paused to gather himself, his voice shaking.

Alan forced himself to continue. "I yelled to another researcher to grab the calf and pull him back up to the surface to see if he was breathing."

In the bloody pool, a diver-biologist cradled the newborn. Desperately he gave artificial respiration to the tiny, gray calf.

"Breathe! Breathe!" the zoo staff shouted urgently.

But the baby beluga's eyes fixed, wide open. He died in the man's arms.

"That baby never took a first breath," Alan finished, choking with emotion. "We just did a necropsy and found out that his blowhole valve was somehow disengaged, broken, maybe in all the intense labor. Otherwise the calf was perfect."

"Perfect," I found myself echoing softly, as if that was any solace.

Alan told me that he'd stayed with Mauyak for hours after the birth as she thrashed about in confusion. All Mauyak did was push her dead calf around in the pool, mournfully. In the wild, a mother cetacean who loses her calf will keep the corpse of her newborn with her, perhaps even until it disintegrates.

"We had to make a terrible decision," Alan explained. "Did we let Mauyak keep her dead calf in the pool or whisk the baby away for a necropsy to determine the cause of death?"

What Alan did not have to say was that in a zoo, the sight of a mother beluga pushing a dead calf around a pool would not make for good audience entertainment.

"Did Mauyak even know her calf was dead before they took him away?" I had to ask. "Did she get any chance to say goodbye?"

Alan lowered his voice. "No," he said. "I think she's very angry with all of us. That's why she won't make eye contact or connect. All she does is push her float toy around the pool, as if this was her lost calf."

He asked me to come visit again. He hoped that maybe Mauyak might relate better to an outsider—or someone she remembered singing with her before this loss.

I made the trip again to Point Defiance Zoo. Though it was still summer, there was a palpable shadow over the zoo. I could feel it in the way the staff didn't greet me but looked down.

"I haven't been back with her since the birth . . . I mean, since the death," Alan admitted as he escorted me to the beluga exhibit. There were very few visitors—the loss of Mauyak's calf had been front-page news. The whole city mourned with her.

The great white whale, with her mouth permanently shaped in a seeming smile, drifted in the chlorinated waters.

"Mauyak won't even look us in the eye," Alan frowned. "She's shunning her keepers. Maybe you can connect with her again."

As we approached the pool, Shikku and Inuk greeted Alan, whom they'd known for over four years, with tweets and a singsong whistle stream. But Mauyak retreated to the back pool. She now balanced a red rubber buoy on her pale forehead.

"In the wild," Alan explained, "if a mother whale can't hold onto the real newborn's dead body, she will find a net, a piece of wood, even sometimes another carcass, to carry as her lost surrogate calf."

It was almost unbearable to witness the change in Mauyak. She swam in tight circles in her back pool, oblivious to any humans or her cetacean companions. Worst of all, she was utterly silent. I wondered if she would ever sing again.

I waited on the dock, hoping she might recognize me—whales have extraordinary memories in those big brains of theirs. I took some comfort in the antics of Inuk and Shikku, spouting water up at me and whistling.

Alan brought me to the back pool where Mauyak swam alone. As I sat cross-legged on the dock and began singing, I noticed that Alan moved away, as if to give Mauyak and me some privacy.

What did I sing that moment, trying to find harmony between species with this mournful mother? I sang what I'd heard at every funeral since childhood—a hymn that is both haunting and healing.

Amazing grace, how sweet the sound . . .
I once was lost and now am found

I've also chanted this timeless spiritual at animal funerals—from a great gray whale in Baja to seal pups riddled with bullets on my backyard beach to LuLu, the great husky dog love of my life. It is a song that is solace to any species.

As I sang, I stretched out my hand. Mauyak slowly swam over to me and lifted herself up with her pectoral fins. I think she recognized me. Rising out of the water, she slid her huge forehead under my hand, like a cat. My open palm again tingled with the cool elegance of whale skin, like wet, raw silk being slipped sensually through my fingers.

I continued singing to her, patting Mauyak's forehead with an elegiac hum between verses. Tears streamed down my cheeks as I shared this mother's sorrow.

I once was blind,
but now I see . . .

Suddenly a stream of ultrasonic whistles ricocheted in rhythm from Mauyak's blowhole as she sounded me. As I sang with Mauyak, mourning the loss of her first calf together, she again opened her gigantic mouth to take my small hand inside.

"Good. Good," Alan murmured. "Keep singing."

The great whale's pink tongue was soft and cool as a baby's face against my palm. Forehead still throbbing, Mauyak opened her black eye wide to bond again with me. There was despair, but also trust. As Mauyak tenderly held my hand in her mouth, I wondered: *Are whales somehow carrying our species in this world—the way cetaceans will mournfully carry a dying calf or lift a newborn up to the surface to survive?*

I felt lifted by Mauyak, even in her grief. As I once again surrendered my open palm to Mauyak's mouth, I believed she held the whole of me—deeply, tenderly. Her eyes also possessed me: unblinking, utterly aware. A great wave of grief washed over me as I finished the hymn, and she stopped her whistling accompaniment. Between us, there was calm and clear stillness.

"I know . . ." I said softly. "I know."

Mauyak gently eased her mouth away and let my hand float in the water near her jaw. She turned on her side, without breaking our gaze. Then she let out a long series of clicks and low tweets. She swam across the pool to retrieve her floating buoy—the baby that will never disintegrate, who couldn't stay in the world with her, the counterfeit calf.

Mauyak brought her buoy-baby back to me and drifted just out of arm's reach, again holding my eye with hers. We kept that gaze for so long it seemed that together we held the whole world between us.

There was a small crowd gathered nearby the beluga exhibit, as if attending an interspecies funeral for the lost calf. "That's her *pretend* baby beluga," one of the children informed the other kids as they watched Mauyak carrying her red buoy.

"The beluga baby is in heaven now, sweetie," a mother reassured the kids.

Another woman shook her head, but sadly, instructing her little boy, "Too bad there's no heaven for animals."

The child shook his head in protest. It reminded me of my own early outrage and disbelief in the narrow dogma that excludes animals from spiritual practice and shared afterlives—a Western concept of heaven, in which everyone but us is extinct. Are we, here below as above, unconsciously enacting a mythical and lonely heaven-on-Earth as we watch species after species die out? How did we get so separated from our fellow animals that many of our religions imagine heaven to be a place where only humans live forever, denied animal companionship?

In so many ways, humans have granted the spiritual realms of emotion and perception to only our species. By denying animals their full range of emotions, by banishing animals from our afterlives, we make it easier to accept a world without them alongside us in this life. That's perhaps why many religions are not deeply alarmed at a degraded earth and ecosystems with massive animal extinctions. Losing animals in our future is akin to destroying them in our imagined afterlives. How clearly does this self-centered world view betray our isolation and solitude here on earth? Our solitary confinement.

Older stories, whether American Indian, Euro pagan, or even Old Testament, are inexorably bonded with animals. Many Indigenous peoples divide their members into animal clans and believed animals were their ancestors, the First Peoples. In some spiritual traditions, like Hinduism and animism, human souls reincarnate as animals. As science at last begins to grant other animals a rich emotional life, perhaps our religions will also begin to accept, as every child knows, that animals belong with us in any afterlife.

Mauyak has had quite an afterlife since she lost her first calf at Point Defiance. Belugas, especially in the wild, have a lifespan of thirty-five to seventy years. A second calf, born in 1992, also died shortly after birth. In 1997, when Mauyak was sixteen, she was moved from Point Defiance Zoo to Chicago's Shedd Aquarium. After giving birth to four calves at Shed, "Mauyak has proven herself to be an attentive and protective mother," says an aquarium manager.

I keep up with Mauyak, and her many calves, in the news and on Facebook links. Mauyak even has her own Wiki fan page. I sometimes watch the YouTube video of her most recent newborn calf swimming alongside her, and I remember harmonizing in elegy with Mauyak over her firstborn—that gleaming white beluga baby who was so perfect, but never took his first breath. In 2019, Mauyak at thirty-eight, successfully gave birth to her latest calf. There is a video of Mauyak and her new-born calf rolling over Mauyak's luminous flanks, the calf swimming so close, face-to-face. What researchers have learned from caring for captive pregnant belugas like Mauyak has helped them in rescue, rehab, and release efforts in wild populations. In 2019, the Shedd Aquarium's Animal Response Team joined with a team of experts in Alaska "to provide triage for a stranded beluga calf that was part of the critically endangered population of Cook Inlet belugas."

As much as I celebrate that Mauyak is alive and has been a devoted mother to many calves, I will always feel the haunting sorrow of her captivity. It would be, for humans, like living in a single bedroom all our lives. Belugas can dive to depths of one thousand feet and travel many miles a day. In 2016, In Defense of Animals cited Shedd Aquarium as number ten on their worst tanks list, which "exposes and represents the misery and suffering of some of the ocean's most intelligent and complex mammals in captivity." I dream of a day when Mauyak and other socially sophisticated and family-loving cetaceans don't swim in endless circles and sing

without their family pods in a cement tank for a lifetime. I dearly wish
Raffi's rhythmic children's song were true for all cetaceans:

Baby Beluga in the deep blue sea
Swim so wild and you swim so free.

The antidote to captive cetaceans is always to witness them free and wild.
When researching the gray whales, I also visited Alaska's Cook Inlet,
which is home to another population of belugas. The inlet's Indigenous
name is Nuti, or "salt water," and the water is murky from glacial silt. In
the long light of midnight-sun summer, several of us posted ourselves at
Beluga Point in Cook Inlet in the hope of catching a glimpse of the white
whales. In the US, most belugas live in Alaska in five separate populations
inhabiting Eastern Chukchi, Beaufort, and Eastern Bering Seas, and
Bristol Bay, in addition to Cook Inlet.

Listed under the Endangered Species Act (ESA) in 2008 as critically
endangered, the Cook Inlet population has ranged between 300 to 1,300
individuals between 1994 and 2000. By June 2023, there were between 290
and 386 belugas, with a medium estimate of 331 in this small, only endangered, Alaska population. Cook Island belugas have declined by about 75
percent, due to loss of food, like shrimp, fish, and seals, as well as chemical
pollution and warming waters. Before subsistence hunting was regulated
in 1999, Tubughana whalers voluntarily ended their subsistence hunt;
other tribes in the US and First Nations in BC continued hunting belugas, with the last US hunt in 2005. The vulnerable Cook Inlet belugas have
not yet recovered, but recent research suggests the population may have
slightly increased by 0.2 percent.

"This distinct population of beluga whales is only found in Cook Inlet,"
explains Mandy Migura, NOAA's Recovery Coordinator for Cook Inlet.
"So, if they go extinct, we don't think belugas will come back to repopulate the inlet."

Residents have organized to help scientists in their annual "Belugas
Count" event to discover the white whale's feeding grounds, study their

behavior, and raise awareness of their plight. There's a particular cove that belugas like to navigate, and researchers always look for the quick surface of that "bright, white hump, against the very gray sediment-filled waters of this inlet," says Danielle Grabiel, Senior Policy Analyst of the EIA (Environmental Investigation Agency). They also listen with hydrophones to the multitudinous vocalizations—gurgles, moans, and squeals.

Because belugas summer so near Anchorage, Alaska's largest city, there is noise pollution from boat traffic that limits the whales' ability to hunt and communicate. It's difficult to determine the health of these belugas because Cook Inlet is so muddy, with strong riptides. Researchers have been limited to studying them at the surface, whenever they can spot them in social pods. But because they lack a dorsal fin, viewing them with binoculars from boats is not as accurate as recent drone footage, especially when measuring and counting the annual birth of beluga calves. Drones help distinguish each beluga by photo ID, a technique used by researchers to identify specific individuals of other species, like that used for pods of resident orcas on the Northwest and British Columbian coasts. Satellite imagery is also helping scientists keep track of the Cook Inlet belugas.

Defenders of Wildlife and Beluga Whale Alliance are working together to help bring this dwindling and isolated population back from the brink of extinction. In 2021, they posted their second annual "Belugapalooza!" YouTube Zoom webinar to talk about what's being done to help recover this precious population.

"Research takes place on traditional land," explains Native researcher Jen Christopherson, "where Indigenous peoples have co-existed closely with these belugas for thousands of years and Native peoples have long been conserving other species." The Tubughana tribe respects belugas as sentinels of the Native village of Tyonek.

Paul Wade, of NOAA's Marine Mammal Laboratory, notes that warmer waters in the rivers, which feed Cook Inlet are causing heat stress. "When animals are not doing well, it takes longer for them to reach full maturity and breed," he explains. Researchers are working against time to figure out why this population is still not recovering. Every year, the public can get involved in seasonal counts and monitoring Cook Inlet belugas. There is a lot of interest in these citizen science efforts; people can sign up for updates and virtually train as volunteers and help report beluga sightings or strandings.

When I first visited Cook Inlet, there were more belugas than there are today. I had heard the chances were very good to spot these gray ghosts. Intently watching from the green shores of Beluga Point, I was very aware that I might be witnessing the last of a population as it struggled to survive. Because of my encounters with Mauyak, I have always had an abiding fondness for belugas. For hours, I sat in the cool, summer sunlight, binoculars hanging heavy on my chest, munching trail mix, and waiting hopefully for a sighting.

After hours of watching, I was just about to give up, declare my vigil an enjoyable picnic, when I heard a blow—quick bright breaths on dark water. The sound of wild cetacean breathing most alerts me to their vibrant presence. My body comes alive when I hear that moist *whoosh* of exhalation, then the deep intake of air—inspiration. A hush fell over the inlet as a huge, white whale surfaced so near, and then a gray-blue calf, swimming alongside in perfect synch, breathing together.

It was as if Mauyak, perfect calf in tow, had returned to the wild, her chilly birthright. For one seemingly eternal moment, the beluga mother surfaced, and I caught glimpse of that great, black, unblinking eye. My hands tingled with the audible memory of Mauyak sounding me—body and soul. Whistles and squeaks carried to shore on the mild breeze, scented with wild roses. Mother and calf spyhopped, spun, and splashed. Listening to their sweet, ultrasonic arpeggios, I wished I could telepath to Mauyak this beluga music of her kin in artic waters.

Heaven still on earth.

LISTENING TO THE
SEA BREATHING

WILL WE EVER break the code and learn the language of other species? That dialogue would transform our relationship with animals. In British Columbia, on a remote, mist-shrouded island of thousand-year-old trees, OrcaLab researchers are listening to Northern Resident killer whales as they glide, leap, and greet each other at gatherings of family clans called super pods. For decades, neuroscientist and cetologist Paul Spong, the founder of OrcaLab, as well as Greenpeace, has been recording these orcas. He has been joined for more than twenty years by Helena Symonds, his partner both as researcher and spouse. They have stayed here on this largely uninhabited Hanson Island studying the orcas who also make this cold, fertile Northwest coast their seasonal home.

I was visiting OrcaLab with Kelly Balcomb, the model for the boy in the famous "Free Willie" movies and son of the respected, late orca researcher Ken Balcomb, who long documented Southern Resident orcas in the Pacific Northwest.

Orcas have much to teach us about sound and communication. We cannot even begin to appreciate their extraordinary skills of echolocation—*seeing* with ultrasound—without OrcaLab's invaluable research on the Northern Resident orcas. Echolocation is a kind of animal sonar that uses sound waves and echoes bounced off their surroundings to better navigate. Bats and dolphins use their superb echolocating skills at night and in dark caves or waters. Some blind people have also developed echolocation to make their way through the world by making clicking sounds and listening to the echoes to move around.

Using a sophisticated system of underwater hydrophones along the Johnstone Strait, OrcaLab researchers can record what Symonds calls "sound sculptures," the complicated vocalizations of orca socializing. These sculptures are so intricate they require a well-trained ear and computers to fathom. Over the decades, Spong and Symonds have learned to identify the signature calls and dialects of Northern Resident family clans.

"Oh," Symonds nods as she hears a high-pitched and rather sweet mewling like distant kittens, "here come the A30s."

Headphones over her silver-blonde head, she sets several giant tape recorders spinning. Her weather-beaten laboratory is so shrouded in fog, there is nothing to see but wet streaks of low-slung clouds. Yet it's hard to feel closed in when we are surrounded by exuberant and rapid-fire bursts, the clicks and eerie arpeggios of ultrasound, some ranging far above our human hearing.

"Remember, this is *live!*" Symonds says. "Just close your eyes and you'll hear the orcas better." Symonds hands me a set of headphones as I take my seat on a rickety lab chair.

I eavesdrop on a wild symphony of orcas calling out and escorting each other through the cold, deep waters along the Strait. Much of the high-frequency conversation is above my hearing range, but I can still sense it as a faint, vibrating echo.

OrcaLab's approach is to listen in, record, and learn to recognize orcas by their voices, adding this to the photo-documenting of their dorsal fins done by other marine mammal researchers. However, they acknowledge that humans may never be able to translate orca vocalizations. But we can try.

These Northern Resident orcas are some of the best studied and most popular of all marine mammals. The killer whale is so well loved in the far Northwest that there is even an Orca-FM radio station devoted to airing the live whale vocalizations for a Canadian audience. With the news in 1999 that orcas off Canadian and Washington State waters were the most heavily contaminated marine mammals in the world, Canada officially declared their Northern Residents endangered; Washington would follow, petitioning for protection in 2005 for Southern Resident orcas.

Half of firstborn orca calves in the Southern Resident pods die in their first year. In Washington State, Southern Resident orcas are also starving because salmon stocks are dwindling; as of 2023, there were only seventy-five orcas left in the cherished J, K, and L pods. In BC, the Northern Residents are also struggling to survive.

As a search for solutions intensifies—removing dams that block salmon streams, decreasing toxic runoff from farming and human pollution, limiting whale-watching boats and container ship traffic—the non-invasive, land-based research at OrcaLab is even more critical.

"Can studying orcas teach us how to communicate better?" I ask Symonds. "How to live sustainably within our own species—and with orcas."

"Listening is such an important skill," she says. "In *any* species. Our ability to understand what we are listening to is our main research tool." Symonds pauses and smiles. "Hear those calls coming through the speakers? That's the A36s."

Clasping the headphones to my ears, I listen to the busy serenade of this orca clan as they cruise by the lab.

"Within each clan," she continues, "there are a number of pods that share an acoustic tradition passed on from generation to generation through the orca mothers," Symonds answers. "Members of a pod are closely related, like an extended family, and they all make the same calls. After so many years of listening and recording these calls, we can tune our ears into their vocalizations. It's just a matter of becoming familiar with their voices."

Much the way we humans recognize a familiar voice, the orcas' calls are so well-known to OrcaLab researchers that they can identify signature whistles by individual. Now, the orcas chirp and send descant echoes around the research station.

Symonds listens intently then nods. "Hear that call? That's very distinctive of the A36s—the mother, Sophia, and her three sons, Cracroft, Plumper, and Kaikash."

We listen intently as the giant tape recorders whirr.

"This orca mother and her adult sons will spend every day of their lives together. Think about that kind of incredible bonding. Only death or capture will separate them. This longevity provides a great deal of stability in orca society. Each orca knows his or her place in the family, the pod, the community. They are very secure."

"Some researchers believe that cetaceans are actually much smarter than humans," I venture.

Symonds smiles. "Orcas have the second-largest brain of all animals, almost four times the size of a human brain and at least as complex. A good memory is certain. Orcas must learn many skills and memorize huge geographical areas. Their range is hundreds of kilometers long, a maze of islands and waterways. All this knowledge is stored and retrieved with ease."

Then Symonds tells me of one August night when a family pod passed the lab. "They spyhopped, slipping up from the surface in a sly, vertical twirl," she says. "They rushed northward as the long, summer twilight finally gave way to the night, and a spectacular show of Northern Lights held us spellbound. Soon the lab was filled with the sounds of whales breathing and calls upon calls, a virtual mirror with the Northern Lights gleaming above us as almost a hundred whales paraded past under a full moon." Symonds pauses. "It's not hard to guess why I stay here, is it?"

The awe in her bright eyes was akin to the reverence I've observed with many cetacean researchers as they study these other "minds in the waters." It's the way I've often felt when swimming with wild dolphins as they escort me deeper into their underwater realms, their sonar scanning my body in pings and clicks as if to imprint upon all my senses their own way of knowing the liquid world.

It's getting late in the lab and several of the research interns leave for supper in the main cabin. But Symonds and I linger to keep listening to the hydrophone symphonies. At last she concludes, her expression pensive.

"Sometimes, when it's late at night, when the sea is smooth and velvety under the moon and the whales are passing by, I just listen to the sea breathing," she says softly. "I believe staying here in one place, listening, not chasing, has changed me. We humans have so few models in our history of successful peaceful coexistence within families and societies. Orcas have all of this. They can teach us—if we can only listen."

Raptly, I listen to orca vocalizations for several days more in the research station. Even our guest cabin is outfitted with speakers broadcasting from hydrophones all night long. It is wonderful to be surrounded by other people who basically live in their headphones. But we are not listening to human music, only the wild vocalizations of orcas.

My last night at OrcaLab, I awaken from a vivid dream of a dolphin pod congregating around the dock below our cabin. I had not noticed the lab's small dock when we first arrived. But in my dream, I see it in exact detail—the mossy wood, a research motorboat bobbing, a few bright, red kayaks. The dream's soundtrack is the exuberant click trains and fast whistles of Pacific white-sided dolphins, accompanied by the rhythmic clunk of fiberglass kayaks against the dock, the shrill cry of seagulls, the thud of the motorboat's floats against wood, the clanging of the anchor chain against its buoy.

That next morning at a robust breakfast with the researchers, I tell them about my exhilarating dolphin dream.

"Yes," Symonds nods, consulting the hydrophone log. "That was about 3:30 a.m. when a super pod of dolphins gathered around our dock. You must have heard them through the cabin's hydrophone speakers," she smiles slowly. "But you also *saw* them in your dreams."

Symonds studies me intently to make sure I grasp the possible implications of my dream vision. My mind is spinning. Did she mean that the cetacean vocalizations also somehow carry images? Is that how dolphins communicate: in high-frequency sound waves that also telegraph pictures? Sound sculptures, indeed.

Think of it as dolphins' acoustic YouTube. Dolphin scientists have already realized that cetacean echolocation is more sophisticated than we can yet grasp. A dolphin can hear so much more than we do. Is that sound also visual?

"So, you're saying that when I was dreaming and actually hearing real dolphin vocalizations through the cabin's hydrophones, those ultrasounds might also carry real-time images?"

"Come down to the dock and see for yourself," Symonds says.

We clamber down from the research center lab to the dock and there it is: The exact picture of the motorboat and kayaks that I'd seen, *not* in my waking life, but in my dream. How had the dolphins acoustically communicated a video scene, a location, a perfect visual replica that was somehow encoded in their calls and whistles?

"It's like an acoustic hologram," I marvel, trying again to grasp the cetacean technology.

"Imagine the possibilities," Symonds suggests.

Perhaps this cetacean communication skill predates the human invention of wireless streaming audio/video now on our phones and our televisions. Cetacean internet.

"Dolphin TV!" I exclaim.

Later that morning as we take our leave of OrcaLab, the A clan accompanies our research boat, leaping and breaching and spyhopping, as if to assure us safe passage on these frigid waters. Two of the orcas, a young mom, Simoon, and her calf, Misty, stay with us. Misty veers off and ventures toward our research boat. We stop and shut off the engine. Misty swims close to the boat in the clear water. She looks straight up at us for a long moment with that huge, dark, and wide-open eye—before swimming back to her mom and her pod.

"Do you think orcas are as aware of you and your researchers as you are of them?" I ask Symonds.

She laughs. "I don't know that orcas pay much attention to us. We're secondary to them. I suspect it doesn't take a lot of energy on their part to take us in. They can easily do it and keep going. I think the most important thing for orcas is themselves, their families, their society."

As if on cue, orcas leave our boat's wake to sail off and dive into the depths of Johnstone Strait. As we head back to Seattle by float plane and ferry, I ponder my dream vision and its evidence that dolphins might communicate both audio *and* visual information in their vocalizations. It seems a simple enough ability, given that they've had millions more years of evolution than humans. What other marvels have those big brains created that we have yet to discover or imagine for ourselves?

OrcaLab researchers may one day finally decipher orca vocalizations and understand another species' language, making orcas no longer so alien. As OrcaLab's Paul Spong says, "The very first time I listened through a hydrophone to the voice of a whale, moving freely through the sea, I knew I was poised just outside a gateway leading to knowledge vital to the human race: We are not alone."

WOLF MUSIC

WE ENCOUNTER WILD wolves not by sight, but by sound—that other-worldly, yet eerily familiar head-thrown-back, the heartfelt howling. It begins with one voice, a wolf solo lingering in rich, lonely mezzo, rising into higher octaves to tremble on falsetto or haunting, tenor half-notes. Then an echoing chorus of wolves joins in with ultrasonic whines, staccato barks and yelps, yipping counterpoints, cello-like bass moans, and a braided, beautifully dissonant harmony, slow to fade. Listening, wolf or human, we want this soul-stirring howling to go on and on. Who wouldn't instinctively respond to such a calling, an invitation, a memory?

We are instantly rapt, attentive, utterly entranced by wolves' voices. Listening to wolves sing changes us in ways that as humans we don't yet fathom, but still recognize. Our bodies instinctively resonate to a wolf howling and we move beyond opinions, politics, prejudice. In some strange way, when we hear wolves, we know that wild companionship still survives. We reorient ourselves from endless and artificial distractions. We unplug and profoundly tune in—for we are no longer alone in these dark woods.

Why do wolves howl? And do these complex vocalizations have a purpose? Howling is one vital way that wolves bond, locate, celebrate, and communicate themselves to one another and the world around them. Howling can be a call to community, a possessive signal claiming territory to alert a rival pack not to trespass; a dinner-call for other family members to come share a kill. The University of Cambridge led a team of international researchers to study the howling repertoires, or "vocal fingerprints" of wolves, in diverse geographical populations. The scientists discovered that wolves could be identified by at least twenty-one different dialects and accents. By studying sonograms and sound wave patterns of wolf howls, researchers realized that, like whales and birds, wolves were "controlling their singing and subject to cultural influences."

One of the researchers, Holly Root-Gutteridge of Syracuse University, wrote a fascinating essay, "The Songs of the Wolves," observing that animals "can be used as a model for humans, allowing us a window into an otherwise cryptic part of our own evolution." She explains that animals often vocalize in complex codes, distinct to their own species. For example, a prairie dog's alarm calls can encode the color and shape of a threatening predator; humpback whales sing across hundreds of miles to signal not only their location, but also call out the identity of their family group. The study asked the question: Is there a shared culture of howl-meanings among wolves? They discovered that wolf howls can transmit intent and meaning, like a musical language. This is a sure sign of culture in any species. Root-Gutteridge concludes, wolves are "like music bands with preferred styles of playing: riff-filled like jazz or the pure tones of classical."

It's difficult to follow wolves in the wild, but in the Cambridge study, scientists recorded six thousand howls from both wild and captive animals throughout the US, Europe, India, and Australia to understand wolf vocalizations. For example, red wolves, now near extinction, have cross-bred with coyotes in their only remaining North Carolina habitat. Red wolves and coyotes have similar howling vocabularies and that "may be one reason why they are so likely to mate with each other," says the study's lead scientist, Arik Kershenbaum, in a story published in the *Daily Mail*. Does this mean that wolves are attracted to howls like their own voices?

When studying other animals, scientists search for evidence that is observable and quantifiable, but artists look at their animal culture. There are quite a few scientists now who are beginning to discuss the idea that other animals, such as whales, elephants, chimpanzees, and wolves, all have a culture. In *The Cultural Lives of Whales and Dolphins*, biologist Hal Whitehead writes, "when culture takes hold of a species, everything changes." The late Alaskan wolf researcher Gordon Haber pointed out that wolves, with their strong family bonds and cooperative hunting skills passed down through generations, were "perhaps the most social of all non-human vertebrates," mirroring many of our human traditions. Every wolf group develops "its own unique adaptive behaviors and traditions; taken together, these can be considered a culture." Wolf howling also has meanings we can only interpret through our own use of language and yes, music. To complement the science of wolf vocalizations, why not ask musicians—those who have spent their lives listening—to help us understand the music of wild wolves?

In my search for musicians who are also listening to wolves, I was delighted to encounter French classical pianist Hélène Grimaud, who in 1996 cofounded the Wolf Conservation Center (WCC) in upstate New York. I asked this gifted musician about wolves: Why do we respond so profoundly to a chorus of howling wolves? Is our attention woven into our ancestral DNA, when we likely once listened out of fear or respect, or our ancestors located wolves on a kill so they could hungrily follow and survive on eating their scraps? Perhaps our human ears are warily perked to help us understand that we've entered territory shared by other equal top predators. Is it an attunement in our muscle memory and even our artistic enjoyment, which allows us to recognize another wilder and more ancient culture, another mesmerizing power?

"Wolves are uniquely individual, so why would we assume that the language is not? You can hear it. Every wolf has a distinct howl," Grimaud tells me in her quick, rhythmic French-accented English. "No two howls are the same. You can easily imagine that there are some wolf dialects that are pack or region specific, which develop from isolation or geographical location. And then it becomes a behavioral and cultural difference, as well. How wolves treat their neighbors, for example or handle family dynamics. So, their howling is an expression of those differences."

Grimaud speaks in thoughtful bursts and riffs, as if following a mindful musical score that is also scrawled over with notes on wolf science. An internationally acclaimed musician, she is known for practicing complex piano concertos not just on the keyboard but in her head. In her memoir, *Wild Harmonies: A Life of Music and Wolves*, she traces her musical development, interweaving it with the natural history of wolves and her own two decades of work with captive and displaced wolves at the Wolf Conservation Center.

"Why do wolves answer our human howls?" I ask Grimaud now.

"Perhaps wolves are generously non-discriminating," she says wryly. "One of the things that makes working with any wild animal so interesting and humbling is that you must interact with them on *their* terms. Often, they are quite forgiving of our bumbling attempts to connect in a proper and dignified way, in wolf terms. It could just be that the wolves interpret humans howling as an invasive threat from another pack. So, the wolves want to advertise that this territory is already occupied."

In the same way that wolves mark territory by scent, they also set sound barriers that other wolves might trespass at their own peril. It's intriguing to imagine what an acoustic map of wolf country would sound like—growls, guttural bluffs and *rubato* boasts, fortissimo barks, possessive, snarling scales, triplets of a groaning Greek chorus, a mournful undertone like a walking bass. And always the sonorous pulse and operatic range of howling wolves. Do wolves ever just sing to make complicated music, as we do?

"One of the most intriguing elements of wolf howling is what scientists call *social glue*," explains Grimaud. "This spreading of good feeling like humans singing around a campfire, feeling closer to one another. It's that same idea—you howl or harmonize and so reaffirm your social bonds with one another. That's not surprising. Any pack animal really depends upon the other to survive."

Certainly, humans are social pack animals. We are also profoundly moved by music, especially by making music together, like wolves. That's why the word "harmony" relates to both music and good, or harmonious, social skills. When we hear human music, we physically attune to that vibration; when we sing together, we blend our voices, matching thirds and fifths, those intervals between notes, like in the *do, re, mi, fa, so, la, ti, do* of C major. Though sometimes we are too close and create a clashing and minor dissonance. In harmony, we try to perfectly fit and find our part in the greater—and sometimes wilder—chorus.

Wolves also harmonize their voices with ours. "Have you noticed," Grimaud asks, "that when a human—who is less naturally gifted in that wolf language—joins in a howl and his pitch lands on the same note, the wolves will alter their pitch to prolong the harmonization? It's very interesting. If you end up on the same pitch as a wolf, he will scale up or down, modulating his voice with yours."

If you listen to wolves singing, you'll hear that wolves rarely howl alone for long before the whole chorus is cued. That chorus is not just about harmonizing. It's also about survival. There's a phenomenon called the Beau Geste effect, in which howling together makes it impossible to identify a single wolf's voice or how many wolves are in concert. Even a family of two wolves can raise a mighty chorus to disguise their small size by creating the illusion of a larger group's voice. In declaring their acoustic territory, the wolf chorus can travel long distances, giving the group the expansive space it needs to survive and thrive.

An interdisciplinary team of Montana State University researchers, including philosophy professor Sara Waller, is studying two thousand howls from thirteen canid species to better understand "how we can learn about the evolution of language." Dr. Waller is studying how animals communicate with one another—and if that influences how humans see them. "Just howls can tell us who is out there," says Waller. She wonders if ranchers playing recordings of wolf howls might be used to ward off wolves from their livestock. "Because I'm a philosopher," she notes, "I work with the group on the big, broad questions."

These more philosophical questions belong not only to scientists, but also to artists. Wolves and their music have claimed territories not just in the wilderness, but also in our human hearts. Throngs of visitors to Yellowstone National Park are thrilled to listen to howling wolves. Social media, film documentaries, and nature channels have hugely popular soundtracks of real wolves howling in the wild. Any online search reveals many audio clips, like the PBS NOVA link "What's in a Howl?" with sound sonography and recordings of a "Lonesome Howl," "A Pup Howl," "A Confrontational Howl," and "A Chorus Howl." Listen in and you can identify the different qualities of wolf song. Hélène Grimaud has even recorded a sonata accompanied by wolf howling.

What do highly skilled musicians like Grimaud hear when wolves sing? What, beyond any survival strategy, are wolves creating in their chorus? Since wolves have a culture, what does their music echo and offer us— if we could listen as fellow artists, with more than simply our scientific ears? I'm reminded of a *New Yorker* cartoon in which a huge whale is chasing a human on the beach. The human is waving his arms and screaming in terror. The whale wonders: "Is that a song?" We moderns, with such acoustic familiarity to wolves howling, are no longer afraid when we hear their singing. In fact, we often try to meet them on their same musical frequency. Does this mean that animals also seek to blend with or are attracted to *our* music?

"When you practice your piano," I ask Grimaud. "Do the wolves join in your music by howling along?"

During her seasons when Grimaud lived next to the WCC in upstate New York, she didn't notice any exact correlation between the wolves howling and her piano. "Their howling was random, coincidental with my playing," she says with a laugh. "But there was one foster-wolf pup who seemed to react to violin music when she heard my recordings. She'd come out of her den and raise her head and howl along to the violin strings. There definitely seemed to be a relationship there."

Grimaud shares some anecdotal evidence of another animal's musical appreciation. When she was living in Switzerland, every time she played Bach, a cow would come close to her window. "As soon as I stopped playing and went over to the window to make contact with the cow, she'd disappear." When Grimaud returned to practicing her piano, the cow would return. "But when I switched to Beethoven," Grimaud says, "she had no interest. Who knows why?"

Researchers have noted that animals do respond to our music. Cows produce three percent more milk when listening to calming music like Simon & Garfunkel's solacing "Bridge Over Troubled Water." Dogs in kennels relax, sleep, and seem less stressed when listening to classical music. Monkeys grow calmer and their appetites increase when listening to Metallica's "Of Wolf and Man." Elephants sway their trunks together to violin music, and there is even a Thai Elephant Orchestra that keeps a more stable tempo on drums than humans do. Cats, who seem to have little interest in our music, will relax when left alone for long hours, listening to "Music for Cats," compiled by another classical musician. Other experiments on how animals react to human music are fascinating and sometimes humorous. There is the YouTube sensation, a cockatoo called Snowball, who dances in perfect beat and screeches along to the Backstreet Boys; or a captive sea lion, Ronan, who jives along to the disco beat of "Boogie Wonderland."

"If you were going to compose a concerto for a wolf audience," I ask Grimaud, "would it be a lament, a love song, a requiem?"

I am thinking about the elegy a composer might create for what are known as the "Judas wolves," those solitary survivors of lethal hunts who are repeatedly radio-tagged so they can be located and tracked down again when the state or feds decide to cull the new pack. Judas wolves, because of their radio collars, betray the location of their next family for a kill. Imagine surviving so much loss of family pack, repeatedly.

"I've never been asked that question before . . ." Grimaud is silent for a while, then says pensively, "Probably I'd choose music with a sense of longing. That's always what I think when I hear wolves howling. Endless longing."

Who is not acquainted with the tender ache, the gravitational pull of longing? A yearning for something so intimate and yet so often beyond us. Like our reach for other animals, other ways of knowing them, other places we might meet.

I ask this musician whose art and life story are so interwoven with wolves, "What if you played a concert for the wolf? What music most embodies for you the wild wolf's spirit and struggle?"

"Rachmaninoff," Grimaud replies without hesitation. She is acclaimed for her impassioned and iconoclastic Rachmaninoff's Piano Concerto no. 2. This is also one of my very favorite concertos for its brave, muscular musical strength and yet moments of sublime longing.

"There is such a quality of being uprooted in Rachmaninoff's music. And again, that intense longing," Grimaud says. "Perhaps it comes from Rachmaninoff leaving his homeland and so becoming a hybrid—one who belongs everywhere but at the same time, not anywhere."

This sounds very much like a wolf's life. Often uprooted in rival battles for territory, wolves must disperse to find another homeland, wandering and searching to belong again.

Grimaud continues with a palpable energy. "If you look at the artistic pendulum, Rachmaninoff was a throwback himself, because the musical movement had evolved, and he wasn't part of that. He refused to compromise. He stayed true to himself—even though he was nearly an endangered species himself."

"There is something inconsolable about Rachmaninoff's work." Grimaud pauses, then rushes on in her quick accent. "In German, we call it *urkraft*—this vitality we feel so deep in our core. The force that enables you to make it through everything—even despite yourself."

Grimaud is talking about the elemental forces in music and nature that shape us all. Like water, the subject of her latest recording. And like wolves, her lifelong passion. We riff about how most scientists are wary of speaking about these mysterious, often deeply emotional connections we can feel with wolves and other animals. They are afraid of being discredited or losing their research grants if they speak out about this extrasensory or nonquantitative world of the wild. But this resonant, powerful human-wolf bond *is* explored through our myths and music. A territory beyond science and even logic. A country best traveled by artists. Maybe wolf howling, like our human music, is a language of love, soulful and sorrowful.

Grimaud continues in a soft patter, her accent deepening. "There's still so much mystery about wolves and our relationship with them. I think understanding wolves is all about acquaintance." In another interview, Grimaud tells the story of her first bond with wolves. In Florida, she met a high-hybrid wolf named Alawa, which means "sweet pea" in Algonquin. "This was a defining moment, a pivot point, a before and after," she says. "I became possessed with the idea that that species needed help."

Meeting Alawa, Grimaud describes, "filled me with gentleness . . . which awakened in me a mysterious singing. At the same moment, the wolf seemed to soften, and she lay down on her side. She offered me her belly."

Such trust is extremely rare for a wolf, especially with a stranger. Once, when the wolf was howling, Grimaud realized, "Alawa isn't howling, she's calling." Alawa was "one of the great presences" of Grimaud's life. Soon more wolves called to Grimaud and inspired her to study wolf behavior and biology with the same intensity she'd given her music. She visited wildlife reserves in America and took a degree in ethology, the study of animal behavior. Grimaud's bond with Alawa endures still in her work with the WCC, where one of the ambassador wolves is also called Alawa. Like her namesake, this Alawa and her brother Zephyr (which means "light" or "west wind") help educate people as part of the center's education programs.

Education is one vital way to speak with those who resist the wild wolf's return, who even want to again deny their right to exist. Grimaud and I discuss the rather counterintuitive polls that show when wild wolves share our territories, there is more hope for coexistence.

"It's all about acquaintance *and* true cohabitation," she says. "In Europe, especially in Spain and Italy, where wolves were never totally eradicated, the farmers have a higher threshold of tolerance. That's because they never lost their knowledge of living around wild wolves. But, you know, in France, when wolves came back from nearby Italy, it was just as bad as in the worst places. After wolves have been removed, people's opposition to them seems to grow even stronger at the idea of wolf reintroduction. Because farmers feel threatened, unfamiliar about how wolves truly function, and unaware of how unfounded their fears are. Everything grows out of proportion in absence. So, wolves fare better in places they've never been eradicated. Acquaintance is everything. What people are afraid of, they have no reason to protect."

Perhaps the hope for future coexistence is to keep wolf populations thriving in our wilderness and never let them be *disappeared* again. That's where education of the next generations comes in. At the Wolf Conservation Center, teaching kids about living with wild wolves in our wilderness is crucial. "One child at a time," says Grimaud. "You never know if that child seeing and loving wolves will grow up to be an environmental lawyer or a wolf biologist. One is never too small to have a role to play and to spread the message about wolves."

"Wolves follow the laws of their nature," Grimaud says. "They can seem merciless, but what wolves do makes sense. While so much of what *we* do doesn't make any sense."

Ethologist Marc Bekoff writes about animals' moral intelligence and sense of fair play in *Wild Justice*: "wild canine societies may be even better analogues for early hominid groups—and when we study dogs, wolves and coyotes, we discover behaviors that hint at the roots of human morality." Even Darwin believed that animals "would acquire a moral sense of conscience."

A moral universe is also what human art is all about. Expanding our kinship system to include other animals means recognizing their individual culture, arts, and morality. When artists, writers, and musicians don't just create "art for art's sake," when they embrace the living world and other animals, it's another way of knowing nature and us. Maybe it's not just going to be scientists or conservationists who help save species; it's also going to be the artists, like Grimaud, who come from a different place, one with a wider range of emotions and ideas, and who inspire and move audiences in ways that conservation may not.

"What might happen if more artists, like yourself, also devoted their time and talent to other species?" I ask her.

"Well, nature is the ultimate muse and the source of inspiration for all art forms," Grimaud answers with her characteristic passion. "And nature doesn't need much of a chance to prove its resiliency. Nature is always there."

Weaving her astonishing musical prowess with her respect for wolves, Grimaud created a video that went viral on YouTube, "Wolf Moonlight Sonata," of her exquisite performance of Beethoven harmonized with wolf howling—shared interspecies music.

We talk about how being with animals is a respite from our own humanity, sometimes even a relief. "At some point," Grimaud says with an audible smile, "we desire to have something in our lives that's *not* just a human relationship."

Grimaud concludes our interview with a poignant story of a group of businesspeople who recently visited the Wolf Conservation Center. When the wolves began their communal singing, "everyone could feel the energy. It was so powerful. You could see it in the reaction of the people, even though they were all being official and dignified."

When we humbly and humanely connect with the music of nature and other species, humans fall into a sympathetic resonance. One definition for "resonance" is "sound produced by a body vibrating in sympathy with a neighboring source of sound." This natural law of resonance echoes throughout nature, physics, and music. Water has a tidal resonance—each cascading wave has a ululating length and width that excites the spacious ocean. In physics, a tuning fork once struck will set another tuning fork vibrating at the same exact tone; and in music, acoustic resonance matches pitches, amplifying sound at the same frequency. In his marvelous book, *The World Is Sound*, German jazz musician Joachim-Ernst Berendt explains, "particles of an oxygen atom vibrate in a major key . . . blades of grass sing." If grasslands and microscopic atoms are singing to us, how much more do we resonate with the wild, compelling harmonics of wolf music?

There is fierce intimacy and a tender tension in our musical resonance with wolves. Sympathy. A symphony. We may only hope that the wild wolf is not simply a tragic song of our nation. But that more of us will listen and join in their gorgeous give-and-take chorus. When we howl together with wolves, we explore a soundscape that is unsettled, wild, and wide open. A territory, a meeting place, maybe even a longed-for reunion. *Ensemble.*

SINGING WITH ANIMALS

EERIE WHISTLES AND mewling of humpback whale songs echoed in the auditorium—ancient voices from another universe traveling here like audible light. I stood before the impressive audience of techies, scientists, and forward thinkers, each with an open laptop.

"Close your eyes and laptops," I asked them. "Listen."

Whale song symphonies ricocheted around the room: haunting, ultrasonic harmonies, warbles, the rubato of baritone stutters, mournful moans, and squealing descants, some riffs far above human hearing. Heads cocked, meditative smiles, as everyone listened. A calm dreaminess came over the faces, the rapt openness that embraces music.

Amid an audience of techies, scientists, and forward-thinkers, I was giving my presentation, "Do Whales Have Their Own Internet?" It was a bit of an outlier for these NPR "Tech Nation" conference goers, but surprisingly well attended. In the Q and A, someone asked, "Those vocalizations, what do they communicate?"

"Whales have their own culture, based on this song-language," I told them and explained: Recent mathematical research has shown that humpback whales use their own syntax to create complex sound phrases. In 2006, the *Journal of the Acoustical Society of America* published a scientific study of how much information was carried in whale songs, which, like human syntax and birdsong, are hierarchical, organized, structured. Another study found that humpback songs "change and completely replace their 'song anthem' every few years, a cultural evolution," akin to any evolving language. Humpbacks have their own dialects, specific to each population, and they "sing the same sequence of the same sounds." They learn new songs as they adapt to their lives and needs.

After my talk, a tall man in the audience approached me and asked if I'd like to visit the Marine Mammal Center in nearby Sausalito. "Come meet a newborn dolphin calf just stranded eight hours ago," he offered politely.

I've spent so many years tagging along with field researchers, I immediately recognized him as that type: khakis, notepad in pocket, tanned face. He also had the rather geeky, clean-shaven look of some of the seminar audience.

"You could be an axe murderer," I grinned. "But I'd follow you anywhere with an invitation like that."

Michael Kleeman is a computer expert and humanitarian with a special interest in the human-to-animal spectrum; he is on the board of the American Red Cross and travels a lot to other countries for disaster relief. His passion is rescuing and rehabilitating marine mammals on the Northern California coast.

As we drove across the Golden Gate Bridge, the fog banks billowed and blew, almost obscuring the towering beams and iconic arches of scarlet steel. California's Marine Mammal Center is the largest marine mammal hospital in the world. Since the mid-1970s, the Center has rescued more than twenty thousand marine mammals, including sea lions, elephant seals, harbor seals, and dolphins. The goal is always to rehabilitate and release the rescued animals back into the wild. This center is the gold standard for rescue and rehab among marine mammals.

Perched on a hilltop near the Pacific Ocean, the Center is a much-visited travel destination. On any day, the center may receive and treat a wounded monk seal from Hawaii or research an uptick in gray whale mortalities (possibly a result of malnutrition from warming waters and not enough food). Education is key to their work; the teaching hospital trains students and veterinary professionals from around the world.

I was honored to be invited "backstage" to the rehab area. All the animals are given names, and their daily conditions posted on the website so people can follow their healing progress and release. As we tiptoed past the noisy outdoor enclosures of sea lions and seals, Michael cautioned me against engaging with the rehab and rescued animals.

"We want them to return to the wild, so the less they know about us humans, the better their chances of survival," he whispered.

Under sheltering umbrellas, so the animals would not get sunburned, there were small pools with several ailing sea lions attended by vet techs and volunteers. Their loud grunts and barks accompanied quiet human voices. From my years watching over harbor seals on my neighborhood beach, sometimes accompanying the most injured to PAWS wildlife hospital, I was well accustomed to the expert veterinary care given these marine mammals. What I was not used to was how professional and impressive this marine mammal hospital was. It was a modern, busy ER.

I was also not quite prepared for how quickly my practiced scientific detachment disappeared when I saw the tiniest porpoise only three and a half feet long—floating flatly in the pool. It was hard not to connect deeply with a calf like Peter Parker, the two-month-old male harbor porpoise who had just stranded off San Francisco's Fort Funston beach. By the time Michael and his stranding team had reached the calf—only six minutes after the lifeguard's call for help—Peter's eyes, flukes, and blowhole had been savagely pecked by sea gulls and his skin was sun-blistered. The tiny calf was too weak to float in the small tank and had to be supported by a round-the-clock staff in a Styrofoam sling. Would this newborn, named in a hopeful gesture after superhero Spider Man, survive?

Michael gently splashed the surface of the pool with one hand. It usually signals cetaceans to respond. But Peter Parker made no move. Drifting on his side, one eye was bloodied, closed.

The porpoise's natural smile does not disguise grief or pain or depression. I'd never seen a calf so lost and lonely as Peter Parker. His image still haunts me. Scrapes and wounds sketched across his pale, gray flank; his pectoral fin was edged as if bitten. Born and abandoned.

"No sign of the mother," Michael said softly.

Separation from the mother, if there is no family pod nearby to adopt and nurse, is certain death for any newborn cetacean. At the center, there was round-the-clock care, nursing via feeding tube, and monitoring of vital signs.

My eyes blurred as I watched the tiny calf listless in the pool.

"The next hours and tonight are critical," Michael nodded. "We're trying to keep him nursed, alert, and engaged. Most of all, we want to make sure he keeps breathing."

· Peter Parker floated flatly in the cool tank. Porpoises and dolphins never sleep. Only one hemisphere of a cetacean's brain rests at a time. In the wild, scientists have observed pods of dolphins in which all those on one side swim with one eye closed; those swimming guard on the other side of the pod, will keep the opposite eye wide open.

There was an ongoing effort to engage Peter Parker in any way we knew. That meant not only medicine, but communication. That meant, most of all, sound. Cetacean acoustic range is impressive, 75 Hz to more than 150,000 Hz. It's like the range of a low hum, to the piercing, almost ear-splitting shriek of a siren, to sounds far above human hearing. Human hearing is usually limited to between 20 to 20,000 Hz. Even a newborn calf must tune down vocalizations to their lowest pitch for us to hear them.

I closed my eyes, better to see in my mind's heart this little life. Instinctively, a soft and low hum arose in my body. "May I sing to him?" I asked Michael.

I'd often sung lullabies to seal pups on my beach, especially if they had been shot by fishermen scapegoating them for approaching their nets to share in the fish catch. One bullet-riddled seal pup had gazed at me for hours as I sang, until an animal rehab volunteer arrived to take him to PAWS. I'd thought it was a death vigil with that pup, but he survived his gunshot wounds and after rehab was successfully released. I'd been able to accompany the pup when he was returned to the sea. The pup circled our boat only once before diving deep. Maybe the same would be true for Peter Parker?

"Well," Michael nodded. "It can't hurt to sing. Maybe it will help."

Michael and I sang to Peter Parker, exchanging the gaze between infant and nurturer that bonds so many species. This is love and assurance made visible: *We care for you as our own.*

I was surprised when Michael joined in my humming, his baritone pitch matching mine in our tender and *sotto voce* duet. We did not want to physically engage any more than medically necessary by touching the newborn. When marine mammal rehab workers are tending to animals, they often wear ungainly rubber suits to disguise themselves, so the animals don't imprint on humans. Sound was our most noninvasive way of touching the newborn, reminding him that he was not alone.

Slowly, the newborn turned on his other side, his remaining eye wide open. "Must have been protected from the seagulls by the sand when beached on his side," Michael said.

I'll never forget that little eye holding mine. It was not as alert as the cetacean eyes I'm familiar with, but it was attentive, even curious. That keen eye held mine, his head lifted, as if tuning in to our voices. The newborn swam closer to us. As much as I longed to touch Peter Parker—what scientists call "the mammalian instinct for touch"—I knew that what touched him most was our acoustic care.

Softly, I chanted a Hebrew prayer, *Kerachem Av*, which translates as "May God watch over you as a parent does a child," and crooned my grandfather's tender, falsetto lullaby, which my family sings to cure fevers.

Peter Parker perked up with my higher-pitched tones—my attempt at a signature whistle. Whenever I sing to other animals, I always remember to also send them visual images. I learned this not only from my own OrcaLab dream of Dolphin TV, but also from studying sophisticated cetacean echolocation and from reading Temple Grandin. The famed author and scientist called upon her own autism to intuit that an animal "thinks in pictures."

I sang on, sending images to Peter Parker of thousand-strong dolphin pods I've witnessed in the wild. I hoped there really was an internet for cetaceans and that somehow, I could enter and join the acoustic conversation.

When I'm with cetaceans, I sing to communicate and try to pay attention to what songs whales or dolphins respond to with the most curiosity. Dolphins appreciate classical music. Once, when a humpback whale, Humphrey, was lost in the San Francisco harbor, he ran away from rap music; but a boat playing Mozart finally led him back to sea. I've discovered, while singing to whales and dolphins all over the world, that they also like the bell-like tones of opera. So, I sang a few lively arias from "The Magic Flute," especially the Queen of the Night's lyric soprano. I also crooned some upbeat Broadway tunes.

When Michael whistled a few warbling notes like birdsong, Peter Parker swam a swift circle around the pool. It was so quick, the tiny splash of his tail flukes startled us.

"Hey, he likes my nightingale call," Michael smiled, shaking water off his face.

One blind eye, a wounded body, but Peter Parker's acoustic skills were intact. His acoustic superpower might save his life and give him a reason to thrive. We kept singing, whistling, humming for what seemed like hours, but was probably just an hour.

When the vets came for another tube feeding, they noted that Peter Parker's vital signs were significantly better.

"Keep singing," the vet said. "Even if he doesn't make it, his last memory will be of tenderness and your lullabies."

As we crooned to Peter Parker, I remembered also singing to the mother beluga, Mayauk, as she so deeply grieved her first calf's death. These two mirrors of mother-calf loss have always stayed with me whenever I hear researchers debate whether animals have emotions or try to fathom an animal's experience of death and loss. In *If Nietzsche Were a Narwhal*, Justin Gregg, of the Dolphin Communication Project, notes that "just because a dolphin can recognize death, it does not mean *she understands her own mortality*." He argues that we humans are the only species who recognize we will die—a "death wisdom" that haunts and shapes our lives.

But I wonder if animals are more keenly aware of their own mortality than we give them credit. As the wounded calf, Peter Parker, floated near us, his one good eye wide as we sang to him, his blowhole opening and closing with each labored breath, I truly believed the newborn understood he might be dying. He was brand new and might now take his leave. For it could be his choice. Since cetaceans are conscious breathers, they can simply decide to quit taking those deep, sonorous breaths. In captivity, many dolphins do just that. Humans breathe, even when unconscious. What if we all had the choice to stop breathing whenever the pain or the loss of bodily functions was too much for us? Their ability to choose death may be a higher consciousness than we can imagine—perhaps an animal's own death wisdom?

Peter Parker rolled over and took a shallow dip underwater, then surfaced with a soft sigh. I knew that any breath might be his last. In my fieldwork, I've often listened to wild animals surrender to a last exhale— what the ancient Egyptians called "the ank," that final, sacred, and mysterious *out breath*.

When I at last said goodbye to Peter Parker, I slapped the water to signal my leave-taking. Suddenly, the tiny porpoise cruised under my hand. Peter Parker whistled out his ultrasonic chirps, then slipped under my fingers, as fast as a bow across violin strings. And like the vibration of musical strings, my skin zinged with sound. When I left the pool, Michael was still softly whistling birdsong to the newborn. Peter Parker was singing back in bleeps, coos, and soft chirps. Perhaps as I was leaving the rehab center he was vocalizing his own name, those familiar creaks, chirps, raspberries, and whistles like a soundtrack of loss and survival.

For weeks, Peter Parker endured, singing, his healing attuned to by devoted schoolkids and many hopeful Facebook followers. But at last, the newborn simply stopped breathing. All of us who'd followed online his struggle to survive, all the vets who valiantly worked to save the newborn's little life, grieved Peter Parker.

We teach our children to mourn when they lose their animal companions. We sing and hold funerals for our beloved pets, for birds fallen out of nests, for urban wildlife as we claim their territories, and for animals killed on our roads. Yet adults rarely formally mourn the wild animals who perish on our shores, in our forests, our mountains, and waters. I've been part of elegies and memorials for orcas, for gray whales stranded in Baja or on my backyard beach, great blue herons and bald eagles discovered dead onshore and in our nearby old-growth forest.

Anyone who observes animals recognizes that they have many expressions and emotions, including grief. Elephants mourn their lost elders; wolves howl in haunting harmonies when one of the family is gunned down. Birds mourn: crows gather, an osprey softly calls out over her empty nest, magpies place bits of grass over the body of a fallen mate. Orcas, the largest in the dolphin family, carry their dead calves for thousands of miles, until the little body disintegrates—like the mother orca, Tahlequah (J35), who astonished the world and made international news in her "tour of grief." She carried her calf for seventeen days, during which time she rarely ate; her family pod took turns carrying the corpse, so Tahlequah could rest. Until finally, the mother orca let her lost calf go. Like many mourners, she had lost weight and was lethargic; but after the weeks of carrying the burden of all she had lost, Tahlequh returned to hunting and seemed to have recovered. She later again gave birth to a calf (J57) who is now crucial to the family pod's survival.

Animals teach us how to survive loss, how to adapt and live on, even when we are heartbroken. We carry the loved one, until we can let go.

Years after I'd sang with Peter Parker, new research documented that calves learn their mother's signature whistle while they are still in her womb. A signature whistle is the name by which dolphins identify each other; after birth, the other dolphins in the pod are noticeably quieter as the newborn apprentices to this maternal signature whistle by listening and mimicking. This imprinting process continues until the calf adapts the maternal signature whistle to develop his or her own distinct sound. Our instinct to sing to this abandoned calf was like trying to continue that intimate auditory bond of mother to calf—to call Peter Parker to live and learn to sing his own name.

Sound is a noninvasive way of holding other animals in our kind embrace. It is a way our species celebrates the lives of other animals. Interspecies singing is part of that celebration. When we listen and lend our voices to other animals, we connect with them in a profound communion that is more of an enduring bond than simple eye contact. Unlike touch or the sometimes too direct and aggressive visual approach, sound is a realm where we can meet other animals more equally. We can benignly seek to blend, not dominate; to harmonize, rather than drown out; to hear others, as much as speak. Interspecies music is humbler, often an elegy, a musical truce, a reunion—acoustic trust.

Sing your name. Close your eyes. *Listen.*

BIRDSONG BLUES

For Merloyd Lawrence

BAGATELLE, BALLAD, DUET, falsetto, flauto, glissando, legato, ostinato, scat—all these musical terms also describe the bioacoustics of birdsong. What is a song but an acoustic echo of the natural world? And what is the most ever-present, but perhaps most undervalued, of all animal sounds? Birdsong. We hear birds first thing every morning and often awake at night to the baritone hoots of hunting owls, the shrieks of great blue herons, the honking of geese. Birds continually serenade us, even if we are not listening.

But for the attuned and attentive professional listeners, which includes legions of devoted birders, the songs of birds are a cherished soundtrack to everyday lives. My many birder friends tell me that what began as a life list of visual sightings has matured into enraptured listening to the winged multitudes who grace our skies, our forests, our backyards. These diverse "soundscapes" are what musician, sound artist, and acoustic ecologist Bernie Krause calls "the great animal orchestra."

Krause has devoted his life to recording the world's wildlife and natural soundscapes; he founded the nonprofit Wild Sanctuary to do just that. "Birds have their own mysterious lexicon," he explains. "As we pay more attention to . . . these voices, and devote some imagination to expanding the language, we will be better equipped to describe the natural world."

Listening to the other voices surrounding us, our own lives are layered with more pleasure and humility; we hear that we are part of something much greater than ourselves. Tuning in, we learn how to harmonize, not dominate. Any musician or singer will tell you that this "blend" is an audio equipoise that is profoundly nourishing. Think of the delight in a symphony's dissonance and the "dark voice" of gifted singers like opera diva

Renee Fleming. Her astonishing coloratura soprano is so resonant, it fills any vast concert hall. So, too, the sounds of birdsong in a moss-hung rainforest or city park entrance us. Our ears embrace what Krause calls "biophony" or soundscape ecology—the study of acoustic relationships between living organisms and the environment.

In *Wild Soundscapes*, Krause teaches readers how to explore our own habitat like acoustic scientists do in the field. He notes that the forest at night is a reverberant theatre or "echo chamber" for nocturnal birds like nighthawks, white-crowned sparrows, or Western screech owls—"their time to sing." You can listen to these sonic habitats, dense and alive with birdsong and vibrations, and try to hear each individual bird's signature sound, like identifying each instrument in a symphony. Discover your own "totem natural sounds—the ones that . . . resonate with your soul." By listening to other voices than our own, we recognize we are only one part of the earth's orchestra. Krause is also using eco-acoustics to study the impact of climate change on biodiversity.

One of the most memorable experiences during the pandemic was that, in our quarantines, with less traffic and jets roaring overhead, we heard much more birdsong—as if there was an extraordinary bioacoustics concert just outside our windows we'd never bothered to attend. On daily walks in my own neighborhood, the trees and bushes burst with birdsong—from the warble of winter wrens to the clever mimicry of Steller's jays. We often fell silent, lost in wonder at such suddenly operatic and vibrant birds. Had they always sung this robustly? Or did our silence simply give them more space to sing? How relaxing and what a relief, realizing that, while birds don't sing for us, we can be their grateful audience.

Humans are primarily visual, but for those of us whose most developed sense is auditory, we experience the natural world and other animals through what German jazz musician Joachim-Ernst Berendt calls "the temple in the ear." The human ear takes in much more than the eye; we never completely close our ears. Hearing is the first and last sense. Babies listen in the womb, coma patients tune in, even when unconscious; and at death, hearing is the last veil to be drawn down on this world. We have evolved delicate lids to close our eyes, but not our ears.

Berendt cites the meditation teacher Bhagwan Shree Rajneesh, who calls the primacy of our eyes the "Adolf Hitler of our human senses" and says that our obsession with television, pictures, and the visual world means people "have lost the democracy of your senses." Berendt concludes, "To hear is to be. And yet millions of people are letting this most noble sense become atrophied."

Perhaps because our human world is so loud, we often are forced to tune out the natural world's lush soundscapes surrounding us. (If alien anthropologists studied the young in our species, they would assume that we have headphones for ears.) It's no wonder we don't notice what we are losing as bird species go extinct and birdsong vanishes from our shared habitat. In a recent article, science writer Ed Yong notes that "by flooding the environment with light and sounds we're confounding the senses of countless animals." Birds are especially vulnerable to noise pollution.

City and industrial noise affect the timing of birds' songs; Yong goes on to say that it affects "the complexity of their calls, and prevents them from finding mates." In an experiment on an Idaho ridge where migrating birds stop over, scientists played a loop of loudspeakers with recordings of passing cars. These highway and automobile noises drowned out the sounds of predators, so "the birds spent more time looking for danger than food." During this experiment, birds lost weight and grew weaker on their migrations, proving that noise alone can dramatically affect and deter wildlife.

The Audubon Society's recent watchlist of North American birds in decline notes that "since 1970 we've lost nearly three billion birds." This translates to more than one in four bird species lost in half a century, or one-third of the avian population. It's not just birds in at-risk habitats like the Arctic tundra, vanishing grasslands, or wetlands; backyard birds are also in decline. About 90 percent of common bird species in many habitats—warblers, sparrows, blackbirds, and finches—are disappearing. There are many causes for these massive bird extinctions—climate change, habitat loss, pesticides, insect declines, outdoor cats, power lines, wireless towers, windows, and wind turbines.

Our springs are quieter as bird communities disappear, and that loss of acoustic diversity detaches us even further from our natural world.

Just as the birds forget their songs, we forget the vital importance of birds in our shared landscape. Mourning this loss of birdsong, particularly in developed countries like America and Europe, a group of a thousand musicians from fifteen orchestras worldwide performed Vivaldi's *The Four Seasons*, but rescored to represent what a changing climate in the future of 2050 might sound like.

Listening to this recording on YouTube, especially the music of a "Spring marred by climate change," is haunting. The violin riffs are sour and off pitch, painful to the ears, the rhythm jarring, the percussion random, off kilter. You can listen to this imagined 2050 version of Vivaldi's masterpiece in various international cities. For example, in the Canadian Saskatoon Symphony Orchestra's disturbing performance "we hear changes in river flow patterns, in snow melt-fed river basins . . . where peak flows are reduced due to warmer winter temperatures, loss of glacier ice." To hear the imminent effects of climate change is a wake-up call. It's like hearing the feeling of loss.

Using music to help us understand the dimming effects of climate change reinforces that the "changes are stark, and irrefutable," says director Tim Devine. Composer Hugh Crosthwaite adds that his *The [uncertain] Four Seasons* rescoring is "meant to put pressure on leaders to act on climate change." He warns, "If we do nothing now, the harmonious environment we rely on for inspiration and nourishment will be forever changed."

Our own present and future generations are hearing far less birdsong than our ancestors. Recognizing this avian extinction is the first step to trying to stop the damage. Listening is a way to begin to tune in to all these bird blues. Is there any solution to limiting our human noise so that other animals might thrive? One man, Emmy-award-winning acoustic ecologist Gordon Hempton, who lives in Port Angeles, Washington, has spent his life "preserving quiet" and listening to the natural world. In *One Square Inch of Silence*, he notes that "natural silence is our nation's fastest-disappearing resource . . . on the verge of extinction."

Hempton asks, "Where have all the songbirds gone?" He mourns that "the landscape of America is sick and losing its voice. The avian choir is not just shrinking but forgetting its repertoire." Like Krause, Hempton has spent decades recording wild voices and soundscapes, and his website offers exquisite audio experiences like "the ocean is a drum" and "global sunrise." Listening to his recordings is a lovely reminder that some of these gorgeous sounds, like the mellifluous songs of Western meadowlarks, are vanishing. His work helps to raise the alarm that birds are going extinct in their natural habitats. Even if some survivors are raised in captivity, songbirds can forget their native language. As birds try to adapt to human noise, like city traffic, they are "losing lower notes and shifting to higher pitches that were less masked by traffic."

The loss of birds and their songs, just like the loss of silence, is a sign that we must pay attention. As Hempton says, "Sound is our warning signal." Hempton's home forest, the majestic Hoh Rain Forest in Olympic National Park, is, by his reckoning and research, the quietest place on earth. The Hoh has some of the tallest trees in the world and the least amount of noise pollution in the United States. "This tall, coniferous forest . . . offers cathedral-like acoustics," he says.

Hempton tracks audio intrusions into this great forest and reports them to those making the disturbance, whether it's an airline's jets or heavy machinery noise. He writes the noisemakers and politely asks that they respect this precious pristine place and "the ear of the animal." Some, though not enough, have responded to this One Square Inch inspiration, including the Federal Aviation Administration, which has sometimes changed flight paths.

In an interview a few years ago, Hempton counterpoints birdsong with his own commentary, including a long note of radio silence. "Walk into the forest with your ears," he advises, adding that you quickly realize, "Earth is a solar-powered jukebox." In his recording of Rialto Beach on the Washington coast, he listens from inside a giant Sitka spruce driftwood log: "wood fibers are excited by acoustic energy . . . the sound of the ocean itself . . . nature's largest violin." His excitement is like that of a child who first holds a chambered nautilus and hears the sea still shushing inside those delicate, white whorls of shell.

All animals use their ears to prowl, hunt, and procreate. Hempton notes that "for all animal life—at least higher vertebrates, listening is our sense of security . . . so quiet places generally tend to be secure places . . .

they calm us." Another remarkable evolutionary connection between humans and birds is that there is a perfect match between the frequencies of human hearing and birdsong. "Why would it have any benefit to our ancestors to be able to hear faint birdsong?" he asks. "Birdsong is the primary indicator of habitats prosperous to humans."

On Earth Day 2005, Hempton placed a small red stone, a Quileute elder's gift, on a Hoh Rain Forest trail log, three miles from the visitor's center. "I hoped to protect and manage the natural soundscape in Olympic National Park's backcountry wilderness," he explains. This 100-percent noise-free space will affect many square miles around, and "quiet will prevail over a much larger area of the park." He explains, "A single origin of noise—say, a jet—can drag a cone of noise over a thousand square miles behind it." But if we protect just one square inch of silence, this will "insulate about 1,000 square miles from intrusions."

Another advantage to tuning in to the voices of the world around us: "When you become a better listener to nature, you become a better listener to your community, your children, the people you work with," Hempton concludes.

After reading *One Square Inch of Quiet*, I decided to take a road trip to the Hoh Rain Forest and mark this quietest place on earth. I've often visited this awe-inspiring forest on trips to the coast. But when planning my trip to see that small red stone and listen to the "silence and the presence of everything," which Hempton so beautifully describes, I realized that my presence would make an acoustic mark, even if I walked lightly on the rain-drenched forest floor. I decided to let that quiet place be. Instead, I walked the crooked hills in the old-growth forest of Schmitz Park in West Seattle, which often seems like the quietest patch in my own neighborhood.

Birdsong in Schmitz Preserve Park is a revelation. Green swallows, robins, song sparrows, and even the zany zip of hummingbirds—these birds adorn the scarlet-barked madronas and ancestral cedar branches. Walking from the busy side street into this virgin forest is like entering a fertile fairy world of dense, evergreen stillness. Birdsong ricochets through trees in riffs and shrills, a concert that would be cacophonic, if it weren't so exuberantly woven into a language that is both foreign and familiar. It's an untamed sound, like a feathered orchestra tuning and tooting their boisterous instruments. As Krause writes, "each resident species acquires its own preferred sonic bandwidth—to blend or contrast—much in the way that violins, woodwinds, trumpets, and percussion instruments stake out acoustic territory in an orchestral arrangement."

One of my favorite acoustic moments is the pre-concert tuning of instruments (I played both saxophone and clarinet in a school orchestra)—controlled chaos and disharmony that changes to attunement, seeking perfect pitch. Finding that perfect harmony is a physical pleasure embodied; it is sensual sound. Birdsong has inspired many musicians. Listen to Beethoven's "Bird Song Opera" and the bright harmonies of Mozart's "The Magic Flute" alongside birdsong—you'll hear why Mozart kept a songbird (a European starling) to inspire his composing.

Birdsong not only offers the joy of listening; it has also been documented to improve mental health by calming frayed nerves. One neuroscience study asked participants to listen to ordinary traffic or local birdsongs for six minutes. The study revealed "listening to birdsong was beneficial; these sounds improved the study participants' moods by reducing anxiety and depressive symptoms." Traffic noises "worsened depressive symptoms." Another study cited in the same *Forbes* article discovered that "people reported greater life satisfaction when there was a greater diversity of bird species living nearby." Perhaps that is because birdsong "is a subtle indication of an intact natural environment that detracts our attention from stress that could otherwise signal an acute threat." The studies tell us that just a "one hour walk in nature reduced brain activity associated with stress."

What if we ensured that all urban dwellers had everyday access to large green spaces; if offices, elevators, and supermarkets were alive with birdsong instead of mind-numbing Muzak; if hospital patients were serenaded by delicious birdsong instead of the harsh and alarming soundtrack of machine bleeps, Code Blue shrieks, and dings? When I was in the hospital in 2017, it was the loudest place I'd ever stayed. Headphones and singing with the nurses were my respite from the cacophony, and every night a fellow patient, a local musician, played his flute in delicate jazz riffs, like birdsong. When my beloved editor, Merloyd Lawrence, was in the hospital during her last days, she opened her window just a crack to make friends with and happily feed a boisterous blue jay she named Henrietta.

During the pandemic, I was deeply grateful to participate in my local chorale's virtual performance of "3 Billion Birds," an original score by our choral director, Bronwyn Edwards, and the lyricist, Pamela Hobart Carter. An elegy for birds, the music ends with a hopeful note of people taking simple steps to continue the love story between people and birds: "Where there are no trees, I'll plant native seeds for you; where grasses grow, I'll allow meadow homes for you. Hey, songbirds, have you heard about my backyard?"

Birds can make a comeback. Proof is the bald eagles, peregrine falcons, and ospreys, who thrived after the devastating pesticide DDT was banned and the 1973 Endangered Species Act was passed. Conservationists and hunters have helped restore America's wetlands, increasing waterfowl like ducks, geese, and swans by 56 percent over the past fifty years. The popular effort known as #bringbackbirds promotes simple actions to help birds, including landscaping with native plants, keeping cats indoors, avoiding pesticides, and putting out bird feeders.

When we take care of and listen to birds, there is delight when that temple in the human ear is aroused and embraced by the chorus of winged creatures. Birdsong is a different language, which calls us "to cross divides," writes David G. Haskell in "The Voices of Birds and the Language of Belonging." In our separate evolutions, mammals' ears developed in concert with water; birds' ears evolved within the soaring element of air. This means that birds and mammals perceive sound vibrations in very different ways. Birds are not as focused on pitch, but on "the overall shape of sound, the nuances among layers of sound frequencies," writes Haskell. But there can be an auditory communion between our species, he adds. "That bridge is made from the gift of our attention . . . opening to the languages of birds in the everyday . . . Our senses learn the language of belonging."

Belong. The word is mesmerizing. Because my father's forestry work moved us every other year, from High Sierra fir to Montana spruce to southern piney woods, the landscape also seemed in motion. To *be long* in one place was to take deep root like other settled folk, or like the trees themselves. After I have lived a long life on the beach that is my forever home, I hope that someone might someday say, "She belonged here," as much as the purple sea stars that cling to rock crevices furred in algae, as much as the seagulls who clamor and cluck outside my windows.

My own everyday birdsong begins each dawn with seagulls scolding like alarm clocks. I awake to the squawk and swoop of gulls, the skitter and staccato stuttering of my indoor Siamese cats hunched down, hidden, hunting birds behind waterfront windows. On my walks along the beach, I often meet Stanley, a birder scouring the misty skies for peregrines, eagles, and red-tailed hawks. Stanley is, by his own admission, "raptor-mad." His devotion to our resident bald eagles and the violet marine mists they haunt reminds me of Northwest poet Denise Levertov's enduring line: "Grey is the price/of neighboring with eagles."

"Seagulls memorize your face," Stanley was the first to teach me, his binoculars hanging like a huge, heavy necklace around his neck. "They know their neighbors."

I stood on the sea wall feeding the flock of gray-and-white gulls who also make this Seattle beach their habitat. Stanley tipped his rather rakish tweed motoring cap and kept walking fast. "Can't let the heartbeat stop." But for birds, Stanley always stopped.

I meet Stanley many days on the beach. We rarely talk; we perform our simple chores. I feed the seagulls and say prayers; he keeps his legs and his heart moving. But between us there is an understanding that these tasks are as important as anything else in our lives; maybe they even keep us alive. The Hopi Indians of Arizona believe that our daily rituals and prayers literally keep this world spinning on its axis. For me, feeding the seagulls is one of those everyday prayers. They caw welcome, their wings almost touching me as they sail low over my shoulders, then hover overhead, midair. Sometimes if it's been raining, their feathers flick water droplets onto my face like sprinklings of holy water. The brave fliers swoop over the sea and back to catch the fruit and leftovers in their beak inches above my hand. Then the raucous riot of gulls crying and crows *kok-kok-ing* as my sidearm pitch sends tidbits whizzing through the air.

Before Stanley scolded me, "Never feed bread to gulls . . . it causes a disease called 'angel wing,'" I had offered tortillas to the seagulls, a few of them skipping across the waves like flour Frisbees. Now, I stick to fish, low-salt nuts, organic chips, spaghetti, and fruit.

I am not the only neighbor who feeds these gulls. For years, several afternoons a week, a green taxi pulled alongside the beach. From inside, an ancient woman, her back bent like the taut arch of a crossbow, leaned out of the car window. She called in a clear, tremulous soprano. The seagulls recognized the sun-wrinkled, almost blind face she raised to them. She sweetly nodded to any passers-by, "Birds know I'm here."

It was always the same driver, the same ritual—a shopping bag full of seeds and bird snacks. "She told me she used to live by the sea," the driver explained to me once. "She doesn't remember much else about her life . . . not her children, not her husband."

Carefully the driver tore each fruit slice just the way the woman requested. "Now she can't hardly see these birds. But she hears them . . . and she smells the sea." The taxi driver smiled, his silk turban wound around his head like a bird's nest. "She tells her troubles to the gulls, who seem to understand."

This bird-feeding ritual, the healing salt-and-mineral sea, this old woman took into her body and soul every week. She lived in the nursing home at the top of our hill. When I saw any ambulance go by, I always hoped it wasn't for Our Lady of the Gulls.

As she murmured and tossed her meager supper to the seagulls, they cried and dived, surrounding her in a feathered halo. Communion. But sometimes after they'd fed, they landed in circles around her, clucking and chirping as if gossiping among old friends. On warm days the old lady found a bench along the beach walkway and gazed at the shining sea, accompanied by her Greek chorus of seagulls. She reminded me of the Spanish poet Vicente Aleixandre's "Old Man and the Sun." The sublime portrait of an old man suffused by sunlight who "went slowly toward nothing/surrendering himself/the way a stone in a tumbling river gets sweetly abraded/and submits to the sound of pounding love."

One fall, when wild hurricanes shook the South and drought seized the Northwest, the old woman stopped coming to our beach. I waited for her all autumn, but the green taxi with its delighted passenger never called again. I took to adding two weekly afternoon feedings to my own morning schedule. These beach meetings are now more mournful, in memory of the old woman who didn't remember her name, and whose name I never knew, who remembered only the gulls.

Not long afterward, my landlady called with the dreaded refrain: *House sold, you must move on.* I walked down to the beach and opened my arms to the gulls. I said a prayer asking that the Salish Sea would keep me near her. One afternoon, I had the sudden notion to drive down the beach. There, I found a waterfront apartment and a nourishing community— as if the home and the neighbors had always been there, just waiting for me to discover or remember them.

Before I moved one stick of furniture into the new apartment, though, I stood on the beach and fed the gulls in thanksgiving. They floated close above my head. I felt surrounded by little angels. Then I realized that these were the very same gulls from the beach near my old apartment. I recognized them: the scrawny gull with that bit of fish line wrapped around a familiar webbed foot, another with a crooked wing, and the distinct markings of a young gray gull, one of my favorite high-fliers.

The seagulls may have memorized my face and followed me. Or I had followed them. But I had also, quite without realizing it, memorized these birds. I knew then I was no newcomer here, a nomad blown by changeable winds. It is not to any house, but to this beach, I have bonded. I belong alongside this rocky inlet with its salt tides, its pine-tiered, green islands, and its gulls who remember us—even when we've forgotten ourselves.

ALLIANCE

*Learning from
Animals*

ANIMALS, LIKE HUMANS, need alliances to survive. They cannot afford the denial of climate change or the threat of predators. Paying close attention and learning about their own habitat are survival skills. Community is essential. Unless a wolf is dispersing to seek a mate or new territory, wolves are rarely alone. *Canis lupus* form packs and feed each other when one of the family is injured. Orcas, sometimes called sea wolves, spend entire lifetimes in family pods. Mother seals share crowded rookeries. Friendships among animals, especially females and young offspring, are vital, like the swinging bachelor pods of dolphins or the two juvenile seal pups, Leopard and Silkie, who hauled out together on my Alki Beach and saved each other's lives.

Then there are the bonds between humans and animals, like the many stories of feral children raised by wolves or dogs or even monkeys. Children understand this ancient alliance between species. They may be young, but their memories and connections with the animals are very old. In my storytelling conservation work and interactions with students in schools, I'm often heartened at how quickly human children identify with other animals. By telling their own animal stories, they are practicing ecology at its most profound and healing level. Story as ecology—it's so simple, something we've forgotten. In wildlife conservation, the emphasis has been on saving species, not *becoming* one with them.

So much of what animals perceive about the natural world is beyond our human knowledge and skills. With our technologies, we are much more distracted and alienated from our own ecosystems than earlier generations were. Our kids are growing up with more screens than forests or waves or wild animals. I enjoy the wonders of technology as much as anyone, but I do worry that we are losing essential survival skills. The ability of animals to focus and navigate the world is astonishing and finally getting its due in popular books like *An Immense World*, by Pulitzer Prize–winning writer Ed Yong.

For those of us who have spent our lives studying animals, it's gratifying to see animal alliance, perception, and intelligence finally being recognized in the mainstream. As Ed Yong writes, "It falls on us to marshal all of our empathy and ingenuity to protect other creatures and their unique ways of experiencing our shared world."

When I watch the stillness of the great blue heron, I am reminded of the ancient practices of meditation and mindfulness. Like a martial artist, the great blue heron is a "still point" before snapping a fish up from the surf. When I listen with my limited human hearing range to dolphins carrying on seven simultaneous conversations or wolves howling in complex harmonies, I know there is so much more being said than I can ever fathom. We are now using artificial intelligence to begin to understand other animal voices and their migration patterns.

The wisdom and astonishing perceptions of other species instructs us to tune in. There is a word for this that is used by both psychologists, scientists, and spiritual seekers—attunement. *Merriam-Webster* defines it as "to make aware or responsive, to bring into harmony (tune)." When we listen deeply to other species, we understand more about our own. What we learn from this connection may seem revelatory or even prophetic. My favorite definition of a prophet is not one who sees the future, but what is happening now, on the ground, all around us. In that way, the animals with whom we share our habitat are prophets. Aligning with the Other, the non-human requires a lot of humble empathy, but taking this leap opens worlds and so many wonders. This attentive alliance, a cooperative relationship, and mutual teaching is the ultimate symbiosis. It begins in our hearts and minds—even our souls.

FERAL CHILDREN AND
THE BIG, GOOD WOLF

STORIES OF FERAL children, those raised and nurtured by other species, have always resonated with me. The most well-known are the "Wolf Girls of Midnapore," sisters discovered in 1920, India, in a wolf den. Amala, who was six, and Kamala, who was eight, had been raised by a female wolf. The twins ran and ate raw meat and crouched on all fours, panting like wolves, howling, and hunting nocturnally. Baring their teeth at humans, "Their jawbones had altered shape, the canine teeth lengthened, and their eyes in the dark had the peculiar blue glare of cats or dogs." Amala died after being taken in by humans. Kamala spent five years in an orphanage, where she learned some words but never the connective tissue of grammar.

There was the "Wild Girl of Songi," captured in a 1731 French royal hunt, who "slept easily in the branches of a tree, sung like a bird, and [flew] up and down tree trunks with the ease of a squirrel." John Sebunya was a three-year-old Ugandan "Monkey Boy," who ran away into the jungle after witnessing his mother killed by his father. He was adopted by monkeys who taught him to forage and live in trees.

A seven-year-old Russian boy, Vanya Yudin, known as the "Bird Boy," chirped and flapped his arms like wings. The Argentinian "Cat Boy" was found surrounded by wild cats who protected him, kept him alive by licking and cuddling him during the harsh winter. In Romania a boy left his family because of parental violence and learned to survive by following stray dogs in the Transylvanian countryside; while in Ukraine a girl, Oxana Malaya, was abandoned by her alcoholic parents and spent six years living with mongrel dogs in a backyard shed. When she was found, she growled, barked, and ran on all fours. The dogs tried to protect her from human rescuers. Taken to a "home for the mentally handicapped," she was nurtured, taught some rudimentary language skills, and now works there. She still runs and barks and spends much of her life taking care of dogs.

These true stories of animals caring for and raising human children, hybrid-people, occur across many cultures. I've wondered what stories the feral children would tell us, if we knew how to listen, instead of forcing them to adapt to our civilization. A documentary was made about Oxana Malaya, who says she longs to reunite with her biological parents. Many of these feral children didn't survive leaving their animal family or the forest and jungles. The scientists who tried to "rehabilitate" these children raised by wild animals ask the same question: "What is human nature?" as Michael Newton, author of *Savage Girls and Wild Boys*, echoes. But I wonder and worry about the animals left behind when a human child they so loyally nurtured is stolen from them. Do they mourn their adopted human who survived because of their forest skills? Do they hope other humans will be kinder to them for saving one of their own?

A few of the children raised by animals have also gratefully told the animal's stories, alongside their own. Marina Chapman was four years old when she was kidnapped in 1952, abandoned, and left for dead in a Colombian jungle. Marina was taken in by a tribe of capuchin monkeys, who taught her to forage and live off the forest and elude predators. She thrived with the monkeys for five years. Found by hunters at age nine, she was sent to a brothel. Marina escaped the brothel, was adopted, schooled, worked as a nanny, and married a British scientist. She authored the memoir *The Girl with No Name*, which was also made into a documentary film. Marina's daughter explains that a typical day in her family life was "us three girls scaling the trees while Dad studied the bark and lichen below (no doubt pulling out his pocket specimen bottles)." Their mother credits the capuchin monkeys with teaching her agility, community, and how to survive in the jungle. Recently, researchers have discovered that capuchin monkeys can help quadriplegics to thrive. Trained like mobility assistance dogs, these keenly intelligent, mobile monkeys assist in daily domestic tasks. Because monkeys can live from twenty-five to thirty years, these "helper monkeys" outlive service dogs.

The real questions is: *Why do wild animals adopt humans?* Why not leave our lost or abandoned children to starve and perish? And what is it about animals in the wild that prompts them to care for another species? There is much to be learned about this symbiosis between species. Don't we owe other animals the same care?

Having also imprinted on many more animals than people in my first, formative five years on the forest, I'd expected to evolve one day to become much *more* than human. When I realized that the deer trophies standing guard over my cabin crib were, in fact, dead—prey and food for my suppers—I had to wonder about the mighty predator who might hunt them. I, too, must be a predator. While I'd identified first with the graceful deer, I also suspected that I might one day learn the stealth and skill of a wild wolf. Not as a hunter, but an animal apprentice, perhaps a biologist—someone who followed the wolves.

Children never forget, and are perhaps most formed by, their first stories. My father's predator-prey hunting tales were my favorite bedtime rituals. At ninety-six, he is still a remarkable storyteller, with just the right balance of animal-to-human drama, paying equal attention to both species. In fact, his animal stories usually outweigh any anecdotes about relatives or people. My whole family continues this devotion to other animals as main characters in our lives and storytelling.

I never liked Disney films with their somnambulistic princesses who had to be woken up by a prince. Or in the twenty-first century—when science has ably proven that wolves benefit our shared ecosystem—Disney's insistence in movies like *Frozen* that wolves are predators of children. My heroes as a child were Edgar Rice Burroughs's Tarzan and the wolf-boy, Mowgli, from Kipling's vivid *The Jungle Book*. Most of all, I exulted in *Julie of the Wolves*, about an Inuit girl lost and adopted by a wolf family.

My family had no pets until I was thirteen, when a feral cat we named Snookums began to stay with us until one day when my mother gave him away to a farmer for his barn. I then brought my little brother the family's first dog, Shadrach, a lively corgi who accompanied him on his early morning paper route. And we always had the Tennessee Walker horses my dad raised and rode. Many summers we spent on my grandfather's Ozarkian farm with his ubiquitous hound dogs, equines, and a fascinating assortment of barnyard animals. I felt truly sorry for those domesticated cows and pigs who never had the freedom of wild animals. Though they were called "*live*stock," they felt much *less* alive to me. At worst, they were prisoners of our hunger and need; at best, they were indentured servants.

A bit of a feral child, I did not take well to being tamed to fit into feminine norms. Any expectations that I would be a dutiful daughter, marrying and devoting myself to children instead of animals, were dashed when I showed more interest in microscopes than dolls. As a kid, my favorite toy was a junior microscope through which I observed and took "field notes" about spiders and snakes, tadpoles in nearby rivers, the finely dusted, incandescent wings of butterflies, the bulbous bellies of frogs. In high school, the only course I ever flunked was home economics and, to this day, my friends fondly tell me that I barely pass as domesticated. Sometimes when I'm anxious or can't sleep, I listen to the primal meditations of animal voices, especially birdsong, humpback lullabies, and the harmonious howling of wolf serenades.

My father noted my disbelief over the Disney films that have done such damage to wolves, a most maligned and misunderstood fellow species. He and I argued the pros and cons of wolf reintroduction, but he did often allow that the predator and prey *belong* together—an evolutionary fit. "A deer's backbone," he said, "it's shaped so that wolf teeth perfectly fit between the vertebrae." This physical bond between predator and prey is evidence of how animals evolve to perfectly adapt and survive. Unlike humans, with our denial of the earth's changes—what psychologists call "adaptive disability."

Though wolves were gone from my birth forest, I believed they would return one day—and I would tell their stories. In 2011, a wild wolf, OR-7, returned to the Plumas National Forest, dispersing from a family pack in Oregon to reclaim the old High Sierra woods and raise his next generations. Named "Journey," for his epic travels that schoolchildren raptly followed, OR-7 was the first confirmed wild wolf in California in eighty-seven years. I was one of the first journalists to cover the reintroduction of wild wolves to Yellowstone for the *Seattle Times* and continue to advocate for restoring wolves to their natural habitat—one that is healthier, more diverse, and more sustainable when wolves are on the land. Apprenticing myself to the wolf as an adult has restored my childhood reverence for their many skills, especially their deep family values.

Alpha males *and* females are strong role models for teaching their pups to play, to hunt, to cooperate within a tight-knit family structure. The family takes care of their injured members, sometimes sharing food with a wolf with a broken jaw; a female wolf will often nurse a pup whose own mother has died. Scientists call this nurturing of the Other "allomothering." Caring for those besides our bloodlines, or even our same species. Feral children prove that animals also practice allomothering with us. We can learn a lot about our ourselves when we study this cross-species adopting and empathy. What do other species model better for us than even our own?

The alpha male wolf is not the rapacious predator of our prejudice and fairy tales. That stereotype comes from a misunderstanding of the real relationships among wolf families. In fact, "the male wolf is an exemplary male role model," famed biologist Carl Safina has written. "I've seen that the leadership of the ranking male is not forced, not domineering, and not aggressive to those on his team."

For my essay "The Big, Good Wolf: Lives of Alpha Males," I interviewed Yellowstone's veteran "Wolf Man," Rick McIntyre, who notes that alpha males demonstrate a "quiet confidence and self-assurance . . . You know what's best for your pack. You lead by example . . . you have a calming effect."

It makes evolutionary sense. Cooperative family members "more sharing, less violent with one another" are more likely to survive than "members beating each other up and competing with one another . . ." concludes McIntyre, who has studied the behavior of generations of wolves.

The first wolf I met face-to-face was an alpha male named Merlin, a two-year-old "ambassador wolf" from Mission Wolf, a Colorado wolf sanctuary, who had been injured before being rescued. Ambassador wolves are those who cannot be returned to the wild, usually because of injuries; they serve as teachers and animal diplomats between species. I met Merlin at a 1997 Olympic Wolf Summit in Olympic National Park in

Washington, where state wildlife agencies and wolf advocates gathered to discuss wolf reintroduction. I was excited about making a first close contact with a wolf. But I was also astonished, after all my work for wild wolves in Yellowstone and Alaska, to find myself somewhat afraid. Why? I knew the facts: no one in North America's history has ever been killed by a healthy wolf in the wild. The wolf is shy and reclusive. Wolves do not seek out people; people seek out wolves.

Perhaps the rarity of this close contact with wolves was why I found myself still afraid. As Merlin prowled our circle, sniffing a woman here, a man there, there was an anticipatory murmur and a palpable, primitive fear also ran through the crowd. It was that thrilling electricity of all our senses heightened, as if our ancient, reptilian brains were still encoded with this memory of wolf: powerful, mysterious, and most of all, untamed.

Sitting cross-legged in a quiet semicircle, awaiting the wolf's gaze and physical scrutiny, many of us leaned forward, hoping to catch the wolf's bright, amber eye. Our yearning to meet this wolf face-to-face reminded me of the words of the naturalist Loren Eiseley: "One does not meet oneself until one catches the reflection in an eye other than human."

When Merlin first entered our circle, he had bounded straight for Kent Weber, the director of Mission Wolf. Merlin stood on his hind legs to slather the man's face with his tongue. It was an astonishing sight, 6-foot-tall man and wolf just as tall standing together in a rapturous embrace.

"This is how he always greets human members of his pack," Kent said, smiling.

There were a hundred humans here, but still there was a tremor through the crowd, as if we were outnumbered. Around the circle, Merlin explored, a lick to the face there, a sniff of the open hand there; the wolf was careful and curious. I realized at that moment, just before the black wolf bounded with a long-legged leap toward me, that as deeply as I longed to be chosen, somehow accepted by this huge wolf, I was also afraid of the unknown. I didn't really know the real wolf, didn't know how to behave. So, I bowed my head, my pulse throbbing in my throat—and waited.

"Wolves, like humans, engage in a lot of eye contact to figure out if an expression says *threat* or *play*," Kent taught us. "So, when you meet the eyes of these wolves, keep an open attitude. Meet the wolf not as an aggressor, but as an equal."

Slowly I looked up, the nape of my neck tingling, as Merlin greeted me with a sniff to my forehead and a slight twitch of his massive ears. Face-to-face with a wolf—so close that all I saw was an amber glow and then the sunlit warmth of black fur against my forehead—Merlin lapped my face, all the while holding my gaze with those pale-fire, reflective eyes that are luminous even in the dark. Warm breath as the wolf sniffed my hair, then again licked my face with a quick tongue.

His touch felt vastly different than being playfully nuzzled by my own husky dog. With his huge paws, imperial and long-legged stance, his direct stare, I knew I was in the presence of a powerful peer. Merlin allowed no Good-Dog pat on the head, interpreting that as a sign of dominance. He only responded to my open palm like a show of goodwill, an offering.

As the wolf held my gaze—his eyes inches away from mine—I was startled by the sheer intelligence blazing there in those brilliant yellow irises. Here was a very astute fellow creature who scrutinized me with all his considerable senses: a perceptive nose that can track prey from a mile and a half away; radar ears that recognize sounds several miles away; sharp eyes that can acutely scan hillsides from a half-mile distance; a delicate tongue that can taste fear in prey before he sinks his teeth into and crushes the thigh bone of a moose; a pace swift and powerful; and a sixth sense honed from an evolution that includes being driven to near-extinction.

Someone snapped a photo of Merlin and me: a majestic black wolf and woman with wild, tousled hair gaze at each other as if in reunion— the forest in me, the wild still in him.

"No need to greet him again," Kent said softly as I again held out my hand to Merlin. "He remembers you."

"And I'll always remember him," I breathed.

I still remember Merlin these two-plus decades later. That photo sits on my writing desk and is also placed in my animal family album. For those of us who remember our childhood bonds with other animals—the animal stories in which we shape-shifted in our imaginations to become more-than-human—the big, bad wolf fairy tale belongs to another time, not our own. We work to tell new stories, especially about wolves, who, like those "helper monkeys" or the wolf families, kindly assist, adopt, and often save human children. The survival of feral children taken in by animals is the scientific antidote to all the Grimm's or other fairy tales that portray animals simply as our predators. Instead of a bad wolf disguised as a human grandmother, stories of feral children reveal humans who adapted and survived by disguising *themselves* as animals.

New stories, especially about wolves, are finding a willing audience. The *Girl and the Wolf* is a recent and beautifully told children's book by Métis poet, filmmaker, and author Katherena Vermette. The story is powerful in its sparse and moving story of "the girl in her red dress and the wolf who isn't really scary," as Vermette says in her author's note.

Vermette radically reimagines the European Big, Bad Wolf tale of prejudice with her Indigenous echo of the wolf-human bond of symbiosis and reciprocity. From the Treaty One territory in Winnipeg, Manitoba, Canada, Vermette's work sings about her people's traditional bonds with the land and animals—whether it's her "river woman," an intimate poem of the Red River ("this river is full/this river is family"), or the gray wolf who gently guides the girl to "take a depth breath." The poem continues, "Close your eyes, then look. What do you see?"

What do we see when we take a deeper look at the animals with whom we share our homelands? When we affix and apprentice ourselves to *their* knowledge and skills? One doesn't have to be feral or adopted by a wolf to recognize that they are also storytellers, top predators, allies, trying to adapt to a changing natural world. They are our teachers and guides, if we can only see. Eye-to-eye.

ANIMAL ALLIES

MY CHILDHOOD WAS blessed with wild animals. To share that, I've written children's books on orcas, wolves, seals, and other animals to bring young people into that intimate bond that is so natural to them. One of my most remarkable encounters with kids and their innate alliance with animals was when I was teaching at an inner-city school as part of a program called Writers in the Schools. Here were kids from all over the city, every color and class, all strangers one to another. Over the next two weeks we would create our own communal story—with animals as the main characters. Our first assignment was to introduce our imaginary friends from childhood. I hoped the kids would identify with wild creatures, real or imagined, as a way of sharing their personal stories.

"My imaginary friend really lived, once," a Latina teenage girl began, head bent, her fingers twisting her long, black hair.

She stood in the circle of other adolescents. This shy, fourteen-year-old girl, Sarah, had struck me on the first day because she always sat next to me, as if under my wing. And though stylish clothes suggested she was a popular girl, her demeanor showed the detachment of someone deeply preoccupied. She never met my eye, nor did she join in the first few days of storytelling when the class of ten boys and four girls regaled one another with favorite animal books, movie characters, fairy tales, or superheroes.

So far, their story lines portrayed the earth as an environmental wasteland, a ruined shell hardly shelter to anything animal or human. After three days of stories set on an earth besieged by climate change, environmental evacuees, and barren of nature, I made a rule: No more characters or animals could die this first week. I asked if someone might imagine a future *healed* world, one that survives even our species extinction. It was on this third day of group storytelling that Sarah jumped into the circle and told her story:

"My imaginary friend is called Angel now because she's in heaven, but her real name was Katie," Sarah began. "She was my best friend from fourth to tenth grade. She had freckles like me and brown hair and more boyfriends—sometimes five at a time—because Katie said, 'I *like* to be confused!' She was a real sister and we used to say we'd be friends for life . . ."

Sarah stopped, gave me a furtive glance, and then gulped in a great breath of air like someone drowning, or about to go down. Her eyes fixed inward, her voice a monotone.

"Then one day last year in LA, Katie and I were walking home from school and a red sports car came up behind us. Someone yelled, 'Hey, Katie!' She turned . . . and he blew her head off. A bullet grazed my skull, too, and I blacked out. When I woke up, Katie was gone, dead forever." Sarah stopped, stared down at her feet, murmuring in that same terrible monotone, "Cops never found her murderer, case is closed."

The kids shifted and took a deep breath, although Sarah herself was barely breathing at all. I did not know what to do with her story; she had offered it to a group of kids she had known but three days. All I knew was that she'd brought this most important story of her life into the circle of storytellers, and it could not be ignored as if *she* were a case to be closed. This story lived in her, would define and shape her young life. Because she had given it to us, we needed to witness and receive—and perhaps tell it back to her in the ancient tradition of call and response.

"Listen," I told the group, "we're going to talk story the way they used to long ago when people sat around at night in circles just like this one. That was a time when we still listened to animals and trees and didn't think ourselves so alone in this world. Now we're going to carry out justice and find Katie's killer. We'll call him to stand trial before our tribe. All right? Who wants to begin the story?"

All the superheroes joined this quest. Nero the White Wolf asked to be a scout. Unicorn, with her truth-saying horn, was declared judge. Another character joined the hunt: Fish, whose translucent belly was a shining "Soul Mirror" revealing the true nature of anyone who looked.

A fierce commander of this hunt was Rat, whose army of computer-ized comrades could read brain waves and call down lightning lasers as weapons. Rat began the questioning and performed the early detective work. We determined the murderer was a man named Carlos, a drug lord who used local gangs to deal cocaine. At a party Carlos had misin-terpreted Katie's making a video of her friends dancing as witnessing a big drug deal. For that, Rat said, "This drug lord decides Katie's got to go down. So, yo, man, he offs her without a second thought."

Bad dude, indeed, this Carlos. And who was going to play Carlos now all the tribe knew his crime? I took on the role. As I told my story, I felt my face hardening into contempt, which carried me far away from these young pursuers, heading deep into the Amazon jungle where Rat and his computer armies couldn't follow, where all their space-age equipment had to be shed, but the others could go, until there was only hand-to-hand simple fate.

In the Amazon, the kids changed without effort, in an easy shapeshift-ing to their animal selves. Suddenly there were no more superheroes with intergalactic weapons—there was instead Jaguar and Snake, Fish, and Pink Dolphin. They were now a tribe of animals, pawing, running, invisible in our jungle, eyes shining and seeing in the night. Carlos canoed the mighty river, laughing—because he did not know he had animals tracking him.

All through the collective storytelling, I'd kept my eye on Sarah. The flat affect and detachment I'd first seen in her was the deadness Sarah carried, the violence that had hollowed out her inside, the friend who haunted her imagination. But now her face was alive, responding to each animal's report of tracking Carlos. She hung on the words, looking sud-denly very young, like a small girl eagerly awaiting her turn to enter a jump rope.

"Hey, I'm getting away from you!" I said, snarling as I imagined Carlos would. I paddled my canoe and gave a harsh laugh. "I'll escape, easy!"

"No!" Sarah shouted. "Let *me* tell it!"

"Tell it!" her tribe shouted.

"Well, Carlos only thinks he's getting away," Sarah smiled, waving her hands. "He's escaped from so many he's harmed before. But I call out 'FISH!' And Fish comes. He swims alongside the canoe and grows bigger,

bigger until at last, Carlos turns and sees this HUGE river monster swimming right alongside him. The mean man is afraid because suddenly Fish turns his belly up to Carlos's face. Fish forces him to look into the Soul Mirror. Carlos sees everyone he's ever killed and all the people who loved them and got left behind."

Sarah jumped into the circle of howling and snarling animals, her arms wide, her voice rising. "So . . . Carlos sees Katie and me and what he's done to us. He sees everything and he knows his soul is black. He really doesn't want to die now because he knows then he'll stare into his Soul Mirror forever. But Fish makes him keep looking until Carlos starts screaming—he's sorry, he's so sorry. Then . . ." Sarah shouted, "fish *eats* him!"

The animals roared and cawed and congratulated Sarah for calling Fish to mirror a murderer's soul before taking jungle justice.

Class was over, but no one wanted to leave. We wanted to stay in our jungle, stay within our animals—and so we did. I asked the kids to close their eyes and call their animals to accompany them home. Some Indigenous South American cultures believe when you are born, an animal is born with you, I said. This animal protects and lives alongside you even if it's far away in an Amazon jungle—it came into the world at the same time you did. And your animal dies with you to guide you back into the spirit world.

The kids decided to go home and make animal masks, returning the next day wearing the faces of their chosen animal. When they came into class the next day, it was as if we'd never left the Amazon. Someone dimmed the lights. There were drawings everywhere of jaguars and chimps and snakes. Elaborate animal masks had replaced the superheroes who began this tribal journey. We sat behind our masks in a circle with the lights low, and there was an acute, alert energy running between us, as eyes met behind animal faces.

As someone who grew up in the forest wild, who first memorized the earth with my hands, I have every reason to feel this familiar animal resonance. But many of these teenagers have barely been in the woods; in fact, many city kids are often afraid of nature. These kids would not have willingly signed up for an Outward Bound program, for instance, or volunteered to go backpacking.

Most of these kids were not environmentalists who worry about saving nature; they don't think about recycling in a world they believe already ruined and, in their imaginations, abandoned for intergalactic, nomadic futures. Yet, when imagining an Amazon forest, too thick for weapons to penetrate, too primitive for their superhero battles, they return instinctively to their animal selves. These are animals they have only seen in zoos or on television. Yet there is a profound identification, an ease of inhabiting another species, which portends great hope for our own species' survival. Not because nature is "out there" to be saved or sanctioned, but because nature is *in* us, in these kids. The ancient, green world has never left us, though we have long ago left the forest.

As we told our Amazon stories over the next week, the rainforest thrived in the sterile classroom. Lights low, surrounded by serpents, jaguars, elephants, wolves, I'd as often hear growls, hisses, and howls as words.

They may be young, but kids' memories and alliances with the animals are very old. By telling their own animal stories, they are practicing ecology at its most profound and healing level. Story as ecology. It's so simple, something we've forgotten. In our wildlife conservation, the emphasis has been on saving species, not *becoming* them. It is our own spiritual relationship to animals that must evolve. Any change begins with imagining ourselves in a new way.

Children, like some adults, know the real world stretches farther than what we can see. They shift easily between visions of our tribal past and our future worlds. The limits of the adult world are there for these teenagers, but they still have a foot in the vast, inner magic of childhood. It is this magical connection I called upon when I asked the kids on the last day of our class to perform the Dance of the Animals.

Slowly, in rhythm to the deep, bell-like beat of my cherished Makah drum, each animal entered the circle and soon the dance sounded like this: *Boom, step, twirl,* and *slither and stalk* and *snarl* and *chirp* and *caw, caw. Glide, glow, growl,* and *whistle* and *howl* and *shriek* and *trill* and *hiss, hiss.*

We danced as the humid, lush jungle filled the room. In our story stretching between us and the Amazon, we connected with those animals and their spirits. In return, we were complete—with animals as Soul Mirrors. We remembered who we were, by allowing the animals inside us to also survive.

A child's imagination is a primal force, just as strong as lobbying efforts and boycotts and endangered species acts. When children claim another species as not only their imaginary friend, but also as the animal within them—an ally—doesn't that change the outer world?

The dance is not over, if we have our animal partners. When the kids left our last class, they still fiercely wore their masks. Even on the bus, they stayed deep in their animal character. I like to imagine those strong, young animals out there now in this wider jungle. I believe that Rat will survive the inner-city gangs; Chimp will find his characteristic comedy even as his parents deal with divorce; and Fish will always remember his truth-telling Soul Mirror.

As for Sarah, she joined the Jaguar clan, elected as the first girl-leader over much boy-growling. When Sarah left our jungle, she reminded me, "Like jaguar—I can still see in the dark."

LEOPARD AND SILKIE:
A FRIENDSHIP

"That is happiness: to be dissolved into something complete and great."

—WILLA CATHER

A CROWDED ALKI BEACH thronged with bright red and blue umbrellas. There were volleyball nets on hot sand, sunbathers slathering oil on burning skin, and kids screaming and splashing in the cold surf. It was a typical weekend on this popular shore in West Seattle. Though I've lived on this city beach for two decades, I avoid its loud multitudes every summer. But I couldn't *not* heed the call from my good neighbor, Nancy Poole.

"Pup on the beach," Nancy's voice was anxious. "Umbilical cord still attached. Pup is already mobbed by people with cell phones. Someone just kicked him to see if he was still alive. Can you come?"

I didn't have the time to interrupt my work; and the last thing I wanted was to engage with the rowdy beach swarm. But for the last several years, a few of my neighbors and I had formed a small cadre of what we called "Seal Sitters" to stand guard over the seals who spend half their lives sharing our shores. It was August, the height of pupping season, and this year we'd had a bumper crop of newborns.

When I arrived on Alki, the scene was chaotic, right out of the film *Beach Party Bingo*. I politely made my way through a circle of curious beachgoers with my plastic tape and a few wooden garden stakes. Pounding the posts in the sand and surrounding the tiny pup in a wide crib of yellow caution tape, like that used in crime scenes, Nancy and I established a perimeter. We'd been taught by the advisors who were part of the "stranding network" at NOAA (National Oceanic and Atmospheric Agency) to watch over the seals who, though not endangered, are still listed for protection under the 1972 Marine Mammal Protection Act (MMPA).

"No sign of the mother," Nancy said, her silver hair in pigtails. "Probably parked her pup here at dawn when nobody was here . . . and she won't be back for hours."

We went over the checklist: *Is the pup plump? How's the breathing? Any sign of the mother offshore? Injuries? Agitated?*

Nancy was sweating and fragile under her floppy sunhat. We neighbors always worried about Nancy's long, devoted hours sitting vigil with any pup. A retired schoolteacher, Nancy was also dealing with a debilitating health issue. But she was determined, as first on the scene, to stay until we could call in other volunteers. That summer, there were only five or six of us on the phone tree list. We called ourselves "neighborhood naturalists," and had grown to be more than neighbors. We were friends, the kind you call in need, especially if that includes other animals on our busy beach.

The tiny pup was alert, the blubbery body round—signs of good health and consistent nursing. But he was startled by noises: trucks, car alarms, motorcycles, and loud voices. We could not stop the noise; but we could courteously ask the people to give him the large space that he needed to rest. The pup was not yet wary or self-protective, more like a little ET on the beach. Who knew how long his mother would be away or even if she would come back with such a mob of people?

"Is it stranded?" a worried mother, hoisting twins, asked as about twenty people pushed at the flimsy tape perimeter for a better view.

"No, seals belong here, too," Nancy answered in her firm, informative teacher's voice. "If you stand back and give the pup some breathing room, you can see better." Nancy handed one of the twins a pair of tiny binoculars.

"Wooooooowwww," the little girl cried out and her twin brother shushed her, then grabbed the binoculars.

"My turn!"

"Let's name him Spud," one of the twins suggested. Right across the street from this beach was Spud's Fish and Chips.

"Good idea," Nancy smiled as if giving the twins a gold star. "If the mother returns and finds her pup surrounded by too many people, she might leave him," Nancy explained. "Perhaps abandoning the pup forever. A nursing pup separated from his mother will not survive."

The idea of losing their own mother seemed to make the twins fall into a hushed alertness. One twin held onto her mother more tightly. The crowd quieted and fell into a contemplative vigil along with us.

This is my favorite time with my own species, when we fall into a reverie of curiosity and kindness for another, not just our own. It is empathy and kinship made visible. You can see this meditative abiding with another, especially on the faces of children, so vulnerable themselves in a bright and sometimes overwhelming world.

With the beach crowds keeping a respectful distance now, the pup seemed to realize he was among friends. Spud rolled on his back to expose his round baby belly—a sure sign of trust in many species. Through binoculars we could see the little black dot of his umbilical cord with no sign of infection. No yellow discharge from his eyes and nose. We scanned to see if there were any bullet holes, gashes, orca bites, or obvious signs of injury. Though Washington State has a healthy harbor seal population, only 50 percent of these newborns will survive their first year. Wild predators, domestic dogs, infection, dehydration, starvation, ingestion of plastics like balloons or bags, or human interference are the reasons so many die.

Not on our watch.

Relaxing deeply, Spud delighted us with a bright red tongue yawn and tiny baby teeth. His silver fur was luxurious and a perfectly mottled camouflage against the beach stones. Most striking were his huge, black eyes fixed on us with that rapt gaze common to all infants. We call this eye contact between human adult and infant *attunement*. When a newborn follows his caretaker's gaze, this is the beginning of empathy and connection.

As the hours passed, Spud sighed, turned on his side, and wrapped his tiny flippers around his robust body. His breathing steadied into deep sleep. I called Kristin Wilkinson, a marine mammal stranding specialist at NOAA. She is as expert as she is helpful. From our description—two and a half feet long and about 25 pounds—she determined Spud was about six weeks old.

"They are weaned at four to six weeks," Kristin explained. "You know, most nursing takes place at night. I once watched over a seal pup for ten days and the mother returned every evening to nurse then go back to sea. You may be there awhile."

We were there for quite a while. In a particularly big crowd, a woman with a camera slung around her neck emerged to ask if she could take photos of this very charismatic, and by now popular, seal. So many people had captured photos of Spud. But after she took hundreds of photos, keeping a very respectful distance from the pup, I asked the woman if she would send me a few of her shots.

"Sure," she said. "I'll send you JPEGs tonight. I'm a photographer."

Oh, right, I thought dismissingly. *Everybody's a photographer.* I'd seen hundreds of blurry, grainy cell phone photos from beachgoers who sent me their images. Hers would probably be just a few more, unusable portraits of a silver blob on the sand.

Skeptically, I studied the slender woman's weathered baseball cap, heavy backpack, and vest with many tiny pockets. She looked like she was outfitted for a long mountain hike, not a beach jaunt.

"Yeah," I said. "I'm a writer."

I was to learn later that this woman was equally unimpressed with me when we first met on that beach over Spud. But that night, when I received a large file of Spud photos from Robin Lindsey, I gasped in wonder. Here was a plump, healthy seal pup, tail flippers lifted, huge, black eyes curious, pectoral fins tucked as he rolled in the sand as if posing for the adoring audience. Robin's portraits were so intimate, so luminous, they took my breath away. I realized I was seeing Spud through the eyes of a brilliant artist. Someone who captures the soul of an animal, not just the science.

"My God, you really *are* a photographer," I told Robin when I called her that night. "Never seen such tenderness in wildlife photos . . ."

In her characteristic, self-effacing laugh, she confessed. "Looked you up online. You really *are* a writer."

Together Robin and I founded an all-volunteer group that began with a few concerned, good neighbors and evolved into a grassroots citizen-naturalist team, trained by NOAA, and now a member of the Northwest Marine Mammal Stranding Network. For the next fifteen years, Seal Sitters volunteers would sit vigil and watch over countless seals: mothers nursing tiny newborns, injured juveniles who suffered from starvation and "failure to thrive," adult seals trapped in fishing nets, seals riddled with bullet holes from fishermen who routinely scapegoat marine mammals for low catches.

We volunteers sit together, watching from a careful distance, binoculars trained on a seal's every move, scanning for wounds or behavioral signs of internal injuries or distress. For up to forty-eight hours, in four- to six-hour shifts, we politely keep people and dogs a hundred yards away from any pup or seal on the beach, as recommended by the MMPA. We explain seal conservation to beachcombers and invite them to join us. Most Seattle city beaches—as along so many coastlines around the world—are lined by concrete sea walls. Alki, however, is a natural beach, and one of the few haul-out sites left in the city where harbor seals can give birth, rest, molt their silver-gray spotted coat, and spend time in community with one another.

The seal's speckled fur is camouflage on rocky beaches. I've watched joggers and clam diggers pass unaware within ten feet of a resting seal. But the seal on shore notices everything: the hoarse caw and the flap of a great blue heron lifting on wide wings, laughing schoolchildren at the bus stop, people digging for razor clams, a fierce osprey hungry for fish spiraling down into the surf, a young girl, tuned in only to her headphones, hip-hopping along the sand.

For many hours, hundreds of seal sitters have sat companionably over seals in the kind of abiding friendship of good neighbors. One teenager did his community service stint by seal sitting and picking up beach trash, like undigestible plastics and lethal balloons that slowly strangle and kill marine mammals. Many who were seal sitters as kids have gone on to become conservationists and study wildlife or environmental studies in college. One of the young girls, Etienne Leche-Rey, an eleven-year-old dedicated seal sitter, was interviewed with me on NPR's national "Living on Earth" series. Etienne told the story of naming her first seal "Forte" because he was strong and had been injured. She did a second-grade science project on her Seal Sitters work. When asked by the NPR host, "Would you spend so much of your time and emotional energy saving an animal if it were ugly?" Etienne promptly answered, "Well, I would. They're still an animal. And they're still a life and they're still part of our planet."

Etienne is now an honors student at Stanford, and she credits her seal sitting volunteer work with expanding her sense of kinships, teaching her about reciprocity, and making alliances in all species.

Over the years, we've trained a thousand neighborhood naturalists to become seal sitters. Robin has taken the lead in these trainings and worked closely with NOAA biologists, who benefit from her wildlife photography, especially in hard-to-diagnose cetacean strandings or pinniped deaths. She also writes the "Blubberblog" on the SealSitters.org website with stories of seals we have kept watch over. Like Jane Goodall with her Gombe chimpanzees, we've named all our West Seattle seals. Naming other animals gives them the respect they deserve. It also characterizes their personalities and engages human interest—because seals are as individual and idiosyncratic as anyone.

Whoever first discovers a seal on the shore gets the honor of naming. Such fanciful names as "Queen Latifah" for the elegantly curved and beautiful harbor seal declared "gorgeous" by rapt beachgoers, or "Neptune" for a week-old pup, so terribly thin, his fur fell in wrinkles around his ribs.

"This one could be in trouble," Kristin said when we called her for advice. "Or, he could be so new that he's only had a few days to nurse."

This newborn was able to hop away from the incoming tide, rest onshore, and warm his little body. But we worried about that shrunken belly. To make sure he survived, Nancy named him "Neptune," after the strong god of the sea, and another volunteer dubbed him "Thorfiin Rollo, the First Earl of Orkney" after a Scottish Hebrides ancestor. Our newborn became "Neptune Orkeny, the First Earl of Alki." He returned to what I call our "day care on the beach" and thrived, delighting many volunteers and beachgoers.

So many stories and so many seals; but for me, the most enduring is witnessing a friendship between two seal pups who saved each other's lives. One morning I got a call from Robin, a very early riser who often patrols the beaches before sunrise looking for seals.

"Got a really thin pup," Robin shouted over the din of boat traffic. "Adorable . . . but he's panting heavily."

She was calling from Seacrest Park, Seattle's most popular dive site and the boarding dock for the Elliott Bay Water Taxi. It is not the best beach for seal napping. Perhaps the pup was not there to rest, but to die. "I'm there," I promised.

Grabbing my tide chart, binoculars, rain slicker, water bottle, and breakfast burrito for a long stay, I speed-dialed a few other volunteers. But it was too early for most seal sitters, who promised to join in the vigil soon. When I arrived on that gloomy gray morning, there was an elder gentleman sitting quietly in a portable chair beside Robin. Fortunately, Seacrest is across the street from a contingent of seal sitters who call themselves the "Condo Brigade." While working from home offices, these volunteers help keep close watch from their windows via telescopes trained on the seals. They also help with dispatch calls and send out email alerts to other volunteers.

Robin was kneeling on the sand using a telephoto lens to take photos of the newborn pup to send quickly to NOAA. "Watch to see if the pup's breathing steadies or if he has any yellow discharge from his nose and mouth," she whispered to the gentleman. "Signs of infection."

That year, we'd already lost several pups to a respiratory virus called lungworm, or pneumonia. Robin's photos were invaluable, not only for evaluating and tracking the pup's health, but also to help NOAA monitor disease and injury among the seal population.

"Here how long on shore?" I asked Robin, as a foghorn blasted from a passing Seattle-bound ferryboat. The keening moan startled the pup, who was snuggled between a mossy boulder and a patch of beach grass. With his golden fur, adorned with constellations of black specks, his unblinking, black eyes wide open, wondering, he was the loveliest seal pup I'd ever seen. Through my binocs, I saw his white baby whiskers twitch and tremble as he sniffed the air for any scent of predators, especially dogs off-leash. As if relieved it was just a few humans, who were keeping a proper distance, the pup stretched, yawning wide, his baby teeth clearly visible. I knew from my NOAA training that the veins of seals are close to the surface of the skin in the fore and hind flippers, allowing them to regulate their overall body temperature. Seals do not have the ability to produce sweat like we do, so this stretching and yawning is their way of cooling down. Constant swimming and foraging for food takes immense energy, especially in the young.

Cloaked in moist fog and marine mists, I shivered, envying the seal pup's dense fur. "He's a real beauty," I breathed. "Like a golden leopard."

"Yeah, but this Leopard is starving." Robin frowned.

For two days we watched over little Leopard and saw his belly shrink, rib and hipbones jutting out against the skin in jagged angles, his fur folding in on itself as malnourishment set in. He was lethargic, sun-blasted, and so weary. No mother in sight. How long had it been since he'd nursed? He was too young to fish for himself. NOAA had trained us to give any newborn pup at least 48 hours before interfering; and, if the abandoned pup seemed viable, to transport him in a small kennel to PAWS wildlife hospital for rehab and hoped-for release back into the wild.

Gazing at a brand-new fellow creature and realizing that I might be the first human this newborn pup had ever met always fills me with a sense of awe—and responsibility. First contact. First love. The ancient Greeks defined several kinds of love: *eros*, for the romance and desire of "intimate love;" *philia*, a more noble bond like "brotherly love," considered the human ideal because it also involved loyalty and sacrifice; and *agape*, which is freely given, universal, charitable, and selflessly offered—even to those we've never met. I would add that *agape* is also for those who are not simply our own kind. *Agape* love is what I've had the pleasure of witnessing with the many altruistic strangers on our beach as they watch in wonder and sympathy for seals.

But little Leopard of Seacrest Park revealed the bond of perhaps all three forms of love. On the third morning, as we prepared to rescue him from his motherless misery on our beach, another seal pup hauled out. Of course, Robin was the first on the scene to spot the luminous white female, a juvenile plump and feisty. She scooted up beach to nestle along-side Leopard in the barnacled rocks. Robin named her "Silkie" for those shape-shifting selkies of Celtic myths who shed their skins to mate and live with humans—before returning to the seal folk, sometimes with their hybrid human offspring in tow.

Silkie was so robust and healthy, especially in stark contrast to Leopard's skinny fragility. She had the most expressive eyes—round, obsidian mirrors that looked up and held ours without fear. A human can get lost in those soulful, dark eyes, just like the old selkie myths tell us. Eyes haunting and somehow deeply familiar. No wonder we fall in love.

Leopard lifted his head, greeted Silkie with a flap of his pectoral flippers, and immediately fell into a profound sleep, as if he knew he was no longer alone. Robin snapped a photo of the two pups together—Silkie with her head tucked into Leopard's sagging flanks, Leopard's tail flippers furled again like a golden sail as they slept, tightly cuddled together. For the first time in two days, Leopard returned to the sea, following Silkie's lead as they both slipped into the surf. Would Silkie be able to teach Leopard to fish or fish *for* him to help nourish them both?

"Probably won't see them again," Robin mused. "Let's hope they stay together and haul out on a quieter beach."

But the next day both pups were back. First Leopard would crawl out on Seacrest shore, his flipper-tracks etched in soft, wet sand like brief hieroglyphics—*I am here!*

Then Silkie. *Me, too!*

It was marvelous to see that in just one day, Leopard was stronger, his belly noticeably rounder. Seal sitters took copious field notes of both pups' behavior and activity. When a rumbling garbage truck startled Leopard from his slumber, he raised his head, glanced around, wide-eyed. One of the seal sitters crooned a soft lullaby, which elicited a sigh from Silkie and a quick return to sleep.

"They look just like aquatic puppies," someone fondly remarked.

Pictures of these seal pups were not only flashed like breaking news across our internet Seal Sitters phone tree, but the sibling-like pups were also so popular that we had to manage daily crowds of well-wishers and local media.

We were amazed that the pups hauled out together every day at 5:30 a.m., like clockwork. Then they would loll around, napping in the sunshine for hours until late afternoon, when they'd ease back into the surf for a night of fishing.

"Wonder how long they'll stay with us?" Robin asked. Her characteristic and rather dour nature giving way, each day, to a kind of wistful hope. She'd seen too many dead and dying seals to be optimistic.

But I, always the idealist, dearly wanted this daily love-in to never end. Would Leopard and Silkie stay together, possibly even mate?

"We can't let it end here," I whispered to Robin one afternoon.

We watched Silkie turn on her belly, her flippers opening to the sunlight. Leopard stretched and leaned against Silkie's outflung flipper.

"They'll be gone tomorrow," Robin predicted, and snapped another multitude of museum-quality photos.

But the next day, they weren't gone. Leopard and Silkie continued to grace Seacrest Park, as if realizing it was safe harbor. They had hundreds of adoring humans respectfully observing and wishing them well. Under such kind scrutiny, and because of their strong alliance, they flourished. Leopard gained weight and energy; Silkie grew even plumper.

Their long naps were legendary, with people setting their alarms to come to Seacrest in the hope of just watching them sleep, their bodies entwined. It was like pure peace and contentment made visible. Something set right again. A world made whole.

For two wonderful weeks, Leopard and Silkie hauled out together. Grandmothers and grandfathers parked themselves in zero-gravity recliners to watch over the sleeping pups; children rode piggyback on parents to get the best view of a golden leopard-spotted seal and his bright white "big sister" who was teaching Leopard how to fish. A local, and somewhat scary, gang made a habit of what I called "drive-by sightings," to patrol the midnight beach and keep the pups safe from drunks wandering the boardwalk after the bars closed at 2 a.m. Divers diverted their underwater explorations to give the pups undisturbed space for fishing. Kayakers kept their distance, drifting far offshore with huge binoculars that looked like antennas. We just couldn't get enough of this bonded pair, this love story of survival and friendship.

One day just as we knew must happen—because these were wild animals, not pets or in a zoo, because they had their own natural lives to lead in the vast Salish Sea, either together or apart—Leopard and Silkie *were* at last gone. There were soon other seals to watch over that summer, but we all were somewhat heartbroken not to rush to the beach and find Leopard and Silkie together. Letting go is always part of the story and bond with wild animals.

"Hey, let's tell their story," I suggested to Robin, "so Leopard and Silkie are not lost, so everyone can meet them." I thought of all the kids in the crowds who lingered longest, who were the most rapt at every bark and funny snuffle, every comic yawn and cozy nap. "How about a kid's book?"

"Ever written one?" Robin asked, dubious.

I'd only written for adults. How hard could it be? I wondered. Just a short story and Robin's stunning photos. Turns out, *Leopard and Silkie: One Boy's Quest to Save Seal Pups* was the hardest book I've ever written. But those two precious weeks chronicling the lifesaving bond of these pups would become my biggest-selling book so far. Seal Sitters grassroots groups gathered on other far-flung shores. Our dispatch volunteers would receive emails from kids in Scotland, Russia, or Iran asking, "Can you come quick? Pup on the beach." Sadly, we'd have to inform them we were only *local*, but they could form their own citizen naturalist volunteers.

One day, Nancy called our hotline. She and her neighbor were watching through telescopes as a seal pup struggled vainly to climb atop driftwood floating in the waves. Repeatedly the pup grabbed hold with front flippers and then fell off the driftwood.

"It breaks my heart that the pup never could find a place to rest," Nancy said.

Her neighbor, Susan, asked her husband to build a six-by-six-foot floating platform for the seals off their private beach. Soon, seal mothers came to nurse their pups, and the young ones napped without threat of predators on this "life raft." We all watched a pup we named Sunny lie on that platform for days, bleeding from a boat propeller gash on its neck.

We thought we would lose the pup, but a week of sun healed him. Susan also witnessed on this float what few people, even marine biologists, ever see: the birth of a seal pup.

These rafts for seals now dot several West Seattle beaches and people worldwide have contacted Seal Sitters for the design to build their own life rafts for wildlife. There is still a raft nearby my waterfront apartment. Some kind neighbor constructed it after my original raft drifted away in a wild storm. Every morning and dusk I watch through binoculars as healthy adult and juvenile seals rest and snuggle together, so they don't have to brave our busy shores.

Much has changed since our early days of seal sitting, including the seals. We've had several years of high pup mortality rates, and fewer volunteers. During the pandemic, all marine mammals got a reprieve from our human noise and manic beaches. But just last weekend, I drove along Alki Beach boardwalk looking for seal pups; the street was as densely crowded as a parking lot, with hundreds of people on the sand. It took me thirty minutes to drive the length of the beach. Every species seeks the sea, and I certainly do not begrudge those of us who long to be in the cold waves on these increasingly hot Seattle global-warming days. But I do worry about how little space there is left to share the shore with seals.

Our Seal Sitter first-responders, Lynn Shimamoto and David and Elaine Hutchinson, have taken the lead now, still devotedly watching over seals who haul out on our beaches. Robin and her partner have moved to Whidbey Island where there is an expansive quiet and many seal pups. Sometimes when I train my binocs on the life raft outside my window, I see juvenile seals napping together, their speckled bodies blissfully plump after a good night of fishing. I remember that newborn pup with golden leopard fur and the blazing white Silkie who found each other in a sometimes dangerous and always chilly sea. Two pups whose lifesaving alliance also taught many children about friendship.

Pups on the beach, I say softly, the mantra that calls Seal Sitters to come. And I sing a little prayer I first made up as a lullaby for Leopard and Silkie as they dreamed on our beach:

May you find many fish.
May you live long and strong.
May you know you are loved.

GRANNY: THE GRANDMOTHER EFFECT

"Know the male yet keep to the female."

—TAO TE CHING, VERSE 28

IT IS PERFECTLY still on the Georgia Strait. Long summer sunlight slants across the quiet waves, illuminating our boat. No generators can be heard. Only the hydrophone's rapid calls of orcas communicating. There is a high-pitched clicking ricochet and then rapid-fire squeaks of ultrasonic echoes like a rusty hinge.

This is orca talk over long distances, almost out of human hearing. Certainly, we cannot see the complex family relationships, because so much of it is under water. But new and exciting discoveries have led some researchers to declare that orcas have their own distinct vocal and behavioral "culture."

As Howard Garnett of Orca Network, an advocacy group, tells the gathered whale watchers onboard: "Orcas practice cooperative hunting, maintain sophisticated family structures, pass knowledge down through generations. These orcas live in sophisticated, matrilineal societies."

Our onboard naturalist, Emily, is like an ambassador, studying these majestic orcas every day. She gives us a laminated sheet of photos identifying the dorsal fins of the southern community—J, K, and L pods, who have been intensely studied for four decades.

Suddenly a mighty dorsal fin rises in the cold waves. An exhalation at 100 mph.

"Granny!" our naturalist happily welcomes the whale. "She's J-2, the oldest whale in J pod. This whale is somewhere between sixty and eighty years old."

We study our orca-identification charts as if sharing a family album. Everyone cries out in excitement as Granny and several other orcas come close to our boat, and then dive together with backstrokes of powerful tail flukes. Soon the synchronized *whoosh, whoosh* as Granny suddenly surfaces again, and we are lost in the warm mists of whale breaths.

I'm thrilled to at last meet this legendary J pod elder who has not only spawned so many generations, but also still leads them through dangerous and dwindling waters. Granny is beloved as the ultimate orca matriarch. In the 1960s when orcas were being captured by marine aquariums for captive tanks, Granny was in her 40s, deemed too old and probably postmenopausal for the solitary confinement, breeding, and the abuse of aquarium captivity. She has enjoyed another five decades in the wild, captivating whale watchers and researchers with her acrobatic leaps.

We applaud one of those breaches near our boat as Granny splashes down, soaking those of us hanging over the railings. I love watching even usually reserved people suddenly turn into kids, calling out and clapping as the orcas rise, spin, and then wave those gigantic whale flukes as they dive again. It's as if we humans can never get enough of this mammalian alliance with a species who has so much to teach and mirror for us.

Howard nods and fondly greets this familiar whale. "Granny here is counselor and guide," he smiles. "The teacher of traditions."

Granny cruises alongside our boat as if guiding us, too. She is huge, about 22 feet long and weighing four tons, with an identifying scoop in her dorsal fin from an old injury. It is astonishing to think about all the human events Granny's long life has spanned. Long before our computers and internet existed, Granny was memorizing the best fishing waters and teaching her many offspring to navigate boat traffic. Granny gave birth well into her elder years and has led her J pod on epic travels, sometimes as far south as Monterey, California, an 800-mile journey from their resident waters off the San Juan Islands near the border of British Columbia. This well-known matriarch expertly found the richest runs of Chinook salmon, navigating her family pod through changing waters.

As Granny and her fifty-one-year-old son, Ruffles, float and loll alongside us, the blast of their breath in perfect synch, I wonder what it would be like to synchronize your breath with another being, for a whole life long. How much close attention and synchrony that relationship would require. When I teach schoolkids about orcas, I always ask them to sit back-to-back and try to breathe together. It's an intimacy, a meditation, that only lasts minutes before we break into our separate worlds of breath and body. Imagine what shared consciousness this kind of orca respiration requires. Orcas, like most cetaceans, do not sleep, they only rest one side of their brains at a time in a waking flow, a marine dream, a floating mindfulness.

Suddenly, Granny turns, gazes up at the people leaning out, our hands reaching for her though we are a hundred yards away. We want to touch, to understand, to be part of her pod. I find myself breathing deeply, as if I can borrow a bit of this cetacean awareness. Whenever I am near orcas, even in research boats much farther away, I always feel less alone, connected with a consciousness I long to understand, but can only try to fathom. I wonder, as I watch Granny's son breathing with her, swimming close, what it would be like to live in a matriarchal society. Granny often adopted orcas from other pods, especially young males whose mothers had died. Whenever Granny took on the care of male offspring—who generally live ten years less than their female siblings—researchers knew the orphaned orca calf had a much better chance of survival.

There is fascinating new research from the Center for Whale Research (CWR) that North Pacific orca mothers make a "lifelong sacrifice" for their sons. "While young female offspring become independent in adulthood," BBC science writer Victoria Gill notes, "males depend on their mothers—even demanding a share of the food that their matriarchs catch." Living all their lives alongside these self-sacrificing mothers, orca sons have a better chance of surviving. But the cost for the matriarchs is high; the CWR research reveals that "for each living son, a mother's annual likelihood of rearing another calf to one-year-old was cut by half."

If a mother orca dies, the chances of her male calf dying is eight times more likely. The fact that orca mothers have been observed literally sharing and feeding their salmon to their sons has gained these male offspring the moniker "Mummy's boys." There might be an evolutionary benefit to this mother-coddling because "the biggest, oldest males go on to father many offspring."

This intense and lifelong bond between mothers and sons might explain why orca matriarchs, like Granny, live on many years past menopause. Only three mammal species go through menopause—orcas, short-finned pilot whales, and humans. Orca females stop reproducing in their thirties or forties, but they can live many years more. Scientists have long wondered what benefit menopause—when females cease being able to reproduce—offers to any species' survival.

"Female orcas and women evolved to live long, active, post-reproductive lives," writes Lucy Cooke in *Bitch*. Cooke romps through new research on female animals' behavior, complex mating preferences, and wily, adaptive abilities. She concludes: "Our human leaders would benefit from a paralimbic lobe transplant—to become more like these wise and compassionate matriarchs, with their unfathomable emotions and supportive, socially inclusive society."

The study of other animals has long been a male bastion with research centered on Darwinian theories of hierarchy and competition—the "king of the hill" point of view. Because there were so few women studying animal behavior, the conclusions drawn then about animal lives and societies were often as biased as the patriarchal prejudices in our own species. But the number of women researchers in the field of animal studies increased dramatically in the twenty-first century. For example, where once there was only the outlier of Jane Goodall in primate research, now primatologists are 50 percent women. As more women study animals, often living for decades in the field alongside them, they've documented how vital females are in animal societies—from the matriarchal elephants, orcas, dolphins, and lions, to the sisterhoods of hyenas and the female friendship bonding among bonobos who "make love, not war," assuring a less violent community.

Recent discoveries about the value of postmenopausal females in both orcas and humans counter the sexist, Darwinian emphasis on male dominance and "survival of the fittest"—that was assumed to mean survival of the strongest male. Now, researchers consider the gift of matriarchs and sisterhoods to any species' survival. "It is a biological cost-benefit analysis . . . whether an older female brings a measurable benefit to her existing family, which outweighs the generic cost of having no more babies."

Any human grandmother charged with taking care of next generations can easily speak to this value. Grandmothers "increase the survival chances of the rest of their family, and therefore their own genes." Because of their decades of experience, matriarchal orcas remember the best salmon runs; their accumulated knowledge makes them natural leaders.

"Older females took the lead more often during years when salmon supplies were low, suggesting that the pod might be reliant on their experience, their ecological knowledge," says Professor Darren Croft, who along with the late Dr. Ken Balcomb, has studied postmenopausal orcas. Individual elders and matriarchs like Granny store this knowledge and can teach the next generations "because post-reproductive grandmothers have more time and resources to share when they're not taking care of their own calves."

These postmenopausal matriarchs lead busy, fulfilling lives and are essential caretakers in the pod's society. On my visit to OrcaLab, researcher Helena Symonds told me, "When a calf is born, the pod takes the newborn on a tour of their range to imprint knowledge of all the special areas. One summer, we observed the oldest seventy-year-old female led the tour. As she swam past, every other orca came up to her, spent a few moments with her, and then moved away to allow her to pass."

Such respect for an elder is an echo of human societies who also value and revere those who have lived long. This "grandmother effect" in orca families is a "powerful evolutionary strategy . . . so powerful that the death of a grandmother can negatively affect a grand-whale's chance of survival even after it has reached adulthood."

Many of our human societies are patriarchal, so learning about matriarchs in other animals is inspiring and instructive. The essential role of mothers, grandmothers, aunties, and sisters in many other animal societies is finally getting its due—and the discoveries are significant. Here in the Northwest, cougars were once considered to be mostly solitary and quite territorial, possessively patrolling and defending their ranges. According to the Cougar Fund, new research has revealed that mother cougars "are dedicated mothers and either pregnant or raising dependent cubs for the majority (over 75%) of their lives." These mother cougars can be "tolerant of slight overlaps in their territories with other females" and will valiantly defend-to-the-death their kittens from hunters, poachers, and a male mountain lion, who will sometimes kill kittens to mate and repopulate with his own offspring. As cougar kittens grow, more females survive than males because of the territorial fights between males.

On the West Coast, we are fortunate to have four decades of research lead by the late Ken Balcomb, a visionary who founded the Center for Whale Research in Friday Harbor in the San Juan Islands in Washington State's Puget Sound region; as well as the Orca Network, founded by Susan Berta and Howie Garrett; and Canada's OrcaLab, where researchers Helena Symonds and Paul Spong have documented the vocalizations of generations of orca family pods. Like librarians and linguists of orca culture and language, these researchers have revealed to the world the extraordinary lives of these fellow creatures.

Less well-known orca researchers include BC's whale biologist and author Alexandra Morton, and marine mammal biologist and poet Eva Saulitis, both human matriarchs and researchers. For thirty years, Saulitis and her biologist partner Craig Matkin studied orcas in Prince William Sound, Alaska, and, before her early death at fifty-two, she cofounded North Gulf Oceanic Society, a research, conservation, and education nonprofit. Studying orcas for half her life, Saulitis wrote movingly about the Chugach orca pods and mourned that "Chugach transients are going extinct. They are leaving the earth under my watch. There will, perhaps in my lifetime, be a last one. How do I accept the reality of the word 'extinction?'"

Saulitis had to witness her beloved orcas navigate the 1989 Exxon Valdez oil spill in Prince William Sound, one of the worst environmental disasters in the US. After swimming through the toxic, iridescent oil sheen and noxious vapors in their home waters, both transient and resident orca pods would never fully recover from the spill. NOAA and other researchers have followed the generations post-spill and found "stark differences." A year and a half after the spill, resident pods lost 33 percent and transients 44 percent of their populations. The transients have never recovered and are listed under the MMPA as "depleted." Resident orca family pods have never reached their pre-spill numbers.

Saulitis, together with Canadian author and activist Alexandra Morton, embody what I think of as a somewhat unsung orca sisterhood. Both women have made extraordinary contributions to the study of orcas. Early in her research career, Morton gave up studying vocalizations in captive orcas, noting, "there was nothing more than tragedy to observe in captive whales." For thirty years, she has documented orcas and salmon in the Broughton Archipelago. She's often referred to as the "Jane Goodall of Canada" for her passionate advocacy to hold BC's farmed salmon industry accountable for the lethal pathogens—sea lice, bacteria, and viruses—their farms generate. The farms expose wild salmon stocks that are already at risk and thus the orcas dependent upon them for food. In *Not on My Watch*, Morton writes: "I had planned a quiet obscure life in the wilderness studying orca, but without salmon, the place I called home felt like it was dying."

Saulitis and Morton, like other women researchers, are mirroring the orca matriarchs, whose long memories and teaching skills assure the survival of new generations of endangered calves.

It is not only the matriarchs who help assure the survival of the family; it is also the many aunties who are midwives, babysitters, and companions if they are not themselves mothers. Researchers Sara and James Heimlich-Boran note in *Killer Whales* that the close sisterhood of juvenile orca females suggests that "same sex may be as important as age in determining relationships" and that "associations between mothers and barren females showed the most stability over time." Because the mother-progeny bond is of primary importance, the strong alliance between barren females and mothers implies that the "relationship is one of kinship." And kinship among aunts and sisters and mothers is centered on cooperation and caretaking.

Not only must the newborn cetaceans be taught to breathe, fish, and understand the sophisticated structures of their society and communication, but newborns often stay all their lives near their mothers to become helpful aunts and later elders in the pod's highly socialized female infrastructure. What might happen if we modeled our own human societies on lessons learned from females of other species, especially cetaceans and their sisterhood of animals? We may thrive in a more matrilineal culture that values communication more than conquest. A culture that reveres matriarchs and sisters as leaders and wise teachers. We could focus on keeping our habitat sustainable for future generations, both animal and human.

That Georgia Strait whale watch was the last time I ever saw Granny, though I followed her life for many more years until 2016, the year she disappeared and was assumed dead. Her passing was news worldwide, from Europe to Asia. "World's Oldest Known Orca Presumed Dead," *National Geographic* announced.

Cetacean advocates, schoolchildren, tribes, and scientists celebrated Granny as a true and dignified elder. Some researchers claimed Granny was one hundred and five when she died, born in 1911. But one biopsy of Granny analyzed fatty acids and suggested that she was born in 1951 and her age range was more likely between mid-sixties and eighties. Still, long-lived and vitally important for her family.

"She was fun to watch," CWR researcher Deborah Giles said. "It's a heartbreaking thing for many of us."

Orca Network held a memorial, a celebration of Granny's life, at Discovery Park. Having written a children's book about Granny, called *Wild Orca: The Oldest, Wisest Whale in the World*, I was asked to speak. Looking around at the crowd, I smiled at the big sign a kid was holding up with a photo of Granny breaching and in big block letters:

GRANNY *for* MAYOR: *Respect Your Granny*

"The world needs more matriarchs like Granny," I began, looking out at the crowd of researchers, cetacean advocates, tribal leaders, and many children. "We all need grandmothers."

A tribal elder held her grandson; she wore a red-and-black blanket with a beautiful orca breaching the water in black silhouette, familiar dorsal fin, that stylized eye, all-seeing, and above the blowhole, delicate abalone buttons like breath. The Tsimshian Hyuk dancers performed a traditional dance, many with children in their arms, and it was like watching matriarchs and sisters weaving their own human pod, the drums like an interspecies heartbeat.

I remembered then my last image of Granny and her son, Ruffles, floating on waves clear as glass. So close to us, we heard every collective sigh, every slap of fin and that sweet staccato of signature whistles, which above water, sounds like cetacean jazz. We all fell silent, not exactly breathing together, but somehow intensely allied. I was deeply moved by this reverence in whale watchers as they witnessed Granny, this great elder, who deigned to linger with us a long time in the summer evening light.

The insights from the Center for Whale Research resonated with many people, like veteran naturalist Mary J. Getten, who devoted decades of her life to leading whale watch boats and studying these Southern Resident orcas. In Communicating with Orcas, Getten took the leap from researcher to animal communicator. And of course, Granny was the animal she most wanted to understand. By going beyond her scientific background, Getten took a risk; but I found her dialogues with Granny to be fascinating, credible. That's because after a life with animals, my dreams are full of other creatures who often offer wisdom from another consciousness. In fact, once when I was in the hospital with pneumonia, Granny swam into my dreams, and I breathed better.

As I watched Granny roll and slap the waves with a huge pectoral fin, gazing up at the rapt people, I remembered Getten's comment that in her first dialogues with the matriarch, she was intimidated because Granny "carries such a feeling of greatness," like a royal commanding our complete attention. Or a spiritual teacher.

When Getten asked Granny why she so often took time to connect with whale watchers, the answer was "direct and clear, almost purposeful," Getten notes. "Her awareness was beyond anything I've ever encountered with another animal."

The matriarch talked about adapting to changing seas and human noise. When Getten asked how Granny felt about all the boats and people, the orca replied: "We sense your hunger to know me and be in touch with us. We give you this contact out of love and service for our planet. Love it. Protect it. Your existence depends upon it."

On that last whale watch with Granny so near us, her eyes easily taking us in with a kind of contemplative calm, I did feel in the presence of animal greatness. I felt awed and grateful. Small, but *seen*.

"Granny loves being alive," one of the teenage boys on the boat whispered.

As if to echo him, Granny leapt high—exuberant and eternal—then did a loud back flop, splashing us all. Granny and her family slipped away through the waves, like brave, black sails.

Granny's Southern Resident family pods are often in the news even now. In spring 2023, the Southern Resident orcas made waves in headlines for visiting the San Juan Islands less than usual. A study showed that numbers of Chinook salmon, their primary food source, were down by 50 percent in the traditional summer feeding waters for the J, K, and L pods. Can the Southern Residents adapt to smaller, less nutrient-rich salmon than Chinook? Their build-up of body mass and survival depends especially on the Fraser River salmon stocks running in winter and early spring.

At the same time Chinook runs are crashing, there is the added stress of more boat traffic from ferries and cargo ships, which disrupt orca echolocation, and industrial pollution in the waters. The study also revealed that "the Southern Resident females have less hunting success than their neighbors up north." The Northern Residents in BC, who have cleaner and quieter waters with more abundant fish, have grown to a total of 300 orcas, while Granny's pods have diminished to 73. The J, K, and L pods are "struggling to survive . . . they're skinny and starving," the study concludes, "and could be plummeting toward extinction."

These dire statistics for Granny's pods are why people heralded news that Lolita (Tokitae), the fifty-seven-year-old orca and member of L pod, would be returning to the Salish Sea, to her family. Captured when she was four, Tokitae had endured five decades in an 80-foot cement tank in Miami's Seaquarium.

Lolita was finally being prepared for the 3,000-mile trip home to a natural sea pen where she would have been reunited with the family from which she was taken so long ago. One of the oldest survivors of captivity,

Toki's ninety-five-year-old mother is believed to be still alive in the wild. But in August 2023, before Toki could be returned to her L pod, the long-suffering orca died suddenly amid accusations of inadequate care, made by former vets and trainers. Veterinarian Dr. Jenna Wallace noted Toki's diet had been reduced for the past two years and so she was suffering from dehydration. "Nobody listened," she told the *Miami Herald*. "She deserved better." Another former trainer said, "What breaks my heart is that Toki died surrounded by strangers." Toki endured a lifetime of solitary confinement, far from her Northwest pod. PETA predicted that Toki's death "would lead to a harsher backlash against marine parks," and called for people to stop patronizing "abusement parks."

I will never forget a video an orca researcher once shared with me of Corky, a SeaWorld captive orca listening to vocalizations of her family pod for the first time in years. At the sound of those familiar calls and whistles, the great whale began to visibly tremble and leap desperately, as if to escape her cement prison and return to her family. It was haunting to watch such an obvious display of grief and yet hope. I am reminded of that video when I heard ecologist and conservationist Chris Morgan in "Eavesdropping on Orcas," on NPR's *The Wild* talk about the new research that "orcas have parts of their brains that are more physically developed than human brains—the parts that have to do with language, emotion, and memory. What can we learn by eavesdropping on orcas?"

Morgan interviews Jay Julius, a member of the Lummi Nation who acknowledges the ancient Indigenous bond with orcas. "Their ceremonies are beautiful," he said. "Their dances and songs are beautiful." When asked what he believed these conversations among Pacific Northwest orca pods were about, Julius responded, "In all honesty and all reality, it's a story of grief."

"The orca story is one of human misunderstanding and generational trauma. But it's also a story of celebration, family, and a sense of place," Morgan concludes. Grandmothers often have a timeless and clear-eyed perspective. May the story they tell their next generations be about more than extinction. And may we, as humans, learn from these grannies and ensure that future generations witness these great minds and hearts surviving in our shared waters.

WOLF EYES

THEIR EYES FIND you first, often golden or dark green, and amber-flecked with a fierce and surprising intimacy. Direct, intelligent, eerily familiar. Though these wolves in Washington's Wolf Haven refuge are no longer living in the wild, there is nothing tame in their gaze. Instead, there is a rich and vivid emotional life that we can somehow read—not just because humans have lived closely with *Canis lupus* since prehistory, but also because the wolves mirror us. Even behind fences, they connect. *First contact.*

One imperial white wolf's stare is stunning. Bart commands our complete attention, even as he rests, with his lean legs almost casually crossed. Lonnie's eyes are shy but steady as he peeks out from behind branches. His expression reminds us that in the wild, wolves are extremely wary of humans and spend most of their lives hiding from us. Delicate Jaque with her flattened agouti-colored ears looks back warily at us as she retreats. Tala, the slender red wolf, steps so lightly and silently out of his hiding place that he startles us. Lowering his sleek, mahogany head, he gives us a quick, searching glance—and then disappears.

Even the abandoned wolf dogs—who this sanctuary's animal care director, Wendy Spencer, says are "caught between two worlds"—haven't lost the wildness or expressive depth in their eyes. Caedus, the lustrous black male wolf dog who shares his life with the delicate and somehow sad-eyed Ladyhawk, stands sentry, his buttery eyes both bold and curious. He might as well be perched protectively atop a remote mountaintop, scanning for his pups and family.

How many of us have ever had the privilege of looking into the eyes of a wolf? How many of us would know if a wolf was secretly watching us in the wild? We wouldn't smell them the way wolves can scent humans from half a mile away. We wouldn't hear them, unless they howled.

Sight is often the only way we sense a wolf, so they are at the advantage when it comes to sensory gifts. And even then, the wolf's unblinking and powerful gaze is unusual in our species. Perhaps that's why we stand riveted at the fence or in the forest when we catch a glimpse of this fellow creature.

"Wolves look right through you, don't they?" a Yellowstone biologist once asked me as we watched the first reintroduced wolves, the Soda Butte family, scamper with their pups and stride across a high meadow. Even from a half mile away, the wolves were keenly aware of our presence.

"Yes, they do," I breathed back then, barely able to hold the telescope, my hands were trembling so.

Yes, I still feel that intense energy running between wolves and humans every time I visit Wolf Haven International and encounter these animals who have found a retreat here since it opened in 1982—giving sanctuary to over 170 gray and red wolves, plus wolf dogs, and even coyotes. We recognize ourselves in wolves—our own hungers, passions, violence, and tenderness. Anyone who spends time with wolves understands that their social dramas—*who's in, who's out*, who's on top, who's struggling to survive, who's ailing or lost, who is thriving—are as fascinating as our own. In the wild, wolves live in close-knit and complicated families; they are affectionate and loyal to their young, and the whole group cooperates to survive together. At Wolf Haven, these often abandoned, abused, mistreated, and misunderstood wolves are given another chance, not only at living, but also at intimate relationships with one another.

All you have to do is hear a wolf howl to intuitively know that wolves always seek community. Just like their profound eye contact, the wolf's howl is a language of loss and longing—and sometimes even joy—that we also instinctively understand.

Wolves, and their domesticated ancestors, our dogs, remind us we are in the presence of an animal who has always belonged very near us. Wolves and humans have coevolved over the last fifteen to twenty thousand years. One long-held theory is that during the most recent ice age, our hunter-gatherer ancestors first offered food scraps to wolves, "who lost their fear of humans and became tame," or "self-domesticated." This theory of wolves as subservient to us, as simply "lazy, opportunistic, outcast-from-the-pack wolves that scavenged at human camps," is not credible, according to author and wildlife advocate Rick Lamplugh.

Like other researchers, Lamplugh debunks this "garbage-dump" model and believes that humans learned from wolves to hunt cooperatively; they "shared the land and its resources and coevolved together." Both species engaged in this "beneficial partnership."

Ancient wolves and our ancestors each had expert hunting skills. Humans and wolves, both top predators, hunted bison, yaks, caribou, and other large prey on the vast mammoth steppe during the Last Glacial Maximum. The wolves' sense of smell, their stamina and speed at tiring a prey, their cooperative culling of game from a herd, could initiate a kill. Then humans, who are taller and can hit a target from a distance, "with bigger brains, better vision over distance, and increasingly improved weapons . . . could have helped wolves kill prey," writes Lamplugh. "Working together, a meal was won using the strengths of both predators. The partners then shared the spoils." Lamplugh concludes, "wolves may have chosen and trained us, much to their own—and our—benefit."

Some scientists, like anthropologist Pat Shipman, author of *The Invaders: How Humans and Their Dogs Drove Neanderthals to Extinction*, believe that our alliance with wolves helped *Homo sapiens* survive, giving humans "an unbeatable advantage over our two-legged competitor (*Homo neanderthalensis*)." When *Homo sapiens* "formed an alliance with the wolf . . . that would have been the end for the Neanderthal." For *Homo sapiens*, the partnership with wolves was a "win-win situation," Shipman explains. These ancient wolf dogs were not a hybrid of wolf and dog but a "distinct group that had characteristics similar to those of today's wolves."

Both humans and wolves evolved together in a symbiotic relationship, says Lamplugh. "We could have, in a sense, apprenticed with wolves and then with our bigger brains and ability to develop technology," mutually thrived. The early wolf-human bond was "both sociable and curious," writes Mark Derr, author of *How the Dog Became the Dog*. The wolves choosing to bond with humans, was "a leap of friendship."

This theory is backed up by new research from Duke University. On *60 Minutes*, Anderson Cooper interviewed evolutionary biologist Bruce Hare on his genetic research into wolves and dogs. Hare believes that the Darwinian emphasis on survival of the fittest is a misnomer. "I think what really summarizes the link between dog and human evolution is survival of the friendliest," Hare explained. His twenty-five years of studying wolves and dogs led him to theorize that "wolves chose us" in the evolutionary bond.

In today's territorial battles between wolves and humans, this ancient evolutionary partnership with wolves has been forgotten or simply denied. Thousands of years of coexistence has turned to conquest with humans' favor of ranches and cattle eradicating wolves from their huge, birthright territories. That's why the way we most encounter wolves now is in sanctuaries like Wolf Haven.

Every time I visit the wolves in this refuge, I realize how much like wolves we humans are. Both our species live in complex social groups, in families or packs that hunt and raise young together. That, plus humans' and wolves' larger brains, our ability to control our emotions and expand our communication skills—all these evolutionary adaptations mean that both humans and wolves share survival strategies.

There is very little modern research on the attachment between wolves and humans. But in one new study at Sweden's Stockholm University, wolves and dogs were reared from birth in identical situations, with twelve Alaskan husky dogs and ten European gray wolves. The study adapted a scientific test originally used with children to research attachment toward familiar caregivers or strangers. Researchers found that wolves, even more than dogs, "showed more affection and spent more time greeting the familiar person and engaged in more physical contact." Wolves adapting to human contact, the study concluded, "could have had a selective advantage in early stages of dog domestication."

The evolutionary wolf-human bond is evident in the fact that all over the world, wolves are returning to their natural habitat—and most humans support this animal ally's return to our often-damaged eco-systems. Yellowstone's decades-long study of wolf generations, as well as the benefits they bring to the landscape and other species, is now an international model for wolf reintroduction. But until wolves can reclaim much more of their natural territory, the most contact we have with these magnificent and much maligned fellow creatures are wolf sanctuaries like Washington's Wolf Haven International.

Wolf Haven is one of fifty-two facilities participating in the federal government's Mexican wolf Species Survival Program (SSP), an effort to raise captive wolves for reintroduction into the wild. *El Lobo*, the Mexican gray wolf subspecies, is one of the most highly endangered of all wolves. Smaller than other North American wolves, these Old-World wolves long ago crossed the Bering Land Bridge to colonize North America. (Siberian wolves wandered the land thirty-three thousand years ago; and ten thousand years ago, these wolves evolved into our Siberian husky sled dogs.)

As a writer and researcher, I was privileged to linger longer than most visitors in the Wolf Haven refuge, studying wolves in their large enclosures. Scientists identify wolves by F (female) or M (male), adding the number of wolf births recorded in any given area. I was especially interested in the wolf family of Hopa (F1222) and her mate, Brother (M1067); they'd just given birth to three male pups in the spring of 2015. Wolves are born blind, and their eyes open after twelve to fourteen days. With their distinctive brown furry capes and tiny, flattened ears, neonatal pups live underground their first weeks, denned up and protected by their mother, who rarely leaves their cool, musty underworld, like an earthen womb. I'd watched these three pups since their birth, gangly siblings who clambered over their mother, rambunctiously wrestled with one another, and learned to howl from their father.

A year later, the federal government chose this family to be released into the wild. The day finally came when Hopa, Brother, and their pups were to be carefully caught up in kennels, driven to SeaTac airport, transported to a New Mexico ranch near the Gila National Forest to adapt to the Southwest landscape that is in their bloodlines, and finally released into their ancestral Mexican homeland. That morning of release, the refuge was afloat in cool mists like a Chinese silkscreen. All the sanctuary wolves were howling—the ancient communal harmonies of high-pitched yips, whines, and haunting keens that we never want to end. Their voices were alert, full of riffs and counterpoints like animal jazz.

One might imagine this "catch-up" of wolves to be a risky and fearsome job. Images of menacing growls, gnashing fangs come to mind. But this catch-up is more like a well-choreographed dance or mime. Everyone in the enclosure is silent. When absolutely necessary, only Wendy Spencer spoke *sotto voce*.

Since Brother and his three sons, now yearling pups, were born at Wolf Haven, this was the first time any of them would ever leave the sanctuary. When he saw the crates, one yearling jumped atop the reinforced plastic kennel and used it like a launching pad to leap into space and crash down on the forest floor. The pups have often played a kind of how-many-wolves-fit-on-the-roof-of-their-wooden-den-box. Answer: all five, including the parents. But this was a morning unlike any other in the pups' lives. The close-knit family took its cue from the matriarch, Hopa.

"Look," Diane Gallegos, the sanctuary's director, pointed me to the screen, where a rather blurry, but still majestic wolf ventured into the remote camera's view. "Hopa is terrified, shaking, but she's poised like the family matriarch she is."

Hopa was lean and almost impossibly long limbed, with an elegant auburn buff on her forehead, intense eyes, and a dark mask shading into a long, pale snout. Surveying her three sons, she looked at once dotingly maternal and yet watchful. Certainly, she could hear the hidden remote cameras rustle in the leaves above as the researchers shifted them slightly for better angles from the trees. A first-time mother, Hopa had quite an impressive history already—and she was only four years old.

As we watched, Gallegos quietly explained what was happening on the remote screen, showing six people, each carrying a lightweight, four-foot-long aluminum pole with a padded Y at the end. The Y-pole gently puts pressure a wolf's neck and haunches, which doesn't stress the animal and encourages them into the kennel. The Wolf Haven vet and staff have been well trained by Dr. Mark Johnson, the wildlife vet for the Yellowstone wolves. Johnson's philosophy is visionary and compassionate. "There is no room for ego when handling animals," he wrote. When catching-up a feral dog or a captive wolf, he asks wildlife handlers to use this as an opportunity to "explore our connection with all things and to explore who we are as a person. This is a profound opportunity . . . exhilarating, sacred, and sad."

The view from the grainy remote camera screens made it look like everyone was silently moving underwater. "The catch-up is quick and efficient," Gallegos murmured as we watched. "Because they're going to endure so much after this. Such a long trip."

"Are they tranquilized?" I asked.

"No," she replied firmly, "they can't be. We don't usually tranquilize our animals unless we must. To fly in a plane tranquilized could be dangerous. You don't want them in cargo, unmonitored, choking. You want them to stay awake. It's a two-hour flight and good, smooth weather, so we hope it'll all go well."

Still in the sanctuary, the mother wolf, Hopa, had denned up. She was the last to be shepherded into her crate. I watched, transfixed, as Spencer almost tenderly reached into the den with her Y-pole. The mother wolf instantly hunkered down at the touch of the Y-pole on her neck. Quickly, as someone else rested a Y-pole on the mother wolf's haunches, Spencer secured a blue head cover over Hopa's face for safety. Covering their eyes and head always quietens wild animals, like horses or animals injured on the road. Something about not being able to see immediately reassures the animals.

Hopa was lifted into the comfort of her own crate, and the muzzle and head covering were gently removed. All five of the family were now ready to go to the airport. The whole catch-up of the wolf family took just one hour. Smiling and relieved, the Wolf Haven staff emerged from the sanctuary, followed by Spencer driving the van. Inside, the wolves, each in their own crate, are utterly still. Mute.

I'll never forget an image of Hopa from this catch-up: Crouched at the very back of her crate, as if to bury herself in the blonde straw, she gazed out, her ears perked to fathom each voice or strange sound; her golden eyes wide, wary, preternaturally focused; her distinctive rust and black fur dense and beautiful. But her dripping black nose betrayed her terror. Her flanks were trembling. Hopa didn't move or thrash or try to escape. She looked hypervigilant but eerily calm at the same time. After all, she had a family to protect from whatever strange journey was being asked of her—nothing less than leading her pups and her mate into the complete unknown. The recovery and resurrection of an entire species awaited her.

When I studied this matriarch's face, I read both fear and courage. I was reminded of the adage that, in humans, the bravest of us are those who feel fear and yet still perform some perilous feat. No one knew that last day we saw Hopa at Wolf Haven that the matriarch was again pregnant. She would give birth to five more healthy pups in New Mexico before the release of her family of eleven into a snowy Mexican forest. I like to imagine Hopa, Brother, and their new generations of pups hunting elk or deer in the lands of their ancestors.

All these years later, I still ponder this wolf's extraordinary face. The photo of Hopa in the crate that carried her to a new life is on my desk. Those by-now familiar amber eyes gaze back steadily. Eye contact is how our human species intimately bond. Wolf eyes equally hold ours, whereas dogs, subordinate, domesticated, often do not. A wildlife vet once told me that in both human and wolf eyes, you can see the heartbeat. Hopa still holds my heart in her gaze, like a wolf spirit that can forever meet our eyes.

THE DOG WHO
DIDN'T LOVE ME

MY UNREQUITED LOVE—ELLA, a sleek and elegant Siberian husky, with icy-blue eyes and the leanness of a racing horse. I first approached Ella, expecting a nuzzle or a lick. Instead, I was greeted with the most skeptical disinterest I've ever felt from any animal—or human.

Ella is the first dog who hasn't returned my affection. Her preferred person—her companion, my neighbor Tracey—kindly shares Ella with me during our daily walks in Seattle. But Ella is Teflon to my devout adoration. Prancing with such startling strength and agility, Ella could be a gymnast. But she deigns to keep pace with us. When we walk down the city streets together, passersby comment on Ella's beauty. Neighborhood bros brake mid-cruise, roll down their windows to offer a rather intimidating thumbs up; elders coo and fawn over Ella and ask us how long we've been together.

"She doesn't belong to me," I say with that familiar pang of pain.

On our daily walks, Ella gazes right past me. Instead, she turns her wolf-eyes up to Tracey with a blazing gaze of belief as if caught up in religious fervor. I think of Saint Theresa of Avila who levitated when she prayed. Ella's expression echoes that saint's fierce grace and possessive zeal. In our love triangle, I am the one who is always edged out.

So, I began my crusade for Ella's affection. Bribes of her favorite salmon treat. Ella eyed me suspiciously, flipped her head, and turned away. What was it about me that Ella found so offensive? She was sometimes friendly with others. We began an experiment to figure out why my love was so unrequited. Why was she so wary of me? Pheromones? Did I resemble someone who had traumatized her as a puppy? We knew that Ella was afraid of teenage boys and skateboards.

I was working on a natural history book about wolves. Perhaps Ella picked up on this energy and, as in all wild wolf societies, was figuring out our hierarchy? After all, Siberian huskies were the last of the modern dog breeds to be domesticated; the black slashes on their thick tails reveal this recent wolf ancestry. They will run wild, no matter how bonded they are to their human families. Research shows that wolves will hold direct and non-submissive eye contact with humans; domesticated dogs will not.

As a pup, Ella was on track to be a champion working dog, a sled dog. But her brother developed seizures, so Ella was taken by another breeder, where she languished—her temperament devolving from alpha to beta in the pack of other huskies. She was almost a year old when Tracey adopted her. I began to watch Ella on our walks and noticed that as I got near her, her ears pricked back—as if I was frightening her. I did not try to touch or engage with her. I could be aloof, as well.

With other people, Ella would often make the first gesture of friendship, sidling along their legs or letting them scratch her ears. Watching Ella allow such affection with others filled me with despair and envy. Sometimes I just canceled our walks if I was already having a rough day and didn't want to be ignored.

One thing I did notice about Ella. When I was quiet and sitting in a chair near her, she'd give me sidelong glances that were thoughtful and penetrating. Sometimes she'd sniff my skin as if snow were falling over us and melting onto her dense fur.

One rainy afternoon, I got a panicked call from Tracey. "Oh, my God," she howled, "Ella got into our garbage full of old coffee grounds, Tylenol, and some cancer meds from my sister. I'm at the vet hospital. Please *come!*"

In the waiting room Tracey was sobbing with guilt and grief. "I've killed my dog," she cried.

Coming from a medical family, I knew this combination was terribly toxic. This beautiful dog's survival was a long shot after such an overdose of our meds and caffeine.

The vet echoed this soberly when she gave us the report. "We've pumped her stomach with charcoal and are watching to see if her kidneys and liver can process such a toxic load. She's on fluids to wash out the poisons. Watching her closely. But it's serious."

Tracey bent her head into her hands and sobbed without any sound, just shuddering. I sat with the dazed stoicism of my medical and military family, nodding at the vet.

"Can we see Ella?" I asked.

"Let me do another set of vitals. Maybe she's strong enough to walk out to the waiting room," the vet answered. "It might do her good to be with her people right now."

As she stumbled toward us, Ella's body seemed flattened out, like a one-dimensional cave drawing. Fluffy tail tucked between her legs, her head hung low. She smelled of charcoal, alcohol, and diarrhea. Her eyes were glazed and weeping, those white eyelashes caked with phlegm. She barely had the energy to lay down at Tracey's feet before she closed her eyes and let out a sigh of utter exhaustion. Tracey stopped crying. I started humming one of Ella's favorite lullabies that Tracey and I often sing to her.

I stayed very still, slowly reaching out a hand to Ella's wet head. No response. Another huff and sigh from her, then nothing. After about an hour, Ella jerked up on her legs, unsteady as a newborn foal. She lurched and then surprised both of us by falling against my knees. Her weight was so light, as if she were fading away right before us.

They say that time stands still in the moment of death. But there was nothing still in the waiting room. Screaming animals and desperate people running around us. The commotion didn't seem to register on Ella. But something made her raise her snout and look directly up at me. In Ella's eyes, with that heart-shaped black mask surrounding numinous blue, there was something startling. I wondered if I would see her pupils dilate or fix like they do right before death.

But instead, Ella's eyes opened very wide, as if seeing me for the first time. It was a fiercely steady gaze, as if she was fixing on some distant, navigational point. As if I were her True North by which this ancestral sled dog might find her way home. Then, she sighed and tenderly laid her head on my knees. She closed her eyes, resting.

I sat very still, not daring to touch her, wondering if these were her last moments. Amazed and humbled that they were with me.

Finally, the vet tech came out for vitals and suggested that Ella might be strong enough to go outside. "Let her sniff the earth and piss out those toxins."

We had to lift Ella up to walk. Outside in that Seattle dawn, the dew-dappled scarlet rhododendrons sparkled brightly; it was as if the plants had dropped acid.

Tracey was calmer now. Ella had made it through the night. These first twenty-four hours had been critical. "Why don't you take her home for now and come back in a few hours for more labs?" the vet tech said. "We'll know more then."

Ella and Tracey took to their bed together, spooning. I took my place on the couch and tried to sleep. Now that Ella was getting better, I was again relegated to wallpaper. No more intense gazes from Ella. No gratitude to show any deepening bond between us. I believed at that moment that Ella would survive. She had returned to her aloof self. I was left out—again. It both heartened and made me yearn for her more. Are there options for unrequited love? What does it teach us about perseverance or the Buddhist philosophy of detachment?

What is unrequited love but the tenderest longing for those who cannot return our devotion? Maybe it's something else—a clarity that allows us to recognize that sometimes we are simply *not* loved at all. Sometimes we are instead tolerated, merely passing through another person's story. An anecdote, a very minor character. When we're not the main character in our love story, what more can we see? What do we learn about ourselves?

I learned that I can still love someone who has very little interest in me. I learned that hope can sometimes be an illusion. Acceptance of what is given is the lesson. I still try to bribe Ella with treats to gain her affection. She's coming around, slowly. Sometimes she even rests her lovely head on my arm. That's when I get a vivid flashback of Ella leaning against me when she was struggling for her life—when she had eyes only for me. It is enough. It is everything.

THE ELUSIVE BEAUTY
OF BIG CATS

I'VE NEVER SEEN a wild mountain lion, or cougar (*Puma concolor*). This is surprising given my childhood on a remote, national forest, endless family camping throughout my early years, and hiking as an adult. Though not so surprising as mountain lions, who are hyper-alert, careful, and reclusive hunters. I did once see the scat and streak (poo and pee) of a bobcat in the Blue Ridge Mountains of North Carolina; and in a Yucatan jungle biosphere, the split-second visage of a jaguar. The jaguar's vertical black slit of pupil in those fierce, golden eyes was both feral and frightening. Just one glimpse of black-and-gold spotted fur, the gaze of regal power, and I well understood why Mayans worshipped jaguars as underworld rulers, showing themselves in a flash of foliage, with a loud, guttural roar. Then, this largest cat native to the Americas simply disappeared from our sight, as if slipping between dimensions. Today jaguars are hesitantly returning to reclaim a range that once ran from the East Coast to the Pacific Northwest to South America.

After all my time spent in Pacific Northwest woods, to have not seen a cougar, our iconic big cat, shows just how elusive they really are. Fortunately, I have two dear friends who follow cougars. One, Laura Bowers Foreman, a wildlife writer, has done volunteer fieldwork with Project CAT (Cougars and Teaching) in Pacific Northwest forests. The other, Dana Kennedy Silberstein, lives in rural Northern California and has encountered a wild mountain lion who was out hunting.

Laura's father was a big-game hunter and US Airforce pilot stationed in exotic locales—from Azores Islands to India to Hawaii. He always brought home animal trophies, including tiger skins, to his wife and daughter of Cherokee ancestry. Haunted by this hunting heritage, Laura trained as a forester on the East Coast with a focus on conservation. After moving to the Northwest, she and her husband raised two children, and Laura has worked diligently for years to save native plants, wildlife, and especially cougars. They live, appropriately, between Cougar and Tiger Mountains, in Issaquah, Washington.

For years, Laura volunteered with Project CAT, an eight-year research study in Washington State to "better understand cougar-human interactions." An innovative program, Project CAT involved K-12 students, local teachers, and community members in three state regions. Volunteers learned to track, observe, and understand how to coexist with cougars. High school students participated in actual radio collaring of cougars, while elementary kids learned how to take field notes, identify animal tracks, and collect scat. They all used a NatureMapping technology called CyberTracker: Tools for the Citizen Scientists to collect data with their cell phones to share with researchers. Such collaborations between researchers and local people of all ages is a way to strengthen the human-animal bond that creates empathy and builds conservation ethics.

In Laura's heavily forested mountain home, she often walked the woods with her kids, looking for signs of cougars. "I wanted my son and daughter to feel at home here," she says. "Connected to nature. In the woods and in life, my kids are more confident. They take risks and are not afraid to be on their own."

Laura has written eloquently about assisting wildlife biologists Gary Koehler and Rocky Spencer, who pioneered Project CAT. To note the slashed bark of trees from a cat's passing, collect their droppings, map their territories, Laura was often called on when biologists were tracking radio-collared cougars. Often schoolchildren watched, enthralled. In a stunning photo on Laura's writing desk, she holds a cougar cub while the biologists quickly record vital signs, age, and health measurements.

Running after big cats, tagging them, doing veterinary checks on new cubs, sampling cougar scat—it was all in a day's volunteer work for Laura. In her *Wildlife Conservation* cover story, Laura notes that cougars were considered solitary animals who came together only to breed. But recent technological advances in GPS and DNA data tests "are illuminating the shadows of cougar life and revealing the softer side of these secretive felines: their altruistic family life."

Once when Laura was helping a Washington State biologist, Ben Maletzke, in the Cascades as they tracked a cougar with a radio antenna, the big cat "bolted from a pile of brush and disappeared into the undergrowth," Laura wrote. "Clearly, she was frightened, not fearsome." Searching the slash pile, they discovered a growling cub. "I took the tiny cat and held him close," Laura said. "Soon his hissing and growling quieted. In that moment, the illusion of a crazed, snarling cougar vanished, and I saw the world through the eyes of a protective mother cougar. I, too, was raising children and understood her anxiety."

While the mother cougar circled nearby, Laura and Ben worked quickly, weighing and tagging the four-week-old cub. When they left, the mother returned to move her cub.

As cougar habitat is shrinking, due to overdevelopment, such community conservation work is vital. "If we leave our children and grandchildren a legacy of learning to live with wild cats, we give them a gift beyond measure," says Laura. "We give them the wild, which is also our human heritage."

Project CAT has ended its work, but Laura continues her own conservation. "Cherokees understood that panthers, as cougars are called in the Appalachian Mountains, were teaching them that by staying alert to their surroundings, they were fully alive."

The Cherokee revered cougars, giving them the name "cat of god." Cougars and owls were the only two creatures believed to ascend to the highest realms of purity and sacredness. Recently Native American communities and wild cat conservation groups are working together to save cougars. The Olympic Cougar Project, co-led by Panthera and the Lower Elwha Klallam Tribe, has tech support to study cougars. Fascinatingly, the technology now being used to research cougars comes from EarthRanger, funded by the Allen Institute for Artificial Intelligence. Wild cat intelligence may indeed seem to us like futuristic AI.

A cougar's extraordinary senses of hearing, smell, and sight all give these sleek, graceful big cats an advantage as another top predator. With keen, far-sighted eyes, cougars see in vivid color to track their prey. Able to leap from the ground to high up into trees and pay intense attention to the slightest sound or scent, big cats are models of astonishing animal perception. These wild cats possess "sight in the dark," according to science journalist Ed Yong in *An Immense World*. The nerve endings in their whiskers are so sensitive, they can detect changes in air flow around them, indicating prey.

Faced with a tiny light source, cougar eyes glow at night. Especially at night or in low light, they can see a wider range than humans—285 degrees vs. our 210. The speed of sight, or CFF (critical flicker-fusion frequency) is also a factor in all animals, especially for capturing prey. "The ultrafast hunts are guided by ultrafast vision," says Yong. Animals see at different speeds as our photoreceptors react to electrical signals to travel to the brain. Think of CFF as "the frame rate of the movie playing inside an animal's head—the point at which static images blend into the illusion of continuous motion." Songbirds and insects like flies, dragonflies, and honeybees see at the fastest rates, up to 350 frames per second (or, also how we measure sound wave length, in Hz). Humans are slow sighters at 60 Hz. Cats are a little slower at 48 Hz and dogs slightly faster at 75 Hz. The concept of fast or slow vision is crucial to understand how we perceive, navigate, hunt, and enjoy the world around us.

What can the study of animals like cougars teach us about how we might pay closer attention to our mutual habitat? As someone who has shared my urban home with Siamese cats for decades, what I most admire about cats, big or small, is their capacity to be awake and asleep seemingly at the same time. Are they dreaming in that alert reverie, with eyes slightly open, keeping ready to instantly catch a fly, or pounce on a prey or toy? Domestic cats sleep sixteen to twenty hours a day. Cougars, especially after a big kill and a full belly, can stretch out on a branch or sunny boulder and seem to snooze for twelve or more. At night, these nocturnal hunters prowl for white-tailed deer, tracking and listening and looking and waiting, in complete, stealthy stillness, for an hour before striking. Once, my niece, who in second grade was in a school play on wild animals, donned the costume of a lion and declared, "Everyone is either my friend—or my food."

The other quality I most admire about all cats, besides their preening beauty, their rapt observation and attention, is their aloof nature. Even though cats live alongside us in the wild or our homes, they seem utterly independent, always untamed. My indoor Siamese are still ferocious predators and growl at strangers. They are champion, Sphinx-like observers. As one born under the bright, but sometimes seemingly languid sign of Leo the lion, I appreciate that meditative detachment, which can embody an almost mystical feline presence. Big cats have power, both symbolically, culturally, and most of all, in our living ecosystems.

How do we benefit when another top predator species thrives alongside our own? Living in harmony with wild animals "plays an essential role in strengthening the resilience and biodiversity of ecosystems," says Mark Elbroch, Puma Program director for Panthera, an organization devoted to the world's forty species of wild cats.

"Cougars are one of those species that is connected to so many other forms of life," adds Elbroch. Like wolves and other top predators, cougars are vital keystone species. Keystone species are those animals who have a crucial and disproportionately large effect on their ecosystems; these species have major trickle-down effects. Cougars control deer populations that overgraze vegetation, and cougar kills feed many scavengers and even insects. "This is a species that should be prioritized because of the net benefit," explains Elbroch. Cougars are in a complex relationship with nearly five hundred living species, "holding America's ecosystems together." Scientists call cougars "biological brokers . . . representing the most diverse number of relationships recorded for any carnivore in the world."

Like the elusive wild cat itself, their essential role in our ecosystem is often invisible. For example, cougars feed on the deer caught in the crossfire of roadways and cars. In South Dakota, after pumas were recolonized to the state, the cost of deer-vehicle collisions dropped by over $1 million. Over the next thirty years, this recolonization is estimated to avert 21,400 human injuries, 155 human deaths, and over $2 billion in costs. Not to mention that cougar kills contribute millions of pounds of meat every day to scavenger communities across North and South America.

Surviving in the wild is hard enough with competition from other predators and the sprawl of human encroachment. But now wild animals must reckon with climate change's increasing wildfires, the flash floods of atmospheric rivers, and weather extremes. Here in the Pacific Northwest, our temperate climate and rain shadow make weather swings even more unpredictable. All animals, human and non-human, must adapt.

Cougars are adapting to shrinking habitat; but they need a lot of open space to roam, since their territories stretch as far as one hundred miles. In the Pacific Northwest, the Olympic Cougar Project tracks cougars, especially as they try to navigate major highways, like Interstate 5, with GPS collars and wildlife cameras. What they have documented is informative.

"One cougar swam a stretch of Puget Sound, reaching an island stepping-stone to new stomping grounds, but was shot there and killed," the Olympic Cougar Project notes. Other cougars try to cross freeways, but if there are no wildlife corridors to open new territory, they are cut off from breeding possibilities and prey sources like elk, deer, coyote, bears, and bobcats. Because their territory is now so limited, genetic diversity, which determines the species' health and survival of cougar populations, is decreasing. The hope is that this new study can uncover correct population data and pinpoint spots where cougars are most likely to try to cross major roadways. Such research could well "reconnect cougars to the rest of the Pacific Northwest."

Wildlife corridors around the West are being reconstructed to connect wild animals like cougars and give them escape routes to better habitat when their own habitats are lost or diminished. Connecting landscapes mean there is a healthy flow of plants, animals, and resources, which in the face of climate change helps us all. Wildlife corridors, like those within watersheds in California, Oregon, and Washington, are not only essential for wild animals to thrive, but they also strengthen people's and other animals' resilience to climate change. A 2019 UN report warned that "habitat fragmentation is a leading cause of the current extinction crisis." The crazy patchwork of dams, freeways, and fences that dissect our landscape makes it difficult for animals to find new mates, prey, and new territories.

Wildlife corridors act as superhighways for wildlife. They "also benefit communities by minimizing the impacts of flooding and improving water quality . . . capturing carbon from the atmosphere and provide shade and leafy cover that buffers extreme temperatures." There are hopes and plans for more national wildlife corridors to restore habitat and "rebuild communities hard hit by recent natural disasters." New research has revealed that "the territories of related [cougar] females are either connected or overlapping . . . GPS data shows grandmothers, mothers, and daughters crossing paths and feeding at the same kill at the same time."

Female cougars sometimes check on their pregnant daughters and have been known to foster orphaned cubs. Recent federal legislation includes the Wildlife Corridors Conservation Act and the Tribal Wildlife Corridors Act. When we preserve the lands and watersheds for other wild animals, like cougars, we are making life more sustainable for ourselves, as well.

Why then, with such benefits to all species, are cougars still so persecuted, sometimes hunted, often killed by wildlife managers if they dare to wander too close to us? When we cull cougars, removing them from the population, especially those adult females who are teaching their offspring or dominant males, young cougars don't learn or know how *not* to prey upon livestock. "Without a strong leader," Project CAT's Gary Koehler said, "chaos ensues because the younger, insurgent lions battle for dominance. . . . Our data shows that the cougars that do make poor decisions are usually young. Often they've just dispersed. Without mom around, a sheep grazing in thick brush is a fast-food dinner for a hungry, inexperienced cougar. But when the young have leadership there is very little predation."

Like wolves and bears, cougars are often misunderstood and maligned. "This species is elusive and often mischaracterized as a vicious, solitary predator, leading to persecution and fueling human-cougar conflict in the United Stated," says Elbroch. Such prejudice demands self-scrutiny and lots of education. And, of course, good storytelling about these big cats.

One of my favorite stories comes from my friend Dana. She is a former Seattle television talk show host and writer who now lives in rural Northern California. Dana and her dog Pecosa roam a former cattle ranch where badgers, coyotes, hawks, buzzards, deer, butterflies, and cougars all claim visitation rights. Following a mostly dry irrigation canal, an old dirt road winds through two thousand acres of oak savanna and chaparral dotted by gray and knobcone pines. When walking, Dana and Pecosa are often accompanied by wildlife. Because she is so familiar with the land and animals, Dana recognizes individual deer, like the one she watched grow over three years from a gangly youngster with rack fuzz to a tall buck with magnificent antlers.

One afternoon, Dana and her dog encountered dozens of buzzards swooping low through branches and unusually close to them. "The birds were so intense that we slowed way down because these scavengers alerted us to pay attention," Dana said. "After all, Peco and I had recently been chased down by two coyotes and my dog had run after a bear . . . but Peco has never caught or injured so much as a rat as we walk this huge ranchland."

Dana had been volunteering at her local wild animal rescue facility and learned a good deal about wild animals neighboring her land. "As we slowed our pace and I leashed Peco, it was that knowledge which allowed me to ultimately identify the beautiful little face with its accompanying stripe turned sideways toward me as though asleep. A badger. Dead with no visible injuries, very thick coat."

She was about to photograph the badger for the rescue center's wildlife biologists, to note that the badger was within city limits. But suddenly Peco sat down, utterly quiet.

"A mountain lion stepped out fifty feet in front of us. I froze. Lion froze. She was small, slim, seemed young. Maybe quite young. She wasn't even looking at us, just staring straight ahead. I signaled Peco to stay with a taut pull on the leash . . . I didn't move a muscle. We waited. Then she turned only her head toward us, pivoted around, and looked right at us."

For what seemed timeless, but was probably only seconds, mountain lion, dog, and woman were utterly still, as if fully taking one another in.

It is that remarkable wild animal-human bond that is as ancient as all our species. Genetic and physical memory. Hunter? Hunted? Threat? Ally? The assessing between animals, whether wild or domesticated.

"Astonishingly, I felt no fear whatsoever," Dana said softly. "I wasn't even that surprised. I've had several encounters with wild animals on the ranch, so maybe there is an internal mechanism in me now that knows this comes with the territory."

Dana calmly noted the mountain lion showed no signs of stress or irritation, the reactions that she'd witnessed in captive wild animals at the rehab center. No twitching or bared teeth, no flattened ears, no growls. "She seemed as relaxed as I felt," Dana continued. "She stuck out the tip of her tongue and released a tiny huff . . . after a few remarkably easy seconds, she turned her head and casually sauntered off."

There was no doubt that the badger was the cougar's kill. "But it's amazing she let my dog and me come so close to the carcass . . . only yards away from her prey. We were no threat to her . . . she did not confront us."

After that encounter with the cougar, Dana and her dog returned often in hopes of seeing the lovely creature again. But all they saw was the badger slowly disappearing. On another of those walks, Dana recognized, lying on its side, neck injured, the buck she'd watched for several years. There were signs that the mountain lion had begun eating the buck's right hind leg, blood fresh and bright red.

"The big cat had to be close by . . . but again, she did not confront us."

Over time that buck carcass also disappeared, until there was nothing left but the antlers, part of a spine, and a few scattered bones. Though Dana still searched for a sighting of the mountain lion, she has yet to see this elusive cat again. But the memory of their exchange is vivid.

"I still marvel at my lack of fear or panic. The lion's calmness. She was extraordinarily beautiful. Her markings like those etched by a fine painter. Her hips moved like greased chain-link, rolling more than hinging. The cat stays with me in the quietest way. I find myself pausing often to look around and see if maybe she might show herself again."

Wild animals, like cougars, have always come with the territories we humans also call home. Why not welcome them, learn to live alongside them, reopen our lands and the expansive territory of our hearts?

GREAT BLUE: A SPIRITUAL LIFE WITH ANIMALS

For Kate Rogers

"The possibility of being present in the world in a whole, undivided way can be a gift of the animals."

—LADSON HINTON, "A RETURN TO THE ANIMAL SOUL"

A PAIR OF great blue herons are on the beach early most mornings, *kraaking* an ancient duet of hoarse caws from the time of dinosaurs. Long, delicate legs lift off with an audible flap-and-swoop, and the whoosh of wings so wide, it's astonishing they can fly. Low tide reveals a sandy spit of tide pools and shallow surf, a littoral zone between land and sea that is perfect fishing for these amphibious birds.

One late spring morning while listening to the news, I watched a stately great blue wade into the Salish Sea, noting her cloak of silver-slate blue feathers, sharp orange beak, and black streak highlighting a fierce, amber eye. Mesmerized by the heron's statuesque stillness, I barely heard the reporter's lament of yet another terrorist attack, ecological disaster, school shooting, record-shattering heat wave. What if stillness—this heron's tranquil focus on the natural world—was also a way to navigate our human tragedies, without denying them? The bird's full attention to the tiniest slippery fish, the shushing waves under a soft, scented wind, and the sea's steady pulse, was a survival skill I might learn.

While contemplating the poise and grace of the blue heron, I saw something I will always remember. A man strolled onto the beach, facing the sea. Eyes closed, the man's palms lifted in a gesture of reverence and surrender. He was murmuring in a low, gentle voice, perhaps a chant. I wondered if he was praying for the world—the human turmoil and despair I'd just heard detailed on the radio.

With a blur of six-foot wings and an otherworldly cry, another great blue rose up and landed near him on the wet sand. After studying the man intently, the heron turned trustingly away to also face the water. With mighty wings outstretched and silver plume rustling like a monk's feathered robe, the bird sunbathed in the bright breeze. The great blue was almost as tall as the meditating man. I remember reading that in parts of Asia herons are divine messengers.

Together, the heron and slender man seemed to hold still a world careening into chaos. There was only the lulling waves, the man's musical chant, the heron's serenity and faith in sun, wind, and human. Perhaps this was what the Taoist sages meant long ago when they taught that one had great lessons to learn from a calm and happy spirit. Perhaps the heron sensed that she was safe to fish and sun herself so close, right in front of a meditating man. As I witnessed the serene self-possession of both human and great blue, my whole body relaxed, rested.

Suddenly there was movement: The man lifted one lithe leg, his arms wide, in a slow-motion swirl of hands, as if he had found his own wings. Thousand-year-old movements, as he gracefully performed the ritual "crane dance" of tai chi. Stepping deeper into the surf, sand sinking under his feet, he kept his balance.

The great blue turned to watch the man's flowing dance, her keen, yellow eyes taking in his imitation of movements that cranes and herons embody so naturally. Other species of cranes, like the Northwest's sandhill cranes, perform stunning courtship dances in the lifelong ballet of their mating. Birds have an intelligence born of the far-sightedness of sky, the knowledge of wind currents, the memory of many migrations. Birds perceive through visual, tactile, auditory, and chemical stimuli, any bird site will note. But what did this heron make of a man trying to dance like her? Perhaps *with* her. Bird and human bonds are as ancient as these cranes. In Japan they tell an old folktale of shapeshifting, the story of the

"Crane Wife." A lonely, poor man discovers a wounded crane in the tall reeds, her luminous flank pierced by a hunter's arrow. Because he is destitute and hungry, the man prepares to kill the crane. But when she lifts her elegant head, silver feathers trembling, those golden eyes holding his, the young man cannot bear to deny the world such bright life.

Tenderly, he lifts the crane and carries her to home. Pulling out the arrow, he heals her wounds with herbs and salve. He attends to her with the devoted kindness that is the best of any species. Soon her wings quiver in anticipation of flight. Wind currents and other birds call her to come home to the sky, to lush and warm wetlands, to their nightly rookeries. Though this crane is the most beautiful being the man has ever encountered, he intuits that she is not his possession, or even his companion. She must be restored to her own wild and radiant destiny. He opens the door, and the crane takes flight. Soaring over the woods, she soon joins the V-shaped curve of other cranes moving like loud constellations in the clouds.

The man is lost without her, remembering the gentle cooing as she cocked her head and listened to him tell the story of his limited life, the flap of her wings as she hopped about his house, the way she watched his every move—as if he mattered. He believes that nothing magical will ever again enrich his life.

But that night, he is surprised by a *tap-tap-tapping* on his door. There in the moonlight stands a stunning young woman, clad in silver and gray silk.

"I am your wife," she tells him simply, her voice flute-like and musical.

He falls back, astounded, as the woman enters his home with authority and such graceful steps she might as well be dancing.

How can a woman so lovely lay claim to a sorry soul like me, the man marvels?

He is so shy he can only watch, awestruck, as the woman takes possession of his meager home. She swoops around, cleaning every cobweb, mending every broken window, setting everything right. The slender woman sleeps in his bed, while the man spends three nights in the ashes of his own fire.

"I cannot support you," the man must admit as they both grow hungry, and he cannot find work. "You deserve a much richer man, someone to take good care of you."

"It is I who will take care of you," the woman smiles, her eyes like sunlight. "But you must not disturb me while I work in my little room."

Of course, he agrees. His life is already so much more wondrous with her. In love for the first time in his young life, he waits outside her door, summoning the courage to whisper through the knothole, "Will you . . . could you . . . marry me?"

A chirp and little cry from inside her room is his answer.

When she finally emerges, she offers him a brocade of silver-gray silk so richly woven, he gasps. Any woman would want this to adorn themselves in splendor. But shouldn't she keep it for their wedding day?

"No," she assures him softly, "sell this at the market and we will want for nothing."

Her silken tapestry, woven with black and gold threads, is so gorgeous that women flock to purchase even small pieces. No one in the village has ever seen such artistry. The man and his new wife grow rich, perhaps spend a little too much, and soon the wife must return to her solitary room and weave more brocade.

"Let me be," she again warns her husband. "Do not disturb my work."

But, like most spouses, the man is too curious. He desires not just the woman, but her soul and her secrets. How does his wife weave such wonders, what is she hiding from him? He leans his head against the door, hears her spinning and whistling. Stealthily, he opens the door to discover—she is *not* human. Transformed, standing on one long leg, plucking her own plume of silver feathers, is that same magnificent crane he once saved from a hunter's arrow. Now, to save them both, she is stripping herself of what she needs to survive. He had not noticed that after each creation of silk brocade, his wife grew weaker. Now, she was giving him her all. And he had broken her only request of him. For privacy, for a room of her own.

His remorse is great, but his loss is greater. She gives him one last, long, and intimate look: then her wings flutter, whoosh, lift. She flies above him, crying—the keen of grief, the caw of betrayal and lost love, the sigh of release.

There are several versions of this "Crane Wife" folktale. In *Tsuru no Ongaseshi*, or "Crane's Return of a Favor," when the man realizes that his wife is sacrificing herself for their love and survival, he begs her to stop plucking her feathers for them. But the crane wife says her gift of silken feathers is for love. "The man says that love exists without sacrifices, but he is wrong. He who lives without sacrifices for someone else doesn't deserve to be with a crane."

These contemplative and often endangered cranes have sacrificed much to share habitat with humans. Here in the Pacific Northwest, as well as worldwide, crucial wetlands are shrinking as we encroach more on their fragile littoral zones; their fishing is also depleted as oceans warm, and fresh and salt waters are polluted by agricultural runoff. In some countries, cranes are still hunted. There is also the never-ending blink and blast of electricity, the ubiquitous din of our species' relentless activity, artificial lights often dominating the night, disturbing great blue heron rookeries and nocturnal hunting birds like northern spotted owls. Natural dark is rare, and so is solitude—the only thing the Crane Wife asked of those who loved her.

But sensory pollution also diminishes people, like stripping off layers of sensitivity, poise, and presence. Many other species are going extinct in this loud, manic, crowded, and deeply distracted world. But what is going extinct in human nature may be our ability to be attentive to rhythms other than our own—the musical lilt and call of birds, the original songs that the wind makes breathing through each tree, the radical silence and hush of stargazing above timberline, the rapt focus of a heron fishing.

During the global pandemic, humans had to stay home, sometimes in solitary rooms, as wild animals reclaimed our deserted cities, towns, and waterways. Like the Crane Wife, we stayed inside, transforming ourselves to create the beautiful fabric of an inner life. With such heightened senses and solitude, how differently did we perceive our natural world? What in our natural world healed, when our own thoroughfares and neighbor-hoods were more populated with animals than people? Our shared eco-systems were more vibrant, more visible, when we were invisible. Wild animals have never really left us. They adapt and abide undercover, until our human quarantines allow animals to reveal their true selves, like in the old Japanese crane folktales, free to spin their silken gifts for us.

Like the Crane Wife, we have stripped ourselves of the very animal senses and protective skills we most need to thrive. For love, for ego, for riches, whatever drives us. We must ask, given such willful deprivation, such an *extinction of attention*: Do we deserve to take up so much space in the same watery world as cranes?

In his wonderful book *An Immense World*, Ed Yong writes about the "radical empathy," which is our superpower. "Empathy toward other species and toward nature is the only way out of our current ecological predicament," he says. This is not new. Folktales like "The Crane Wife," mystics from Lao Tzu to Christ, Buddha, and the Dalai Lama, have taught compassion as a spiritual path—*and* a survival skill. What's new in the twenty-first century is that mainstream science is finally embracing such spiritual traditions.

The first stories that we tell our children teach empathy and close atten-tion to other animals. "The deepest layers of our psyche still have animal characters," notes psychologist Ladson Hinton in his essay "A Return of the Animal Soul." Children naturally commune with animals. They include animals in their bedtime prayers; they easily shapeshift to imag-ine becoming animals; and they have imaginary friends who *are* animals. Eighty percent of kids' dreams are about animals. That bond has fallen to 10 percent by adulthood, when one's life is burdened by busyness and distraction. Imagination and empathy are often sacrificed to greed and the grind of getting ahead. The crane husband lost the great love of his life when the mystical animal bond was broken.

As I watched the man doing *Tai chi* on my beach in communion with the great blue heron, I recognized the swirling circle of his arms, like wings, as the "silk unreeling" of my own decades of *Tai chi* practice, a reminder of the silk weaving of the Crane Wife tales. I wondered what the great blue heron made of this man's subtle dance, what the Dalai Lama calls "spiritual mindfulness." Did she feel connected to the man in some cross-species recognition of the dance, the stillness? Certainly, she allowed his presence and perhaps shared his reverence.

Most wild animals flee or hide when humans are near, when we come crashing through underbrush or racing motorboats across waves. Why did the heron accept such intimacy, such abiding closeness? Man and bird stood only ten feet apart, but they were not separated in their seamless quality of attention and meditative presence. The heron's bill was not pointed down to instantly pounce on a fish in the shallow surf; she was standing on one leg, her eyes fixed on the distant horizon. As if sensing the bird's reverie, the man also ceased his dance, his palms resting on his belly. Both human and bird stood in absolute calm, gazing out across a sea so glassy and sunlit, a shining path that shimmered from shore to horizon.

Our species rarely cultivates such calm—the kind of animal stillness and scrutiny that is the opposite of fight-or-flight stimulus. And yet, in such meditative moments, we often see the world most clearly. The *clear seeing* of man and heron. Contemplation and the inner life are antidotes to fear and mindless distraction. As the Taoist writer Huanchu Daoren writes, "Best be very calm yet radiantly alert." To answer the Crane Wife folktale, this reverent and compassionate man, who included another animal in his own spiritual practice, certainly deserved to be with a crane. She had chosen him, to abide together, though just for a while, because great mystics also teach impermanence.

We may well be an impermanent species; our consumption and exploitation of nature and other animals foretells the unintended consequence of our own extinction. But perhaps the pandemic and our mandatory retreat gave us a far-sighted glimpse of how much nature and other species will recover from our overstep, our breaking of all our treaties with the earth. The contemplative Time Out we endured might also help us imagine another future than extinction for ourselves and other animals. The man and the heron dancing together on the beach will always be for me an image of a healed, restored world. That is what we must imagine, a future in which the Crane Wife doesn't leave—because we help heal her and honor her needs, what Ursula Le Guin calls her "serene, inexhaustible fullness of being." Only then can we stay and survive together. Cranes, after all, mate for life.

A foghorn moaned in the marine mists. With the slightest wisp and whisper of wings, the Great Blue lifted, her legs dangling one more moment in the surf. The man turned to give the great bird a deep, slow bow—a gesture at once grateful and glad. With a mighty flap, the heron lifted, circled above him, called out in that timeless caw, and then was gone. Into the great blue.

ADAPTATION

*A Change Is Going
to Come*

I MEASURE MY life in animals. Other people might categorize their lives by mates, children, jobs, or homes. The way we remember our personal histories tells us a lot about our core character, our passions, and with whom we share our worlds. I also measure my life in books. Animals and books are how I define my decades. They are the guides to change and how I must adapt.

Much of my work as a writer has been protecting animals, which means that I've had to be more of a warrior then I might've wanted to be, simply because I live in a time of massive animal extinctions. Wild, endangered animals particularly call me to listen and tell their stories. More than my human companions, animals have taught me most about both play and rest. As the lovely poem "Change of Life" by Judith Collas concludes, I have never ended up "sleeping with the wrong dog."

Animals have their own sense of humor so often overlooked, whether it's the "pup sitting" wolf in Alaska inventing a tug-of-war game to teach reluctant pups to cross sharp gravel, or the trickster raccoons taking over our urban neighborhoods. Crows covet and play with shiny objects, and river otters romp on sea walls like Keystone cops. Researchers have only recently discovered that rats laugh, and bees enjoy playing with balls. As Martin Buber writes, "Play is the exultation of the possible."

In *Animal Happiness*, poet and philosopher Vicki Hearne writes, "animals have a greater gift for accepting happiness than we do . . . all happiness is animal happiness." An animal trainer for over twenty-five years, Hearne delights in the "different kind of mind" of animals and "the radiance that is sometimes possible" when we "acknowledge that others exist."

Climate change is demanding that we change, whether we believe in it or not. Polar bears swim miles farther between shrinking ice floes. Caribou alter ancient migration paths by recognizing subtle shifts in temperature. Hungry grizzlies must accurately time their hibernations with budding fauna, streams, and spawning salmon. Dolphin super pods respond to rising seas by fishing farther offshore.

My friend ecologist Joseph Meeker suggests we adapt our ways to imitate the animals, who have always been more interested in surviving than in killing their own kind. Survival, not death, is what makes us truly heroic and adaptive—and perhaps happier. The longer I survive, the more I see change and play as a skill that contributes to longevity. Animals have taught me as a nature writer to be less a tragic hero and more just someone who bumbles along, adapting. On one of my recent birthday cakes, a friend wrote, "I play, therefore I am." My relationship with animals is now more about play, intimacy, and wonder, the simple gifts of animal happiness.

THE SECRET CITY LIFE
OF RACCOONS

IT'S DARK, AND I'm driving a Seattle neighborhood side street so perfectly domesticated with trim lawns, well-tended shade gardens, and recycling bins lined up like green guardians. Darting across my headlights, a round animal, a hunchbacked dash, scoots across the street, toppling those tidy bins. Dog? Cat? No, feral, amber eyes stare right at me as a raccoon chomps and chows down on a burrito. Two more tiny hunchbacks scramble across the street and study their mother's garbage feast: limp french fries, peaches, a half-eaten Starbuck's bento box. Those furry, striped bandito faces are so frightened, so endearing, so brand new, I think: "Oh, let them be. We've all gotta eat."

Idling, so as not to spook the kits, I watch the mother raccoon defy gravity and climb straight up the side of a tall garage. Not a tree, but a spacious flat for three. One of the kits quickly follows her; but the runt of her litter keeps slipping off the slick gutter pipe and sliding back down. The grounded kit's hands and feet still can't get a toehold on the pipe. She cries out, a sound like high-pitched hissing screams that trails off into a weird little whistle. The mother raccoon coos back, encouraging. After all, raccoons can safely fall as much as thirty to forty feet and stick the landing. Slowly, with much chirping—like animal terror made audible—the last kit inches up the aluminum pipe to the roof. The two kits survey all below them with an expression that is at once proud, possessive. This is their home, too.

"Urban wildlife," that's what scientists call raccoons who are now thriving in our cities. I think of them as Raccoon People. Even though wild animals have a natural fear of humans, many are now adapting to and sharing our habitat. New research reveals that raccoons prefer urban living and, as they move into our cities in record numbers, they are fascinating scientists. They stay close to their many dens—usually traveling in a three-block radius. Raccoon mothers are affectionate and devoted to their kits; females often den together in what is aptly called a "nursery."

Raccoon mothers, like busy single moms, also share the chore of kit-sitting their babies, in something like a raccoon playground. To watch raccoon mothers and kits in a backyard or favorite green space is to witness animal play at its most comic. While the rest of the world sleeps, raccoons roll and wrestle, jump and race around each other like furry gymnasts. Backyard planters, gardening tools, even a scooter can tempt a raccoon to invent new games for nocturnal fun. Friend and wildlife photographer Robin Lindsey once discovered a raccoon kit at dawn thumping around a soccer ball someone had left on the beach.

After only twelve weeks, raccoon kits begin to wander away from their mothers, and yearlings are fully independent by eight to fourteen months. They spend the rest of their brief two- to three-year lives foraging, mating, and if female, raising new kits.

Because a raccoon's front feet are nimble and nearly as manipulative as human hands—and they are so remarkably curious—their brains are developing in complexity to meet the challenges and secret pleasures of city nightlife. So they are a lot like us, beings who have evolved by exploring, hunting, problem-solving, play, and manual dexterity. Researchers who study raccoons have documented that raccoons are more intelligent than dogs and some toddlers; a raccoon "can remember solutions to tasks for up to three years." In studies, "they were able to open complex locks in less than 10 tries." Some scientists theorize that the dark mask around those intense eyes is an evolutionary gift that deflects glare, giving this fellow creature enhanced and enviable night vision.

Some people wrongheadedly feed raccoons, which deprives them of the dignity of making their own living. Some people fear raccoons as rabid, but only one person in the US has ever died from a raccoon transmitting that dread disease. Some people mistakenly call raccoons "nuisance animals," but to disrespect raccoons is to lose what is most wild about our cities. In "Let the Postpandemic City Grow Wild," Ben Wilson, author of *Urban Jungle*, proposes making our cities even greener. Instead of more concrete and asphalt, we can create in our cities "a unique eco-system that offers us protection against climate threats and a vital, visceral connection with wildlife." He imagines cities with large urban woodlands, creeks, wetlands, gardens, all "enhanced by exuberant wild-life." Restoring these green spaces in our cities means welcoming back urban wildlife, like racoons, to their birthright territories.

Why not consider these sometimes rowdy, nightlife-loving, and always entertaining raccoons as a sign of a healthy urban wildlife habitat that we can all share—like good neighbors?

HUMPBACK HIP-HOP:
SPEAKING IN SONG

For Linda Gunnarson

IN WATER WARM as blood, our sea kayaks glided silently through the afternoon "vog" of Hawaii's big island. This haze of volcanic gas, fog, and smog clings to the skin, smells slightly smokey, and obscures all horizons, as if we were paddling through a moist, dark cloud. Disorienting, but then so was air eighty degrees warm in winter. My friend and I had journeyed to this familiar refuge from a waterlogged Seattle. Far above us, Pele was erupting in hot, black plumes, sending bright orange and yellow lava flows hissing into the sea.

I'd come here to Kealakekua Bay for several years to happily reunite with the resident wild dolphin pods and to observe the spring humpback whale migration. These island waters are home, and holy to me. I was covering the issue of ocean noise pollution, especially the military sonar being tested around the world and especially in these tropical islands. These low-frequency underwater sonic blasts and 235 Db (decibel) pressure waves are so loud that the sound has been compared to the ear-splitting drone of a jet engine, or the metallic shrieks of jack hammers. Listening to this sonar through hydrophones, people instinctively cover their ears to protect from what *Scientific American* called "rolling walls of noise." And our puny human hearing can't even register the full horror of this lethal sonar.

Such unbearable noise disorients cetaceans; they panic, propelling themselves to the surface in a vain attempt to escape the sonic stress. Rising so quickly, cetaceans die from the bends. Military sonar vibrations can rupture lungs, and above 210 Db, this lethal noise can bore straight through the brain, until the delicate tissue hemorrhages. After these military sonar tests cetaceans are often found beached with bloody, shattered ears. A deaf whale is a dead whale.

The late Ken Balcomb, of Friday Harbor's Center for Whale Research in Washington State, called this military sonar, an "acoustic holocaust." Balcomb was one of the first to document mass strandings of deep-diving beaked whales off the Bahamas and in Pacific Northwest waters. Sonar waves at these dangerous frequencies, he explains, cause "tissues to tear, much as a wineglass will shatter at a particular pitch." Whales and dolphins have no defense against military sonar. If cetaceans survive a military sonar test, the disorientation can still cause temporary hearing loss, which affects reproduction, communication, and the mother-calf bond. Humpback whales stop singing.

On the Big Island, it was like witnessing war games in a whale nursery—killing with sound. We'd already documented the heartbreaking sighting of an abandoned calf, something one long-time researcher, author Leigh Calvez of the Ocean Mammal Institute, had never seen, since humpback mother-calves are so deeply bonded. Humpback calves are usually safely tucked between a mother's pectoral flippers, never wandering more than 180 feet from the mother. After the Navy's sonar tests here in the islands, Calvez's research team recorded 230 breaches by the calf—almost one frantic breach per minute. They also noted 671 pectoral slaps, signs that this calf was in trouble, on the edge of exhaustion. The orphaned calf had been without a mother for seven hours. Weary, drifting too close to shore, the calf slapped flippers in the surf near sharp, dangerous lava rocks.

"We never saw the calf again," Calvez said sadly.

Such documented damage to cetaceans in Hawaii was also seen off the California coast after military sonar tests, in which Navy scientists themselves documented gray whales changing migration routes to avoid the sonar tests; and blue whales decreased their vocalizations essential to finding mates by 50 percent.

In 1999, I was one of the first to break the story of military sonar's lethal effects on Hawaiian humpbacks in an essay published in the *Seattle Times*. A *New York Times* op-ed writer immediately called me to get more background on my story. He was appalled at the sonar tests and promised to get the word out to a larger audience. When that editorial never appeared, he apologized. "The editor said I had to choose between my heart and my head," he admitted. "My editor warned me *not* to become some animal rights' bleeding heart."

In a poignant echo of the editor's fear, the *New York Times* reported a 2023 summer stranding of 100 pilot whales on the coast of Australia. Before they fatally beached, the whales "gathered in a heart shape," floating in the surf.

Earthjustice was one of the first to sound the alarm in the Northwest. "In May 2003, a group of about 20 killer whales and dozens of porpoises were forced to flee the waters near the San Juan Islands in Washington State, after a Navy ship passed by with its active sonar blasting." The Center for Whale Research has audio recordings of military sonar testing that the public can listen to on their website.

This acoustic trauma in our waters is mostly out of our earshot; many people assume the seas are silent. Because we can't hear it, we assume the sound doesn't exist. It's ironic that the US Navy's acoustic research in the 1970s Cold War was the first to document what were initially seen as mysterious whale vocalizations. That discovery led to researchers Roger and Katy Payne, with Scott McVay, recording a bestselling 1980s album, *Songs of the Humpback Whale*, that inspired countless other humpback song albums.

Like the Paynes, scientists can do more than simply report and analyze. They can get involved in conservation. Dr. Lindy Weilgart of Nova Scotia's Dalhousie University, a leading expert in whale acoustic communication, gave testimony against the military sonar tests before a Hawaiian federal judge. In a *Christian Science Monitor* op-ed, she wrote: "As a scientist—and as a mother and fellow inhabitant of this fragile planet—I am alarmed at this new threat to our oceans. I cannot imagine why we would subject marine inhabitants, the majority of which are highly sensitive to sound, to yet another source of pollution."

In that first Hawaiian research trip, and amidst all these threats to cetaceans, our mood was solemn and apprehensive as we paddled far out
from the Big Island's shore. From our little beach shack with its screens
for walls, a place owned by a Hawaiian family who'd lived here for generations, we'd already seen a few humpbacks breaching and playing. Of
course, we couldn't protect them from the underwater shrieks of military
sonar; but we could witness any damage and report on it.

With field notebooks in hand, we were adrift in sorrow, expecting to
witness the worst of what our species does to others. Floating on decep-
tively calm waters—we were not prepared for what happened next.

We heard the humpback singing before we saw her. Long, operatic
trills punctuated by percussive chirps and whistles rising beneath our
boat—vocalizations that vibrated the fiberglass kayak's hull. Floating in
this melodic embrace of humpback song, my hollow bones echoed with
those elegant, ultrasonic chants. My body simply a musical instrument
for such astonishing scales, from flute trills to bassoon-like bass notes—
this humpback's serenade. Closer now, but still no sighting. We listened
and looked at the horizon as late sunlight eased through misty veils.

"Two o'clock," my friend said very softly and lifted her paddle to make
less noise.

I turned my kayak to see the humpback breach close by, the body like
a silver skyscraper rising in the sea, as if the ocean itself was building
this behemoth from the bottom up. Her massive snout with its flap of
ventricle folds, like a huge accordion of skin, was impressive, but above
water, the singing less audible. She hung mid-air, pectoral fins flung out
wide from the heavy bulk of her barnacled flanks, which streamed seawater like a waterfall. Her endless mouth was fringed with plates of baleen,
made of keratin like that of human fingernails. Then, a sudden tilt backward, her huge tail flukes slapping the waves on her way back down to
coral depths.

Stunned, silent, we smiled. It was the closest encounter I'd ever had
with a humpback whale, having mostly seen them from research or whale
watching boats, or from shore. Was this humpback simply breaching or
was she trying to escape the underwater sonar we knew the military was

testing in this whale nursery? I took out my notebook to jot down the
time and activity to give to the cetacean researchers monitoring this bay.

But the humpback was not done with us. More accurately, we didn't
matter at all to her. We were not the main drama or characters in her
world. Just as I was sketching her identifying color patches, the constellations of barnacle scars and teeth chomp marks on her tail flukes—she
suddenly breached again. *Almost on top of us!* So close, I was eye-level
with her; and her black, unblinking eye was surprisingly small for such
a mammoth being. But there was nothing small about the awe ricochet-
ing in me, body and soul. To be met with such keen presence—a regard
that I can only call conscious, intelligent, alien—is to be forever changed.
Taught that ours is not the only consciousness at work in our blue-circled
water world.

I gasped. Only then did I realize I was gulping seawater because the
fountainhead of the humpback's breach had tipped my kayak sideways.
With my head underwater, her voice was so much louder, as if the ocean
herself were singing. Soprano scats, whirs, and calls that descended into
chirrs, rumbles, and melancholy moans. Songs zinging and vibrating in
underwater rhythms like humpback hip-hop. My skull was zinging, as I
listened underwater. I was inside a greater body now.

Where I'd expected to feel only sadness because of what was happening to these endangered humpbacks, I felt inexplicable happiness, an
expansiveness of spirit. I was more than a little human bobbing about in
a warm sea. I belonged to all the tragedy and beauty of being.

Just then my friend reached over and helped me right my kayak. She
laughed when she saw that though I'd lost my paddle, I still clutched my
small notebook in one hand.

"Good thing it's waterproof," she said drily. "Look . . ." she pointed at
the tip of the humpback's dorsal fin, all that was now visible above the
water.

But right next to her swam a smaller fin slipping up and down, almost
comically.

"A calf!" I tried not to shout.

"Yes." My friend shushed me and then whispered, "All that wild breaching before must have been her birth labor. We were just caught up in it."

"Midwives," I nodded, still feeling joy pinging up and down my spine.

The calf was taking her very first breaths, arcing up awkwardly and flopping back into the waves as the humpback mother cruised closely alongside. To be there at the beginning of a great life was a blessing. Again, I leaned over in my kayak, dunking my head into the water to keep listening. Humpback mothers sing welcoming songs to their calves. This whale's lullaby was exquisite with otherworldly wails, staccato *chirp-chirp-chirps*, bird-like calls, stuttering grunts, and then a lingering, low murmur. It was as if the humpback rejoiced and yet keened for her whole world, even as one species seems determined to destroy it.

Humpback songs have been heard all over the world. This radiant music has become a soundtrack to my own daily life, whether it was listening while quarantined in the hospital when I had pneumonia or daily napping in my little apartment on the Salish Sea. "The longest, liquid song," that's how musician and philosopher David Rothenberg describes humpback songs. "Evolution does not just encourage the survival of the fittest," he writes in *Thousand Mile Song*. "It produces wondrous beauty and strange ways for animals to be in touch." That this music also profoundly touches us is a sign that humans can tune in to other voices than our own. "Deep listening," as my friend Justine Willis Toms, a New Dimensions radio host, calls this attention to the natural world and all sentient voices.

Like Rothenberg, Tobias Fischer and Laura Cory, in *Animal Music*, posit that "there must be some emotional reason we and the whales need music." Perhaps it is an adaptation that both humans and whales have made because music is important to our own survival. They explain that humpback whale brains have three times as many spindle neurons as humans. Spindle neurons are the ones associated with emotion, memory, reason, communication, problem-solving and adapting to change. The facts that a male humpback's song changes from season to season, that their songs can echo across half the world; and that humpbacks sing the same song, adding riffs and self-identifying counterpoints, reveal a much more nuanced purpose for their singing. "Perhaps we are tuning into a secret life, a sonic landscape that whales rely on to create meaning . . . like folk songs in human history . . . a desire for self-expression, creativity, and perhaps an appreciation of aesthetics."

Neuroscientists have explored many theories about the evolution of music and its importance to "social capability . . . that can promote human well-being by facilitating human contact, meaning, and imagination," explains Robert Jourdain, author of *Music, the Brain, and Ecstasy*. "Music deeply engages both hemispheres, including the areas where language, spatial math, and emotions originate. [It] is a social instinct that engenders cooperation, emotional connection, and cognition, improving levels of the neurotransmitter, dopamine, in the reward centers of the brain." Musicians' brains are, indeed, different than those of non-musicians. Science has discovered, notes Jourdain, that "early musical training affects children's linguistic expression, and perhaps they are more sensitive in neonatal development."

Bone and ivory flutes date back forty thousand years to when *Homo sapiens* were first making music. Music is so essential in human development that "we probably sang before we spoke," neurologist Oliver Sacks writes in *Musicophilia*. "We humans are a musical species no less than a linguistic one."

Music has been such a constant theme, a soundtrack, in my life. Of course, I apprentice to the singing of other species, like humpbacks. When we listen to voices besides our own, we expand our own cognitive and social evolution to embrace what Sylvia Earle calls "dancing in their three-dimensional world."

We in the Pacific Northwest are fortunate that the Salish Sea is welcoming the return of more humpback whales than we've seen in generations. Twenty-five years ago, there were *zero* humpbacks seen off Seattle's coastline; in November 2021, five hundred humpbacks and a record number of calves were officially sighted. In 2022, humpbacks again broke all records, with more than 270 days of sightings. The Salish Sea offers migrating humpbacks their last opportunity to feed before they travel to breeding grounds near Hawaii and Mexico for winter, where they mate and give birth. These days, I watch humpbacks breaching near my backyard beach.

In April 2019, President Joe Biden designated 116,098 square nautical miles off Washington, Oregon, and California as critical habitat for three populations of endangered humpback whales. This protection is long overdue and perhaps one of the reasons humpbacks are coming back. "To recover West Coast populations of these playful, majestic whales, we need mandatory ship speed limits, and conversion of California's deadly trap fisheries to rope-less gear," noted the Center for Biological Diversity, whose lawsuit helped achieve this conservation victory. We also need to monitor ocean noise pollution like deep-sea seismic surveys and underwater explosions, and to limit military sonar testing.

The welcome rise in humpbacks and their calves is also happening in the South Atlantic, where populations had fallen to as low as 450 whales twenty-five years ago; but in 2019, the count was 25,000—"an estimate now close to pre-whaling numbers." Scientists have documented that when we preserve habitat for species who are threatened, they are twice as likely to recover as those without those critical protections. When we help endangered species like humpbacks to rebound, what more can we learn about this other animal intelligence?

Some researchers are using twenty-first-century technology to study cetacean culture, especially whale songs. Karen Bakker, author of *The Sounds of Life*, is on the forefront of animal communication. When scientists use bioacoustics recorders and computers, "it's like taking off the blindfolds and opening up your ears," Bakker explains. "We are on the brink of inventing a zoological version of Google translate," she predicts, because we are finally breaking the barriers to animal communication.

For example, right before humans almost drove sperm whales to extinction, scientists realized the whales were communicating in a kind of Morse code with individual words or syllables. Humpbacks were one of the first species to awaken humans to how whales communicate over the mysterious SOFAR (Sound Fixing and Ranging) channel—those deep ocean layers that broadcast their songs vast distances.

Humans are at last listening and using our technologies to begin to fathom animal language. "Not only what we can say to animals, or they can say to us," Bakker points out. "But what they're saying to one another."

Before we developed telescopes to see the stars, our ancestors believed Planet Earth was the center of the universe. Many people still believe humans alone have culture, language, and music—that we are still the center of Earth's ecosystem. But we can choose to humbly listen to other songs like the humpbacks, to honor the vital role all other species play in our planet's well-being and survival.

"The sea has ears," writes naturalist and wildlife filmmaker Tom Mustill in *How to Speak Whale*. Anyone who's seen a sound spectrogram of a pod of orcas vocalizing is most likely impressed by the complexity: impressionistic white squiggles rising, jig jazzing, merging, shooting up then down, lines overshadowing and swirling around each other, all etched against a black background like an artist on acid. An illustration in Mustill's book shows a 2019 award-winning "Craziest Spectrogram" image that looks chaotic to our uncomprehending eyes. But with these technologies we can now "use synthesizers to generate new sounds and make microphones capable of recording sounds we cannot hear," like whale ultrasound or elephant infrasound. We can document individual whales using photo ID and generational histories.

Sometimes I wonder if one day we'll develop new technology to recognize that humpbacks have also long laid down their songs as recordings on conch shells or coral reefs or undersea caverns. Maybe we'll discover valuable whale song libraries that generations of whales, and now humans, can at last hear. I believe that I've been acoustically imprinted on the voices of other animals, especially cetaceans. Maybe some future MRI or CAT scan will recognize that these mammal kin engraved echoes in my body, inscribing my brain and body musically. For those of us who've had close encounters of the whale kind, maybe one day we'll be able to recognize and translate these embedded acoustic tattoos. In another life, I'd like to be a translator for whale songs.

If a humpback whale can sing a song that Roger Payne has estimated travels thirteen thousand miles, why can't they also invent ways of archiving those songs, the way we do with CDs and vinyl and computers?

Those big brains, larger than and sophisticated as humans', have had millions more years of evolution. What underwater libraries are they creating, what tales are they singing that we may one day hear and understand in ways that change our world? How will we one day adapt to speaking with animals? When our own AI is advanced enough to understand the intelligence of these highly sentient fellow beings, we will be living in a new world.

The generous whale mother in Hawaii, who could have easily killed me with a tail or pectoral slap, sang instead a lullaby of the deep, a song that can be heard across oceans. May these songs endure for thousands of years.

SCENT OF SNOW

WHILE I'VE SPENT most of my adult life researching and writing about wolves, I began life as a prey animal. Children are like prey—small, helpless, powerless, and at the mercy of adults, who are usually benevolent, but can also be predatory. I still have memories of staring up at the deer heads above my crib, those graceful snouts, shining black noses, doe eyes; impressive racks of six-point antlers on which my mother gaily strung knickknacks like a tiny Smokey Bear toy, holiday ornaments, and even a small coconut head with googly eyes. Hunting mobiles, tinkling above in the mountain breeze, to amaze and amuse me.

I believed these deer trophies were devoted relatives, the first faces I ever loved. Imprinting on these ungulates left me with a lifelong fascination with deer, elk, moose, caribou. It was a complex bond because I soon grew up and realized that I was both prey and predator.

Since I didn't often accompany my father and later, my little brother, on their hunting trips, my first glimpse of wild caribou was when I met my father at the Alaska Wolf Summit held in February 1993 in frigid Fairbanks. I was covering the event as a journalist, and my father was attending as the Director of IWA (International Association of Fish and Wildlife Agencies).

The summit was a raucous affair with a thousand-strong observers, orange-clad hunters mostly booing, yelling, and stomping boots in makeshift bleachers set up over an ice rink. Scientists and wildlife advocates took their turns speaking against the aerial hunting of wolves by federal and state wildlife agencies. My father had advised me simply to take off my press badge and accompany him to meetings, where I took notes, listening to wildlife managers playing poker with top predator animals like wolves and grizzlies.

Outside the chilly ice rink, the cold was breathtaking as we walked down paths delved six feet deep through snow. Pro- and anti-hunting protesters yelled at us, waving signs like "Eco-Nazis Go Home!" and "Iraq—Want Some Wolves?" There were a very few protesters with signs: "Dead Wolves Kill Tourism," and "Wolf Hunting is Bad Science." One hunter was dressed in a fur bikini under her parka; another wore a wolf skin draped over his wide shoulders.

"It's a circus, not a summit," complained one of the Game Board members.

The Defenders of Wildlife speaker had told the riotous crowd, "What makes the deer so fast? The wolf's tooth." I remembered my father explaining that the deer's spine has evolved its delicate notches to exactly fit the wolf's fangs. Deer don't survive being knocked unconscious. As prey animals, they've learned how to die quickly.

During the chaotic days covering this Wolf Summit, I was fighting off real fear. "Ever feel like you're also prey?" I asked Renee Askins, who founded the Wolf Fund.

She glanced around the ice rink and said softly, "Remember, these hunters are terrified of us—that's why they're so angry. We wolf advocates are a real threat to their way of life, their dominion."

This Wolf Summit was a collision—a violent clash of cultures. Each side was in the other's cross-hairs. Any minute, I expected gunshots to ring out. What I wanted most was to escape this fracas into the cold refuge of mountains.

Journalists were the prey at this Wolf Summit. My friend, the Alaska poet Peggy Shumaker, found me on the very last day of the Wolf Summit, hiding under the bleachers, wearing my noise-cancelling headphones and hunched over field notes. Those of us who have long admired Peggy's poetry call her the "Sensualist of the Far North"; and her collection *Wings Moist from the Other World* is a perennial in my library and my teaching. As noted in a review in *Publisher's Weekly*, her poetry is known for its "almost treacherous emotion" as well as a "hint of serenity well-deserved."

"Looks like you need rescuing," Peggy said wryly, and we were off in her tiny, but intrepid truck.

She drove us along ice-rutted switchback roads way up into the expansive Brooks Range. The brief Alaskan sunlight had given way to a rather rugged-looking moon. According to the *Farmers' Almanac*, this fading New Year's moon was called a Wolf Moon. In that wan moonlight, we waited, watching.

Below us, crossing a frozen valley, was a vast herd of caribou. I heard the distant thunder of hooves crunching through the deep snow, and was awestruck by the pulsing, headlong, strangely synchronized movement. With my binoculars I caught the blur below of thick tan-and-buff fur, the syncopated stride of powerful legs. The caribou herd trotted together in a slow-motion stampede. Their jagged, curved antlers, like bone antennae, were raised high as they scented the chill wind for wolves.

Were wolves also watching this slow wave of prey below us—the throbbing heat of fur and bodies so tightly packed together for protection? Perhaps a hungry wolf family was poised nearby and calculating the risks of tackling any caribou straggler in such a huge herd. How much stamina to chase and take one down? Was it worth the risk of life and family?

"Amazing," I murmured. My breath haloed the air with a quick warmth.

"It's good to get up here," Peggy nodded with a faint smile, her face blister-red and chapped with the cold. "You can see a lot farther." Her poem "Caribou" describes what we witnessed:

Hoof—

one hoof
through fresh snow
touches,
breaks
the light crust pushing deeper

to hard pack. Haunch deep.
Only then can she
move on.

The change we need so delicate
so crucial

it might be
silent, it might be this quiet
step, breath.

"We can see what the wolf sees," I said, regarding the herd below with narrowed eyes, like a predator. Here in the Brooks Range, it was the wolves who were the aerial hunters. Not us. Maybe it was the hangover from the contentious Wolf Summit, but the magnificent sight of thousands of caribou inspired in me both wonder and sorrow. Perhaps that is the contradiction, an ambiguity for those of us who understand that we are both skilled predator and prey. We comprehend that we are utterly dependent upon our own keen senses, our own home ground, for survival.

We stood on that mountain, mesmerized by the mighty caribou herd traveling in single file for what seemed miles. Their concave-shaped hooves are adapted like natural snowshoes to deep snow. In rivers, these hooves are paddles. Caribou have been clocked running as fast as 50 miles per hour; and when they sense danger, a caribou gives off a scent that warns the others in the herd to flee. But these traveling caribou (the herd is most often led by a cow) seemed unhurried, efficient in their minimal use of energy to cross the tundra. In certain European regions, calm, nonaggressive caribou have for centuries been domesticated and called reindeer.

Caribou migrations are legendary but still somewhat mysterious. Theirs is one of the longest and last great wildlife journeys, akin to that of Arctic terns and humpback whales. In spring, caribou migrate north to the Arctic Coast. In fall, they journey south. They winter between Alaska and the Yukon. The herd we witnessed midwinter were using their remarkable sense of smell and forward-thrusting antlers to sniff under snow drifts for any food—grazing on moss, lichens, grass, shrubs. Herbivores, caribou are prey for many Arctic predators: bears, lynx, wolverines, golden eagles, and humans. Caribou herds, like reindeer, exist worldwide, especially in cold climates of Russia, Scandinavia, and Siberia. There are a few remnant caribou left in northern Idaho and Montana. Their estimated worldwide population is five million.

Caribou need a lot of land to roam. Accomplished swimmers, they will often simply paddle across lakes, instead of navigating around them on shore. Their thick fur traps air to keep them afloat, like a life jacket. Recent research reveals that caribou "are one of the few mammals on the earth that can perceive UV light," which may explain their keen adaptation to knowing the right time to migrate. Sensitive noses track not only smell but subtle changes in temperature that cue the caribou when it is time to migrate. When the winter temperatures drop, signaling snowfall, the caribou decide to migrate. When conditions change, say a warmer winter or less snowfall, the caribou might slow down, seeking more lichens and foliage, especially for the pregnant cows who need those rich nutrients to give birth.

Weather profoundly affects caribou migrations, as does climate change: there are more forest fires now. Caribou must arrive in their Arctic birthing grounds each spring. But a changing climate can throw off their timing, threatening the birth of calves. Some researchers wonder if warmer weather might work to increase caribou ranges, but more abundant foliage is also a possible predator trap for caribou.

A caribou's relationship to snow is primary. They are animal weathervanes as we study climate change: "the climate system, namely snow, icing, rain, solar input, temperature, wind, clouds, and seasonality, vary dramatically in their importance to the ecology of different caribou populations," notes the National Park Service's study on climate change. Deeper snows mean more energy needed to forage down and find winter foliage. These conditions can reduce pregnancy rates, affecting pregnant cows' ability to feed, as well as lower calf births and the survival of offspring. Climate change also influences insects, parasites, diseases, and predation.

Scientists using NASA's Earth Observatory are tracking caribou migrations by satellite telemetry, and a video created by the University of Montana Wildlife Biology shows the complexity of caribou herd migrations in Northern Alaska and Canada. According to a recent Canadian government study, some caribou "are less social and do not migrate." Other massive migrations still leave scientists "perplexed." Also of concern are the declining populations of Arctic caribou, what scientists call an "ecological chain reaction." Their natural range is vanishing due to logging, mining, oil drilling, human development, new roads, and increased predation. In Canada and the Lower 48, caribou are declining, "not faring as well as moose and wolves in the same areas." Researchers are trying to figure out how to manage caribou populations.

According to data surveyed in the NPS study, "Indigenous Peoples are forced to grapple with mounting threats to food security, cultural traditions, and infringed treaty rights." First Nations tribes like Inupiat and Gwich'in rely upon caribou migrations. The Gwich'in call themselves "Caribou People." Their villages in the Arctic National Wildlife Refuge subsist on caribou. It is vital to their culture. "We will not survive without the caribou," said the late Vuntut Gwich'in leader, Darias Elias. Before his death in 2021, Elias represented Yukon's northernmost community, Old Crow. As tribal storyteller and legislator, Elias advocated for his people and for the Porcupine caribou herd. He worked to support wilderness declaration for the Arctic National Wildlife Refuge in Alaska, which is on traditional Gwich'in lands. Elias told the story of camping one morning near the refuge as a park warden for Vuntut National Park. "There wasn't a cloud in the sky," he said. "I heard rumbling, so I stopped and saw a cow caribou and a calf come over the pass and, in just minutes, I was surrounded by about twenty thousand caribou . . . a sight, experience and a power that I will never forget . . . long live the Porcupine caribou herd."

The legendary Porcupine caribou have been studied extensively. On the round-trip migration between the southern wintering territory and the spring calving grounds, "one of the cows traveled 3,140 miles—the greatest distance recorded for any land mammal."

Science, government, tribes, and conservationists are all helping to understand and protect the caribou for future generations, animal and human. In my own family, the hunters are now too old and too environmentally minded to head north to prey on caribou. My brother, a lifelong military man, stopped taking hunting trips with our father twenty years ago.

"Things have ends and beginnings," writes poet Charles Wright in *Caribou: Poems*. "Cloud mountains rise over mountain range. Silence and quietness, sky bright as lake water . . . Grace is the instinct for knowing when to stop. And where."

On a recent midwinter family Zoom, my brother Mark reminded our ninety-six-year-old father and the gathered family about their one-time caribou hunting trip in Alaska. Mark called in from Florida wearing a light polo shirt. My father was in coastal North Carolina bundled up in his flannel shirt and fleece vest. I joined in from Seattle, wearing finger-less mittens and a down vest in the unseasonable cold. Weather is always a hot topic during our weekly family Zooms.

"A bush pilot flew us into the middle of nowhere," my brother began. "It was 2000 and I was the youngest hunter, in my early forties. Dad was in his early seventies. Gary Morrison, the director then of Alaska Fish and Wildlife, was hunting with us. We camped for about five to six days and had only brought enough food for several days because it was so heavy to carry. We expected to just live on the game we killed."

My brother paused with the characteristic self-effacing smile of a born storyteller. "Our base camp was rough tents; we knew grizzlies were around. But one of the hunters in our camp had just killed a caribou and hung the carcass up in nearby trees. That worried me. I asked Gary, 'Won't they lose their meat to bears?' I told him I was sleeping with a .38-caliber pistol.

"'That pistol will just make a grizzly angry,' Gary teased.

"'But what do we do if a bear gets into our camp?'" my brother asked.

Mark shook his head, grinning. "I thought I was going to get wise advice from Fish and Wildlife. But after a long, thoughtful moment, Gary concluded, 'Well, I guess we just hope the grizzly goes to *another* tent.'"

Everyone on Zoom laughed and pleaded for the story to go on. I am proud to come from a family tradition of storytellers. In fact, I'm the quietest one.

"What happened?" I asked. "Did you get your caribou?"

"We walked about two miles out," my brother continued. "You know, caribou can see and sense a hunter approaching from far away. So, we had to sneak up on a big herd. Found one resting in the sun, his back turned to us. We navigated around to get a better shot, since it's hard to kill an animal from behind. Both Dad and I fired at the same time. But the caribou only had one bullet hole—a clean heart shot. Dad's a better shot than I am, so it was probably his kill. But then we had to butcher the carcass right there, because we couldn't carry such a heavy caribou all the miles back to camp. We deboned it first; the meat weighed fifty to seventy-five pounds between each of our backpacks."

Dad was nodding in his little Zoom square. Behind him hung his favorite Atlantic Ocean painting. Nearby in the living room, I knew there would be his racks of antlers—moose, elk, deer, or caribou.

My brother took up again. "Now, this is where the story gets interesting. It was starting to get late. But in Alaska, the sun doesn't go all the way down, so it's still light at eight o'clock at night. Even with the midnight sun, we couldn't find our way back." He paused, then admitted what most men often don't. "I was really scared. We got lost!"

Then my brother playfully reminded our father that he often quotes Davy Crockett, "I ain't never been lost—I was misplaced for three days, but never lost."

We all laughed, fondly remembering that our father had never once admitted to getting lost on any of our many cross-continent moves.

My brother continued, "I told Dad that we should shed these heavy backpacks, and all the meat. It was going on 9:30 at night and we really didn't have any idea where we were. They sent out a search team for us, firing shots in the air. We followed the sound of gunfire and finally made our way back to camp. . . *with* our caribou meat. Eventually, we had it made into caribou steaks, burgers, and salami and shipped to us all."

"I don't remember what caribou tastes like," I admitted, not having eaten caribou since midlife when my father would fly down to Seattle from Alaska carrying coolers of fresh game.

"When we ate the caribou in base camp, we added olive oil and butter because it didn't have enough grease," my brother said. "It's very lean. Not one bit of fat."

"Yeah," I said. "Because caribou are always on the move."

We then engaged in a lively discussion about the difference between antlers and horns, in which Dad informed us, "Antlers are shed seasonally and then grow back. Horns are usually smaller." Someone else piped up that both male and female caribou grow those impressive antlers.

My brother's story stays with me for the theme of humans getting lost. Only a few miles from camp, hunters were disoriented by fading light and the heavy burden of their packs. I had to wonder: Do caribou ever lose their way on their long migrations? Or does their ability to sniff out foliage under snow and to track the temperature changes that trigger their thousand-mile migrations orient them? What is their future, and ours, with the profoundly shifting snow and ice of the Far North?

Climate change, well, it changes everything, for everyone, human and animal. In such drastic global extremes of weather as the world is experiencing—rising seas, fires, floods, sinking coastlines, thawing Arctic ice, and in 2023, some of the hottest temperatures ever recorded on Earth. Most climate change is human caused, from our consumptive relationship with the earth. But we are also the prey tracked down everywhere we live, at the mercy of now inescapable effects of climate.

We are truly lost. Scientists galore have sent up warning shots of clear, predictive data to try and to call us back to some base camp of safety, of sanity. But are we listening? Facts don't seem to truly engage our senses. A recent study by glaciologist Martin Sharp of the University of Alberta uses a novel technique to help humans tune into the *sound* of climate change. For those of us who listen more than look, these extraordinary recordings of glaciers melting can be heard in the *New York Times* 2023 piece, "The Poignant Music of Melting Ice."

Microphones buried in Canada's Devon Ice Cap, which is the size of Connecticut, were used to record and monitor the rate of melting ice. As reported by the *New York Times*, the researchers were surprised to hear that "as deep ice gradually thawed, an unexpected symphony unspooled . . . air trapped inside the ice, perhaps for centuries, exploded incessantly, creating an allegro of snaps and pops that conjured the electronic productions of Autechre and Aphex Twin."

Anyone who has heard Autechre's space-age whines and eerie drones or the British contemporary composer Aphex Twin's snappy, synthesized percussion and idiosyncratic techno piano riffs can experience the sounds of ice melting. When Sharp played the glacier recordings to his students, he said, "It gave people a different way into what I was talking about, other than just showing slides. The sound conveyed what it was like to *be* there."

This study's ice music has often gone viral. It includes "the laser-like phenomenon of someone skating across thin ice, the shootout sensation of ice being dropped into a frozen hole, the meditative sighs of ice forming and popping inside a Swedish lake." The scientists, by asking us to use our imaginations and tune in to melting ice caps, provide some hope. "If more people can actually hear climate change through the once-unknown songs of failing ice," Sharp concludes, "can they be inspired to help prevent it?"

Other scientists and musicians are recording melting Arctic ice to inspire us to listen to these once monolithic, now calving glaciers as they splinter, fracture, and slide into the sea. Norwegian musician Jana Winderen creates "poignant musical postcards from melting and cracking masses of ice." She realized that photos of icebergs were meaningful to our mostly visual species, but sound embodies the experience: "the brutal noise [an iceberg] made while breaking free from a glacier, however, could be harrowing . . . as the frozen world gave way to heat."

Young people seem to be listening to the soundtrack of melting ice and climate change and heeding its warning. They are the generations who must adapt most to our changing world. What more will they recognize, like the caribou who track temperature to change their migratory times and routes? Every animal has a superpower. For caribou, it's the scent of snow, the lichen buried deep under frozen snowfall. For humans, it may be our imaginations, just as much as our science, that helps us find our way back.

When I listen to glacier music, the memory of standing on that icy ridge watching thousands of caribou travelling together always comes to mind. Peggy's caribou poem is even more prophetic today than it was at the turn of a new century on that ice-clad mountain as we observed another world and a herd traveling in one beautiful, heartbreaking body:

The change we need so delicate
so crucial.

WHEN WE STAYED HOME

WHEN A LETHAL disease quarantined us during the global Covid-19 pandemic, animals reclaimed their territories. As we isolated and sheltered inside, the natural world was wild again, unburdened by our noisy, busy dominion. Fascinated, we watched animals inhabit land and seas where we had encroached. It was astonishing how quickly our absence freed other animals to return to their rightful habitats. Humans were the species now in cages; we were the captives. I couldn't help but wonder if there was joy and even some triumph as wild animals took over our empty cities and neighborhoods.

On social media, millions of people posted videos: Coyotes exploring a beach near the Golden Gate Bridge or gallivanting on golf courses in Florida, an alligator crawling through a mall in South Carolina, penguins waddling along South African city streets, kangaroos *boing-boinging* along Australian sidewalks, peacocks shrieking and strutting in Mumbai parking lots. In Argentina, a sea lion slept on a sidewalk; on Oregon beaches elk herds galloped across sand; in Brazil, baby sea turtles hatched on bare beaches, safely scooting to the sea. In Japan, deer wandered down steps into subway stations, no trains to catch. In England, sheep spun on a merry-go-round. Wild boars in Israel snorted and hoofed through a city. All over the world, people heard more birdsong than ever before.

With far less traffic on US highways, there was 58 percent less road kill. Bird migrations during the pandemic's first spring were less interrupted by airplanes; oceans suffered much less noise pollution and there were fewer boat traffic collisions with whales. Scientists called the sudden decline in human activity during the pandemic "anthropause."

Here in Seattle, the Pacific Northwest's biggest city, there were so many sightings of urban wildlife that one *Seattle Met* reporter declared "it's *Jumanji* out there . . . reports of a turkey wandering around West

Seattle, of a mad squirrel attacking a child, of midday coyote sightings, of rats alternately frolicking in the parks or turning to cannibalism." In my neighborhood, raccoons reigned; those hump-backed mammals were no longer just rowdy night life. More people than the usual birders observed "a dark cyclone of crows" circling a tree. Murder of crows, indeed.

In Glacier Bay, Alaska, migrating humpback whales, what one scientist calls "a chatty bunch," weren't so drowned out by the loud cacophony of cruise ships. Listening with hydrophones to humpbacks *whup* and whistle, researchers documented sounds two months into the pandemic that were half as loud as those in May 2018. For orcas off Vancouver Island, this meant a once-in-a-lifetime lull in ferry and cargo ship traffic. Normally, the underwater noise from sixty thousand commercial vessels worldwide creates "an oceanic smog" that disturbs all marine life. Researchers in an article said that "this momentary quiet will lead to a better understanding of how noise affects them."

For those of us who also consider animals our good neighbors, the pandemic rest of our species showcased the benefits for other animals, especially the wild ones. From our forced retreats, we watched with wonder, while the whole world again belonged to animals.

Because of this time out, we've had a chance to consider our imprint on nature and wildlife, the fact that, as the *New York Times* declared, "animals are running out of places to live . . . wildlife is disappearing around the world, in the oceans and on land . . . humans are taking over much of the planet, erasing what was there before." With a human population of over eight billion, our species dominates climate and environment, prompting scientists to describe this twenty-first century's geological age as the Anthropocene. A 2022 UN biodiversity convention is aiming to slow humanity's "war with nature," noting that "humans have significantly altered 75% of the Earth's land and two-thirds of its oceans." Mass wildlife extinctions and the loss of biodiversity is staggering for all future generations, human and animal. One scientist predicts, "We might already be looking at a much-reduced set of species." We already are.

The pandemic gave us an empathic glimpse into what a much-reduced set of humans looked like. During the pandemic there were over one million deaths in the US and three million deaths worldwide. During quarantine, I once again read Alan Weisman's remarkable thought experiment *The World Without Us*, in which he imagines the world after human extinction. Writing in 2007, Weisman's vision of a world sans us is eerily prescient. In the chapter "Lost Menagerie," the author envisions "your familiar landscape swarming with fantastic beings . . . deer with antlers thick as tree boughs . . . furry rhinoceroses, big hairy elephants, and even bigger sloths . . . wild horses . . . panthers with seven-inch fangs and alarmingly tall cheetahs. Wolves, bears, and lions so huge."

Imagining a future world where wild animals dominate is both bracing and instructive. "Animal species we consider the most intelligent—dolphins, elephants, pigs, parrots, and our chimpanzee and bonobo cousins—probably wouldn't miss us much at all," Weisman theorizes, noting that "although we often go to considerable lengths to protect them, the danger is us." "We're the alien invaders," he admits. "Every time *Homo sapiens* went anywhere else, things went extinct." Weisman's research of a future without humans is not dystopian; it's from nature and the animal's points of view. In his chapter on the "sea cradle," he interviews a scientist studying the bleaching of coral in Australia's Great Barrier Reef, who points out, "The great majority of sea species are badly depleted, but they still exist. If people actually went away, most would recover."

People going away—it's not that impossible. A pre-pandemic 2016 study found that "A typical person is more than five times as likely to die in an extinction event as in a car crash." Scientists predict that in six generations, by 2085, human populations will decline. Is the global pandemic a preview of our diminished future? Will we see other species repopulate their natural territories? Or will animal extinctions outpace ours?

The global pandemic gave us a pause, a time to reflect on our own endless abuse of our home planet and all other animals. It added depth and urgency to those of us already contemplating our own demise. For me, the return of wild animals to their rightful territories, their birthrights, was illuminating. It reminded me of my early days in the wilderness of the High Sierra when the little cabins of our neighbors dotted a vast forest and animals outnumbered us. That brief return of animals restored some balance I always believed in. The myriad images of wild animals returning to their rightful habitat, wrote author Helen Macdonald, "open up a space for us to imagine the new world that will come when this crisis is over, a space that might allow us not only to rethink how we relate to the natural world, but to one another."

How will the time during quarantine and after change our lives and our bond with other animals? Was this pandemic perhaps a dry run or practice for when *Homo sapiens* disappear? Will we find new ways of cohabitating now that we've witnessed how easily the natural world repopulates without us? There are ecopsychologists who posit that, like animals, we have an "ecological unconscious" that longs for the land and other sentient beings. We endure a deep "homesickness" when we are separated from nature and fellow creatures. Many conservationists are working now not just to rewild habitat and wildlife, but also to "rewild the psyche." Perhaps this pandemic offered us this more generous embrace of ecosystems and all other animals. The revered biologist E. O. Wilson believed that human beings have "an innate tendency to focus on life and lifelike processes." Perhaps the millions of humans lost during the pandemic forced us to pay more attention to life—*all* life, not just our own.

Unlike the transhumanists, I don't cheer for humanity's end. I always hold out hope that our species will have learned from the pandemic and will welcome more wild animals back to their rightful, shared homelands. I work for that interspecies family reunion. I tend to be more aligned with Weisman, who concludes: "Is it possible that instead of heaving a huge biological sigh of relief, the world without us would miss us?" I also wonder: Would the animals miss us? The pandemic revealed that other animals thrive without us. When we rest, they can come out and play.

APPRENTICESHIP TO ANIMAL PLAY

DURING ONE OF the darkest times of my life, I often found myself lying flat on my studio floor, face-to-face with my Siamese Manx cat. As I wept over my many losses, Isabel would leap onto me as if my prostate grief were a posture to invite her kittenish pounces, her purring growls, and tiny tiger attacks. If she were a kitten, I could have better understood her sudden playfulness, indeed her mania for play. But Isabel, a homeless cat I'd adopted, had never played with me before. Why, when I was my most grief-stricken, would she mistake my sorrow for high-spirited cat games of stalk and bat-the-birdie, and braid my hair with claws tenderly tucked?

As I lay snuffling on the old blue carpet, a desultory hand stroking this small, bobtailed cat who threw herself into dazzling cartwheels over my legs, I found myself smiling. Soon I was checking out cat-play toys like the bright purple "bird" that whizzed through the air around Isabel, inspiring her acrobatic leaps and midair somersaults. Her movements were shocking in their grace and complete abandon.

One morning as I was crying my eyes out over the end of a long romance, I had gone through a box of tissues when Isabel leapt onto my chest, her slanting blue irises oscillating. Tail twitching, she stalked me with ferocious glee, snatching the tissue and shredding it all over my face. This flimsy foe vanquished, she turned tiny tail and hunkered down next to me, awaiting the next fabulous threat.

It was only then that I wondered if something about my grief had engaged my cat's imagination so deeply that her response was new behavior: this inspired play. Isabel's history was lost to me. I knew only that she'd been feral for the eight months my neighbors fed her where she cowered under their back porch. She'd never allowed them near until one day she had what my neighbor Pamela describes as a "kitty nervous breakdown."

"That's all I can call it," Pamela explained as she pleaded with me to take Isabel into my own home, where I already had an older, much-beloved Siamese Manx named Ivan, and Ziggy, a burly chow-chow/Newfoundland mix a park ranger once called "a bear on a leash." There was really no room for another animal.

Pamela continued, "This little rag-tag Siamese just sat in the middle of our driveway and screamed her head off as if to say, 'I can't take one more homeless day. I can't hide in the dark one more night from raccoons. I'm not letting humans come near or touch me—but please just pick me up and put me out of my misery!'"

I knew the feeling.

"Besides," Pamela coaxed. "You love Siamese, and Isabel looks a lot like your big Manx, Ivan Louis. Cats live longer with mates."

I brought the tiny, matted cat into my home, where Isabel proceeded to perch on my bookshelf, watching the birds on a branch outside. From this safe post, she endured my other curious animal companions. Surprisingly, she began engaging with Ivan, though he sometimes swatted her away. At night, Isabel often stole into my bed, but during the days she kept her distance. She was silent, sneaky, and except for an essential sweetness to her nature, she seemed what we would call "shut down."

"It's trauma," the vet diagnosed. "Imagine what she's been through out there, lost and homeless. Who knows what she's seen, what she's survived? It may take her many months to know she's safe and sheltered." The vet stroked Isabel's matted, dull fur and clipped away another of the greasy globs of furball that knotted her body like tumors. "She may be just too traumatized to ever play again."

"So play is a sign of good health?" I asked the vet, intrigued.

"Oh, yes," he said. "Both physiological and psychological health. In any animal, it's a sure indicator, not only of good health but of their chances for survival. When an animal never again engages in play, we don't hold out much hope for full recovery."

For over two years after I took Isabel in, she had not played. I had given up hope, or just decided it was not in her nature anymore. When her unexpected, wholehearted playfulness coincided with my own whole-hearted grief, it took me a few weeks to notice. But at last, I recognized that, for some reason, her trauma was over even as my own began. Isabel was not *trying* to balance me, though she did. Perhaps she'd perceived my horizontal crying bouts as a delicious new game in which her humans were at last supine, at her level. Whatever the explanation, her clowning was so serious that it literally eased my dark moods into musing, companionable play. It was a perfect exchange, for which I shall always be grateful. We had slowly nurtured each other out of deadening despair and into some daily delight in living.

I've always placed a high value on play. My decades of studying and encountering wild dolphins was an apprenticeship to play, a time spent learning the lessons of another intelligent species that spends three-quarters of their lives playing. What are our big-brained mammal cousins learning during all that playtime that might teach us how to better survive the stresses of our lives? Dolphins in play, like many other species, learn vital survival skills: astonishing navigational teamwork with their family "pods," communication abilities that at times seem almost telepathic, and a buoyant resilience. We humans respond to dolphins with a surge of pleasure and sometimes joy. In Hawaii, I watched even a boat of serious scientists burst into laughter when a pod of spinner dolphins flew over our bow, twirling like silver corkscrews. Ken Norris, the respected spinner dolphin researcher, finally concluded after his decades of study that dolphins spin and somersault simply for the fun of it.

In a *National Geographic* article about "Animals at Play," physician Stuart L. Brown concluded that play is an indicator of psychological health, well- being, and even survival. Just as my cat Isabel's vet had said. In the mid-60s, Brown's research linked mass murderers with their "absence of a normal play pattern" in childhood. It is a chilling commentary to note that decades later in America, random mass shootings are now commonplace. Brown noted a striking 90 percent of young men committing mass shootings showed dysfunctional play "like bullying, sadism, extreme teasing, or cruelty to animals." Such abnormal play was rooted, says Brown, in an inflexible, black-and-white morality where "problem-solving" allowed two possibilities: conquest or defeat.

This research led Brown to expand his study of play to include other non-human species. He also theorized that humans have much to learn about play from other animals. Brown cited primatologist Jane Goodall's decades of chimpanzee research in Tanzania's Gombe National Park. Goodall has often described chimpanzees as champions of play. She noted that a sure sign of depression in infant orphaned chimpanzees was that they stopped playing at all.

Play doesn't end in childhood or in the animal kingdom. Play is also about developing a lifelong imagination that is flexible and responsive to the surrounding environment. True play calls forth from us, both animals and humans alike, the highest creativity and inventiveness. Visionaries of all species are often champion players. They don't win finite games; they imagine infinite possibilities. Visionaries look over the next hill; they find a new way of swinging from a tree to ford a river that one day might rise to a flash flood. They mate in new ways. They do not always support the status quo. This play is often risky behavior for many animals, because while a dolphin is spinning, a monkey is swinging, or lions make love on the open savannah, those individuals are at risk from predators—and sometimes even at risk from their own species.

When we play, we let go of our wariness, breaking down our walls and psychological barriers. Some scientists believe that those who play the most in any species are also those who contribute the most to evolution. If play were not somehow essential to evolution, why would natural selection have permitted, and even promoted, such unabashed and unprotected play? There are researchers who conduct play workshops to help people recover from addictions or post-traumatic stress disorder. A therapist I know tells me that he always asks: "When did you stop singing, dancing, and playing?" And yet we cannot structure play as just a means to an end; we can't teach ourselves to play simply as a chore or a prescription because "it's good for you."

Play that is goal-oriented will soon become tiresome and just another kind of work. Play, as any apprentice to animal play will affirm, is most rewarding when it is pure and spontaneous fun. In *The Comedy of Survival*, Joseph Meeker says, "Play allows us to most easily cross boundaries between human and animal, between male and female, even between enemies." Meeker always assigned his students the homework of writing a "Personal History of Play." He asked for daily details of play that is timeless, pleasurable, nourishing, and restorative. "In at least a dozen species," Meeker explains, "the ratio of play to non-play in a day is the same as the ratio of REM sleep—and you know what happens when humans are deprived of those deep sleep rhythms of REM. We literally go crazy."

The cat story of Isabel that began with sadness ends with an eerie and almost amazing happiness. The reason this homeless Siamese cat adapted so well to my other Siamese, Ivan, was because, as I finally discovered, they were, indeed, litter mates who had been separated at birth. They looked so much alike because they were, in fact, siblings. Through a strange series of coincidences, Isabel had gotten lost several miles up the hill and finally found her way back to the beach and her brother. Isabel and Ivan became inseparable; and bonded pairs of animals live longer. My two Siamese enjoyed long lives, finally passing at twenty-one and twenty, even though they were both diabetic. They began a tradition of Siamese cats that includes two more bonded pairs, Loki and Tao, and my current cat family of Tako and Rita, popular on my Facebook page for their feline "WrestleMania."

I could go on and on about the value of play to us all. But my cats are already jumping on my desk looking for that elusive birdie; and my neighbor's dog is restless, eyeing her squeaky ball as if it were all that mattered in the world. Time to get outside, to enjoy this brief hiatus from Seattle's rain. And as we walk along the Salish Sea, I'll look out over the waves for the happy rise and dive of dorsal fins—more playtime.

BRINGING BACK BEARS

SOME CHILDREN HAVE teddy bears for companions and touchstones. My early childhood in the national forest cabin was filled with stories of Smokey Bear, a real-life survivor of the Capitan Gap Fire in New Mexico in the summer of 1950. This black bear cub was no fairy tale; he was a brave orphan found by firefighters near the fire line. The firefighters were also caught in the fire storm's path, and they lay face down for over an hour on a rockslide as the fire burned over them. The cub had sought refuge by climbing a charred tree, but his paws and hind legs were singed, painfully. The firefighters rescued the cub, and one of the base camp's cooks slathered the cub's paws and legs with butter—some locals say bacon grease—before he was flown to Santa Fe, where his burns were treated by a New Mexico Department of Game and Fish ranger and his family, who cared for the cub.

As a child I'd seen vivid, scary photos of this bear cub curled up with his tiny paws in white bandages. Every time my own father went off to fight forest fires, I prayed that this little cub who was growing up strong would protect him and all the other wild animals from the flames. Animals and people on fire, running through a burning forest, their skin or fur aflame with red-hot, hungry tongues, was one of the most haunting nightmares of my childhood.

The Forest Service soon named the cub Smokey Bear, and he became an endearing and enduring symbol of fire prevention. The poster with Smokey pointing a scarred paw and the words "Only You Can Prevent Forest Fires" was burned into my consciousness. To this day, I have Smokey Bear swag—flannel sheets and salt-and-pepper shakers, T-shirts and a giant stuffed teddy bear—reminding me of my duty to the forest and all wild animals. I am still afraid of fire and constantly nudge everyone to turn off Christmas tree lights, snuff out candles, stamp out campfires—anything that might burn down the house or forest. I am always reminding my friends when they trek off camping that nine out of ten wildfires are caused by humans.

Smokey Bear lives in me so deeply that when my father was chief of the Forest Service, he asked me to write a kid's book with Rudy Wendelin, illustrator of Smokey Bear. I still have those original drawings buried somewhere in my storage unit. In my first memoir, *Build Me an Ark: A Life with Animals*, I wrote the story of Smokey Bear, who lived in the concrete caves of the National Zoo in Washington, DC, with a female bear, Goldie, until he died in 1976. I had hoped as a child that Smokey would be rehabilitated and returned to the forest. It's probably where my years of writing about wildlife restoration took root.

In the summer of 2021, I was transfixed when firefighters rescued another bear cub from the devastating Antelope Fire in the Klamath National Forest on the border of Oregon and California, only a few hours' drive from my Plumas National Forest birthplace. Clinging to a tree near Antelope Creek, this cub was also badly burned. Eerily, the rescue was on the seventy-seventh anniversary of the original Smokey Bear. Wildlife biologist Sarah Bullock found the young bear, who had been either orphaned or abandoned.

Poignant photos of Bullock in her yellow hard hat holding the cub went viral, her hand cradling the bear's paws. Especially poignant was the image of the cub hugging the base of a tree, his hind legs lifted just off the ground. With second and third-degree burns on his nose and paws, the 16-pound cub was taken to Gold Country Wildlife Rescue facility in Auburn, California, where he was attended to by veterinarians from my alma mater, University of California.

"He is eating well and taking fluids on his own, which the doctors consider a positive sign for full recovery," news reports reassured those of us who eagerly followed the rescue.

Bullock and California Department of Fish and Wildlife biologist Axel Hunnicutt had first tranquilized the cub, and several drivers transported the injured bear two hundred miles to the wildlife rescue facility. Gold Country Wildlife Rescue often receives animals found alive after wildfires, "with the ultimate goal of reintroduction into the wild whenever possible." Unlike the original Smokey Bear, this young survivor of one of the deadliest Western wildfires had a chance to return to the forest.

This remarkable wildlife facility in 2021 rehabbed three bears from the Antelope and Dixie Fires. Their stories are not the stuff of Three Bears fairy tales, but of devoted wildlife rescuers, who work to heal the damage climate change has brought to the West with its devastating cycle of fire and floods. Photos of these three bears cuddled together in a wooden bunk are featured on the facility's website. But sadly, when I wrote Gold Country Wildlife Rescue to inquire about the cub rescued from the Antelope Fire, they reported he did not survive. Two other burned cubs did live and were released in the spring of 2022, "deep in the mountain wilderness."

Smokey Bear has made a comeback now after Woodsy Owl and other Forest Services characters failed to capture the public's imagination as much as that singed little survivor. Kids can still write Smokey Bear at Washington, DC 20252. Current television ads again feature a Smokey Bear character who is witty, as well as instructive, when advising us to always extinguish our campfires. This twenty-first-century Smokey Bear has a lot to do to educate us as devastating wildfires consume Western forests. Smokey's Only You campaign now includes environmental lawyers for states and cities. A *Grist* article in the spring of 2023 reveals that "A third of the West's burned forests can be traced to fossil fuel companies." Added to how much worse corporate emissions have made wildfires is the complex factor of climate change, "roughly doubling the acreage burns over the last 40 years." A laborious crusade is finally heating up to hold companies like Chevron, Exxon Mobile, BP, and Shell accountable, by suing them for wildlife and environmental damage to our forests. Studying how "thirsty" the atmosphere is, scientists can study how "hotter temperatures cause moisture to be pulled out of vegetation, turning forests into tinderboxes just waiting for a spark."

Because Smokey Bear was the icon of my forest childhood, bears are also a kind of animal totem for me. My parents' home is decorated with Smokey

Bear memorabilia, from carvings to an original painting of him with a shovel in one giant paw and a Bible upraised in the other. As in all the official Forest Service posters, in this painting, Smokey wore blue overalls, belt, and hat, but he is standing next to a portrait of my father, who was still a bear of a man into his late eighties, often testifying before Congress on forest and wildlife issues. Now ninety-six, he no longer camps or treks around the Alaskan tundra on his hunting trips.

Growing up, we camped in so many of the West's great national parks and forests that I'd often tease my father that my childhood was "camp-or-die." One of my favorite bear encounters was in Montana. My father had long before taught me what to do if I met a bear in the woods: raise up to my full child's height, wave my hands above my head to look taller and fiercer, and holler out, "I'm a human being! A predator, too. I'm as big as you!" Sometimes when we camped or hiked, we'd tie silverware to our mess kits and that percussive clang and clatter let the bears know it was our turn on the trail.

One year, camping in Glacier National Park with my grandmother, we had our first close grizzly bear encounter. My three siblings and I had seen grizzlies only at Forest Service dumps, where we'd watched from a safe distance. But the past winter had been especially cold and the ravenous bears' emergence from hibernation coincided with our spring camping.

"Bears have been denned up all winter," my father warned us. "They're just waking up and will be hungry. So be on the lookout. Even if they're groggy, grizzlies are dangerous."

He gave us one of his wildlife lectures. This camping trip, it was all about hibernation. Black bears and grizzlies were the biggest hibernators, but squirrels, rodents, some birds, skunks, bats, even ground hogs all curl up in trees, caves, even cliffs to snooze. "Not much food . . . grass, fish, berries, insects . . . for them in winter," my father explained. "So, they rest up in the winter months."

"Are they really fast asleep?" my little brother asked.

"No, it's like a kind of physical pause," my father said. "Bears stay warm and survive off all the food, fat, and water they've stored from eating so much in the spring and late fall. That's why bears are really big. Sometimes mother bears hibernate curled up with their cubs."

The image of a giant bear and her cubs stowed in a mammoth tree's knothole was the stuff of children's books illustrations that we always hoped to see in real life. I kept an eye out for bears clambering down from the treetops.

That spring morning in Glacier National Park, while my parents and Uncle Clark were in the nearby woods hunting for kindling to start a breakfast fire, Grandmother Elsie laid out a picnic table with fresh bread, thick bacon, campfire skillet–blackened scrambled eggs, and her famous homemade apple butter. Grandmother's apple butter, along with her recipes for Wolverman's relish, chowchow chopped pickles, black-walnut divinity, and cherry fudge, were her finest legacy. My grandfather even made up a word, "larrapin," for Grandmother's most delicious culinary delights. We positively lapped up her cooking, especially the luscious, darkly sweet, tart apple butter, which had the slow consistency of molasses with succulent chunks of bright apple flesh and skin.

This morning, the homemade jam brought us kids to the wooden picnic table more surely than any breakfast call. We followed our noses to Grandmother's apple butter the moment we heard the whoosh and pop of the Bell jar wax break open. Other noses must have quivered at the scent of such a sweet treasure, too, because while we kids were saying grace with our eyes open, heads bowed over the toast and apple butter, I saw a big, blurry shape out of the corner of one eye. It was a gigantic grizzly bear raised up on his hind legs and lumbering toward us as we said our prayers.

Not one of us did what we had been so carefully taught by our father, draw ourselves up and look big. But at least we did not cower. We froze, like possums, standing utterly still in the presence of such absolute animal power. This grizzly was so splendid in his reddish-black shaggy fur, with his paws the size of my little brother's head. We were more awestruck than afraid. Our paralysis was as ancient as if our reptilian brains had memorized this image: giant bears hovering over barely human beings.

There was no talking to this creature, no bargaining or boisterous argument about sharing top predator status. We were in thrall and insignificant to this bear. Eerily human-like, he walked on strong back legs toward our table. He did not roar, perhaps appreciating our sudden silence while Grandmother continued saying grace. I remember clearly being impressed by the bear's black, sniffing nose raised high with a surprising delicacy, as if this bear, too, understood the joy of homemade jam.

It did not seem odd to feel complete reverence for this grizzly. Mouths open, eyes agog, we kids just stared as the grizzly moved toward us, his feet so big the ground thundered beneath us. But my grandmother, who had lifted her head after a firm "Amen," let out a whoop.

"*You! Shooooo!*" she yelled at him, shaking her finger.

It was the way she'd discipline us if we tried to steal her apple butter. Grandmother was so possessive of her recipe that she hadn't even passed it on to my mother. She was darned if she would share her jam with a bear.

"*Shooo! Shooooo! Shoooo!*" she yelled in her old-lady wavering soprano.

With each admonishment, she flapped her flowered apron at the bear. "This is my last batch of apple butter," she informed the grizzly. "It's not going to be gobbled down by any big bear. Go on with you now! *Git!*"

I closed my eyes, expecting to hear the bear decapitate my grandmother with one massive blow from those paws with claws huge as rakes. My sister remembers that my grandfather rolled up a newspaper and smacked the grizzly on the head; all I remember is the grizzly poised over my tiny grandmother and her jam. The grizzly bear gave one last, almost longing sniff and then, with a huge harrumph and sigh, turned around and fell on all fours. The grizzly did not run away but strolled pigeon-toed nearby and shook his massive head back and forth, grunting. I wondered if we had hurt the bear's feelings by not sharing our sweets.

It wasn't fear we felt now, as the grizzly lingered nearby, his nose still sniffing the air. Especially since Grandmother had reprimanded the grizzly as high-handedly as she often did us. I felt grateful that the bear had left us alive. We attacked that jar of apple butter with our own animal hunger. It wasn't until Uncle Clark came back, waving his arms and screaming for us to hide under the picnic table from the lingering grizzly that it occurred to us we were in grave danger.

Uncle Clark quickly packed us into the station wagon to wait for my parents to return. Squeezed in the back seat between camping gear and a giant cooler, I watched the grizzly. With a vengeance, he turned the picnic table upside down, licking the wood where I'd spilled some apple butter. I was pleased that he had at last gotten a taste of Grandmother's glory.

Maybe the grizzly was still too drowsy to take on my fierce grandmother. Perhaps hibernation had taken its toll and the grizzly was more interested in the fragrant, fresh flowering trees or salmon leaping in the nearby river. These many years later, animal hibernation is still a scientific mystery. It is considered "an amazing trick of biology." How does such a large body shut down for six months and yet emerge again in the spring with all its physical functions still working? If humans hunkered down for that long without food, water, exercise, we'd suffer dehydration, starvation, oxygen deprivation, bone decay, major organ collapse—we'd probably perish.

But bears' bones are *stronger* after hibernation, their bodies profoundly rested and restored. The ultimate winter nap. "Hibernation defines the outer limits of what's possible in terms of mammalian function," writes Brian Barnes, a University of Alaska Fairbanks zoologist. Scientists are now studying the physiology and adaptive ability of hibernation in bears as a possible key to helping humans heal from osteoporosis, cardiac events, Parkinson's disease, stroke, and Alzheimer's. Barnes explains, "heart attacks and strokes greatly reduce the supply of oxygen and nutrients to the brain. That lack of supply would be much less damaging if doctors could rapidly reduce the demand by putting a patient in a state of hibernation."

A bear's hibernating brain and central nervous system accumulates proteins, explains Yale neurophysiologist Elena Gracheva in *Smithsonian Magazine*. "Could it even be possible to give human patients a similar awakening" and rigorous spring cleaning of such vital brain proteins?

A recent study found that when mice were induced into hibernation and awakened, their memory and brain connections improved markedly. This induced hibernation in humans may one day help Alzheimer's, stroke, and Parkinson's patients. Studying hibernation for humans is also crucial for space travel, which would require many metabolic changes and biological adaptations. Science fiction assumes hibernating for perhaps hundreds of years to explore planets light-years away.

Studying bears not only gives us insights into possibilities for human hibernation, it also serves as yet another wake-up call to our own earth's changing climate and ecosystems. Bears time their spring wake-up on weather and temperature. Researchers are documenting how our warming world is affecting how long bears hibernate. So far, they seem to be adapting. Bears are thriving in Florida swamplands, Mexican forests, and in southern Europe, where winters are now much less intense. In Greece and Croatia, some bears "skip hibernation entirely. . . unless they are pregnant."

What's equally as crucial to bears thriving is the relationship between us and *Ursa*, the genus of bears. Like wolves and other top predators, bears have been relentlessly hunted to make way for our farms, ranches, and cities. In 1975, the "keystone species" of grizzlies were so diminished by hunting and federal or state killing campaigns that the populations had fallen from an estimated 100,000 in North America to only 150 in the Western US. Protected in 1973 under the Endangered Species Act, grizzlies are slowly on the rebound. Today about 700 grizzlies roam Greater Yellowstone. As a keystone species, their presence is a linchpin to health and recovery of the greater ecosystem.

When I was conducting research in Yellowstone in 2016, I interviewed several tribal members, including Blackfoot, Cheyenne, and Sioux, who were working tirelessly to protect grizzlies and continue their conservation as a "threatened species." But grizzlies were about to lose their protection with some states petitioning to delist them and restart the hunting of grizzlies.

David Bearbow Bearshield, of the Cheyenne Nation and Chairman of GOAL (Guardians of Our Ancestors Legacy), a coalition of fifty federally recognized tribal nations, explained the ancient and sacred bond between Indigenous peoples and the grizzly, a relative, protector, and guardian. Lean and clean-shaven with closely clipped black hair, and wearing a striking silver bear medicine necklace over his jean jacket,

Bearshield looked more like a movie star than wildlife crusader. Yet he was as articulate as he was fierce about the grizzly. Trophy hunting of bears, he said, is murder.

"Ninety percent of tourists to Yellowstone come to see a grizzly bear alive, not dead," he said. Because grizzlies are habituated to people in Yellowstone, they often come to food sources, trash, or the side of the road. "The bears expect a telephoto camera lens," Bearshield grimaced, "not a gun."

In an interview with *Hungry Horse News*, Bearshield explained that the bear in Indigenous ceremonies is often called "grandparent." He was hopeful that sovereign territories would be "linkage zones between two main grizzly populations." Bearshield and other tribal leaders, including Blackfoot and Iroquois Confederacy leaders, had just gathered in Glacier National Park for a grizzly bear summer ceremony and to protest delisting—removing grizzlies from federal protection. "Delisting ensures that the grizzly bear will never be a recovered species," Bearshield warned.

Over several meetings with Bearshield and GOAL tribal members in Yellowstone, I learned more about grizzlies than even my early years on national forests had taught me. "We call the grizzly The Ancient One," Bearshield said, then added with a frown, "scientists call her *Ursa arctos horribillis*." The pejorative is in the Latin name for the species, and it is detached from any intimacy or ancestral relationship. "Hopis have the longest association with the grizzly of anyone on the planet," Bearshield continued. "Hopi Bear clan is the parent clan of all. Grizzly bear is the physical embodiment of the spirit of the Earth. Grizzly bear medicine people are very powerful healers."

He went on to talk about wildlife conservation in the West. "Hunting and fishing licenses only pay for six percent of wildlife management," he said. A fact that the general public doesn't know because hunting and fishing licenses are often lauded to pay for conservation.

My years growing up in the Forest Service and writing about wildlife as an adult have taught me much about the divide between management and conservation. A majority of the public approves of restoring wildlife like wolves and bears, while "less than a third of Americans approve of hunting for a trophy," according to a study by the Association of Fish and Wildlife Agencies. State and local on-the-ground managers are often dominated by hunters and ranchers, rather than wildlife advocates. Many hunters, like my own father, are staunch conservationists.

In an interview with a reporter for a local Cody, Wyoming, newspaper, Bearshield noted: "In protecting the grizzly, we protect our ancestral lands, our cultures, and ourselves . . . the grizzly is considered an ancestor, a grandparent, teacher of healing and curing, integral to creation narratives, ceremonies, and practices. These narratives to traditional tribal people are the equivalent of scripture."

Bearshield and other GOAL leaders were also working with organizations like Wild Earth Guardians and Apex Protection Project to talk to locals and Yellowstone tourists about why bears must be restored to their birthright territories. "There cannot be delisting of grizzlies without conservation," Bearshield insists.

In any conversation about grizzlies, tribal peoples' spiritual bonds with wildlife are as important as management policies. "There are many different paths to the Creator," Bearshield concluded. "It doesn't matter which one you are on; it only matters that you are on one."

Here in the West, there are many researchers and conservationists who embrace the return of the grizzly bear. In 2023, the Fish and Wildlife Service conducted a status review of grizzlies, after Montana and Wyoming petitioned the ESA, asking that protections be denied and that all grizzlies in the Lower 48 be removed from federal protection under the ESA. These petitions on the part of trophy hunters and ranchers have been denied—so far. Seventeen Tribal Nations, Sierra Club, Earth Justice, and NRDC were among the lead plaintiffs in restoring ESA protection for grizzlies. The federal court declared that the petition to delist was based on "political pressure by the states rather than having been based on the best scientific and commercial data."

In British Columbia, other Indigenous nations are also deeply involved in grizzly bear, orca, and salmon conservation. The Great Bear Rainforest, a magnificent and pristine preserve of 6.4 million hectares (the size of Ireland) is a vital network of marine zones, ancient forests, and the Great Bear Sea—those waters surrounding the Great Bear Rain Forest extending along the North Coast of BC down to Alaska. "First Nations stewardship of these lands dates back more than fourteen thousand years," said Christine Smith-Martin of the Coastal First Nations. "We can take care of our territories."

Indigenous communities are holding the government accountable, not only for the damage from clear-cutting and marine degradation, but also to assure future genetic diversity and to adapt to climate change. The plan is to fulfill Canada's hope of protecting "30% of its land and oceans by 2030."

Dallas Smith, president of Nanwakolas Council and negotiator for the Great Bear Rainforest plan, says that Indigenous communities have been able to take back the narrative long dominated by outsider groups who haven't reflected "Indigenous knowledge and values." Smith concluded that the government is "going to have to dance with us, instead of making us dance for you."

In the Pacific Northwest, where grizzlies were trapped and hunted almost to extinction in the 1800s, the last official sighting of a grizzly bear this side of the US border was in 1996. There were plans begun to bring grizzly bears back to the North Cascades ecosystem, but the Trump administration stopped them. Now, Fish and Wildlife and the National Park Service are again investigating reintroducing grizzlies to the North Cascades. The bears will be designated as an "experimental population" on the "threatened" species list for protection. This reintroduction has bipartisan support, with a majority of Washington voters approving plans to restore grizzly bears in the North Cascades. Ninety-one percent polled on the Grizzly Bear Recovery Plan agreed that "grizzly bears are a vital part of America's wilderness and natural heritage."

This reintroduction would restore "a piece of the Pacific Northwest's natural and cultural heritage," says Don Striker, Superintendent of North Cascades National Park. "A first step toward bringing balance back to the ecosystem."

The proposal is to relocate grizzly bears, seven bears a year, from the Rocky Mountains and Canada to the North Cascades. Like wolf reintroduction in Yellowstone, which serves as a model worldwide for wildlife restoration, bringing back grizzly bears will enrich our wild heritage. But grizzlies, unlike wolves, are having trouble getting here on their own, so require reintroduction. "The thing about the Cascades is that it's the only potential landing spot for recovery or restoration outside the Rocky Mountains," explains Conservation Northwest's international programs director Joe Scott. "If we cannot accommodate them in this minuscule percentage of their former range, what does that say about us as a species?"

What do we restore in ourselves when we bring back wild animals like grizzly bears? A balance of top predators on our land, a mature relationship of respect with other creatures, a harmonious understanding that we need the wild, both in our ecosystems and in our imaginations.

Bears continue to roam our imaginations. Every year, I work at my desk with one screen focused on Explore.org's live Bear Cam at Alaska's Brooks Falls. The sight of mother brown bears teaching playful cubs to catch salmon as the scarlet fish leap up the waterfall, accompanied by a soundtrack of seagulls and rushing water, is a Zen-like accompaniment to computer-bound days. In 2022, a wildlife camera, this time in Boulder, Colorado, accidentally captured hundreds of "bear selfies" that quickly went viral. Though there are no known grizzlies in Colorado, the usually solitary and elusive black bear, one of 17,000–20,000 in the state, was caught "preening, posing, and cavorting for the camera like a diva, seemingly taking a cue from Madonna."

As much as bears teach us about rest and play, they also sometimes offer comic relief, whether it's the eternal Yogi Bear of cartoons, Winnie the Pooh, or the surprise smash hit *Cocaine Bear*, a ridiculous and hilarious film based on a true story. In it, a 500-pound black bear on an island in Georgia gobbles an illegal drug stash and runs roughshod over the clueless campers. My friends Tracey, John, Greg, and I emerged from our pandemic hibernation midwinter and delightedly streamed the antics of this CGI-enhanced, coked-up bear. Like an anti-superhero, the bear romped over people's tents and territories to reclaim the forest. It was like watching Smokey Bear go full-on demonic Joker. None of us could remember laughing so uproariously since before the pandemic.

The Great Bear still occupies a primal place in our human stories. A sort of genetic cue or reminder from our ancestors who knew the power of top-predator peers, bears are darkly comic and playful, cuddling our children yet capable of casually killing people with the swat of a huge paw, just like that long-ago grizzly who coveted my grandmother's rich apple butter—but decided to let us live.

SUPER POD

WHEN I LEARNED that my friend Jane Goodall had never encountered dolphins in the wild, I asked my cetacean naturalist "podmate," Doug Thompson, to set up a cruise for Jane. Doug has studied whales and dolphins since the 1970s. Today he also still leads whale-watching trips through his Summer Tree Institute in Southern California.

"Your job, Brenda, is to call in the dolphins," Doug informed me with a grin, the night before we would set sail with Jane. "You'll really have to meditate, since they don't always come to our boats."

That night before our cruise, I was anxious about my meditative task. Dolphins in the wild approach us *only* when they wish an encounter. They are just as likely to briefly explore a boat or swimmer, and instantly vanish. Was it presumptuous of me to call in these sentient beings to whom I had long apprenticed myself? After all, dolphins are busy with their own lives, their complex family relationships, their sophisticated communications, their daily dramas.

But my decades of studying and encountering wild dolphins has also convinced me that dolphins, with their big, complex brains, might best be met in meditation. Some scientists theorize that dolphins spend much of their time in the slower, more reflective brain wave called "alpha," or "delta," which we humans experience as the deepest, restorative meditation or dreaming.

Author Diane Ackerman shares my fascination with cetaceans. In *Deep Play*, she writes about how dolphins "bridge worlds" in a "dolphin dreamtime." She explains, "Dolphins are often portrayed as seers and savants who can peer into our hidden depths, those dark emotional oceans inside our psyches." Why couldn't this contemplative cetacean awareness tune into our human dreams, what Carl Jung calls "the collective unconscious."

That night before our dolphin cruise with Jane, I wondered if the dolphins might grace me in a dream, as they so often do. I prepared for sleep with my regular nightly Taoist meditation, and before dawn I had a familiar lucid dream: I am underwater, buoyant, breathing as I once did in the salty womb and again when I almost drowned in a Pacific Ocean undertow as a toddler. Spinning around, I hear the far-off chatter of dolphins—watery crackle and popping patter—then the creaking as dolphins venture near me. Ultrasonic whistles and trills signal their arrival before I can see them. As in waking life, the pleasurable pings of sonar from these dream dolphins echoes, zings, and vibrates along my skin, probing inside my belly and brain like an audible aurora borealis. There are shimmers of violet-blue, pale strings of lavender and rose, some otherworldly colors I'd never seen before.

Dolphins may live in a world of synesthesia—all senses blurred so that they see sound, hear colors, taste textures. With their highly developed and sophisticated brains, dolphins may intertwine their senses to experience their underwater world multidimensionally. In my dream dimension, I could almost gain access to their perceptions. There were audible maps, geometric grids, that ricocheted and zoomed around me in zigzags of sound pictures. It was like listening to a topographic map come alive, like watching Google Maps pulse with visual music.

Deep underwater now in the dream, I opened my eyes wide, breathed in the fluid flow of the sea and suddenly there they were: Hundreds of dolphins swimming straight toward me. A multitude of sleek, silver aerodynamic bodies streaming at warp speed—a *rush hour of dolphins*. I was in their way, too slow to move and save myself. *Well, if I had to die, this was certainly a unique way to go.*

I braced myself, difficult to do underwater, anticipating that the darting dolphins would run right into me, much as they use their strong beaks to ram sharks. Closing my eyes, I awaited the collision of cetaceans and stretched out my arms in surrender.

Suddenly, I felt a loud whooshing inside my ribcage. Each dolphin who passed through my heart left an audible imprint. It was as if I'd laid my body against a high-frequency speaker, thrumming with sound. I was just a doorway for these hundreds of dolphins, passing easily through my body without doing me harm. My wide-open heart chakra was portal to a parallel world.

Maybe I was dying—the dolphins were accompanying me to the next world, as they have been thought to do since antiquity. Or, maybe I was really living the full spectrum of what dolphins must experience in a fluid environment that creates as many inner worlds as outer. When I awoke, my body still vibrated with sound and my heartbeat was much slower than ever before.

That dream affected me profoundly. I was still in an altered state when we clambered aboard the research boat the next morning to take Jane and her friends out to sea, but I no longer felt any anxiety about "calling" the dolphins. They had called me. Nor did it surprise me when, after hours of sailing and encountering not one, but eleven blue whales, the largest animal on earth, we found ourselves in the middle of what seemed like an infinity of zooming dolphins.

"*It's a super pod!*" our naturalist, Doug, shouted above our delighted screams. "Must be two thousand bottlenose dolphins."

The dolphins were surfing our bow wake and zipping alongside us. Mothers, calves, aunties, maybe a bachelor pod of scouts accompanying the matriarchal multitudes—their fast, aerodynamic bodies jetting by so close to each other and to us. It was a sleek ballet of silver fins, slivering through waves, the *twhoosh, twhoosh* of their breaths as they inhaled then dived in perfect synch, only to surface a moment later still in close formation, flying together in midair. The whistles and bleeps of a super pod, a concerto of click trains and ultrasonic trills.

Our naturalist explained, "Dolphins are one of the only animals on the planet to see three-dimensionally. Much of their big brains are used to echolocate and listen to what they see underwater. Hear those whistles? The first thing a dolphin will say is his signature whistle—his name."

I leaned way out over the bow. Speeding dolphins splashed me, their tail flukes flickering like rudders to navigate so near, but never colliding. No wonder they had so effortlessly flowed through my chest in a dream the night before. I was simply an energy field, an open human mind. It was during this super pod encounter when I first came to believe that dolphins not only see and hear in three-dimensions, they also slip *between* dimensions. Their long evolution of consciousness has allowed them to crossover between other worlds. It's what our physics can still only theorize about, not mathematically prove—parallel universes.

Never or since, except in my dreams, have I ever encountered so many dolphins. Had I presciently seen and felt them the night before, as I once had acoustically dreamed and visualized the dolphins at OrcaLab?

This super pod dolphin encounter, which our group recorded and posted on YouTube, has changed the way I encounter dolphins. I'd long since made the decision not to swim with dolphins, even in elective captivity, and I encounter them now only in their wild habitat—and in my meditations. But now I was fascinated by the seemingly extrasensory survival skills cetaceans might teach us.

Researcher John Carlyle, who has studied dolphins for twenty years, once told me of his favorite experiments with dolphin echolocation. Trying to discern the limits of dolphin sonar, Carlyle placed blinder eyecups on dolphins and then asked them to recognize certain symbols only by echolocation. In an experiment that had taken him months to design, the dolphins learned the symbols in five minutes.

Pat Weyer, a glass artist, educator, and researcher, has spent years as a scientific illustrator, researching spotted dolphins in the Bahamas with Wild Dolphin Project. Weyer theorizes that dolphins acoustically create geometric, visual maps, much like our human experience of virtual reality. She wonders if sound waves might carry pictures for these sentient and sophisticated cetaceans—sound maps created through a pictural and acoustic language to better navigate their underwater worlds. Imagine what an ultrasonic sound map would look like in three dimensions, with color and movement? These kinds of revelations informed much of the true cetacean science in my sci-fi novel, *The Drowning World*. The rest I simply imagined.

As I continue to encounter cetaceans and speak with researchers, their sense of excitement over dolphins' skills has only increased. Denise Herzing is executive director of the Wild Dolphin Project. Her own thirty years of research rivals that of Jane Goodall's. "By observing dolphins in their natural habitat, we learn much about conflict and cooperation, respect and learning, and civility toward each other," Herzing says. "Values that are greatly needed in the world today."

Like many who have spent much of their waking life studying cetaceans, my dreams are often populated with dolphins and whales. Researchers and cetacean scientists tell me, off the record, that their work with dolphins continues, especially when they sleep.

"All day I record their vocalizations," once scientist tells me. "And at night there's what I call a 'dolphin download' that always adds insight to my research. I can't publish these findings because they are labeled metaphysical, not scientific. But sometimes I wonder if cetaceans, with those big brains and such a fluid environment, ancestral hands now evolved into flippers, haven't developed their own kind of telepathy. Sometimes we humans are humble and attentive enough to tap into something besides, and perhaps beyond, our own consciousness."

I cherish my lifelong cetacean bond, this apprenticeship to another animal who has so inspired and taught me how to live in this water world. On a recent research trip to Hawaii's Big Island, I was kayaking in a warm-water bay. Suddenly, I was surrounded by a wild pod of sleek spinner dolphins, including mother-calf duos accompanied by babysitting aunts and sisters.

"We're in the middle of their nursery pod," our naturalist guide whispered as we paddled slowly through calm waters.

Six dorsal fins swam close behind me, their *twoosh, twoosh* exhalations like musical, rubato sighs. Thirty or so spinners swam close, circling me. At the sight of so many wild dolphins, I leaned over in awe—and promptly capsized. Plunged underwater, I heard that familiar high-pitched click and whirr that sounds like a cross between a Geiger counter and rusty door. I floated, holding my breath like a free diver as the nursery pod encircled me.

The dolphins surprised me with their tenderness. With my head now above water, I tried to synchronize my breathing with them, and several spinners leaped up, somersaulting, and then dove back into the sea, their wake splashing over me. Back underwater, I attempted my human version of a dolphin signature whistle, complete with rapid-fire gurgles and bleeps. It seemed to amuse and interest the nursery pod because they all suddenly cruised closer in a dazzling display of acrobatic dolphin dance.

Imagine dozens of dolphins speeding by in a blur of silver and gray skin, ultrasound, and curved fin, streaking past, in one breath, as if one body. Their speed and sound registered like a trillion ricochets, tiny vibrations echoing off my ribs, within each lobe of my lungs, and spinning inside my labyrinthine brain like new synapses.

Then I was alone for a moment as I drifted through the depths. Dolphins seem to cherish these meditative underwater moments with their human companions the most. Suddenly I saw out of the corner of each eye, three dolphins flanking me and then several tiny dorsal fins—newborns guarded by the nursery pod. They had accepted me into their pod. I was surrounded by fast spinners who slowed to accompany my pace, and they kept me in their exact center for what seemed an hour. It was only then I understood what it feels like to be fully adopted into the deep, welcoming alliance of dolphins.

I am pod, I felt, with no sense of my individual self. *I belong*.

I am often visited by these otherworldly dreams of dolphins—super pods sharing their water worlds and wisdom with me. Not only am I an apprentice to this cetacean species and other remarkable animals, but I am also somehow imprinted. Perhaps that is what happens to those of us who devote much of our lives to another animal. There is a bleed-through of ways we understand, experience, and intuit the natural world. After all, we share this blue planet. Why not learn from each other how to survive and change, to cherish our habitat, our only home?

Acknowledgments

JUST AS THERE are so many animals to thank in *Wild Chorus*, there are also animal people who have lent their voices and visions to this book. My parents, Max and Jan Peterson, gave me the invaluable gift of a Forest Service childhood with more animals than humans; my sister, Paula, and brother, Dana Mark, always inspire me with their stories. I am very grateful to my own pod of friends and animal allies, including Tracey Conway, Vanessa Adams, Mindy Exum, Dan Miller, Greg Garrison, John Keister, Mary McKinley, Maureen Michelson, Robin Lindsey, Doug Thompson, Haleh Nekoorad and Jon Long, Linda Hogan, Joy Harjo, Jane Hirshfield, Sy Montgomery, Leslie Meredith, Christy Ottaviano, and Mary Bisbee-Beek.

I'm grateful that animal advocate organizations, many of which are profiled in this book, are conserving wildlife: Seal Sitters, OrcaNetwork, OrcaLab, Marine Mammal Institute, Wolf Haven, Wild Sanctuary, Belugapalooza, OrcaSOS, Living with Wolves, Wild Dolphin Project, Raincoast Research, BirdLife International, Jane Goodall Institute, The Cougar Fund, NRDC, Center for Whale Research, SummerTree Institue, and Conservation Northwest. If you want to help, contribute to and/or volunteer with your favorites.

My longtime literary agent, Elizabeth Wales, and editorial assistant, Adrienne, were the first to help me envision *Wild Chorus*. I've found happiness and harmony with Mountaineers Books editor in chief, Kate Rogers, who always lets me know what animal stories work best. Editor Laura Shauger is an abiding editorial ally, copyeditor Erin Moore polished my prose, creative director Jen Grable and designer Melissa McFeeters generously worked to make this book intimate in the hands and lovely for the eyes. Glorious animal art by Levi Hastings graces the cover and pages. My kids' books agent, Anne DePue, offers editorial wisdom and guidance. My coauthors and master illustrators Wendell Minor and Ed Young bring my animal stories to vivid life. Alaska poet Peggy Shumaker graciously lent me her "Caribou" poem. Thanks to my blood brother, Krystian Jeszka, brilliant Dr. Raya Mawad, and Taoist healer, James Dowling. My creative consultant, Anne DeVore offers intuitive inspiration. My late editor, Merloyd Lawrence, still sits on my shoulders—like wings.

My writing students always hearten and delight with animal stories of their own. And I feel gratitude every day for my feline companions, Tako and Rita, the endlessly entertaining "wrestle-mania" Siamese cats, and Ella Bella, the husky who likes me just a little more after daily walks and endless bribes.

References

Epigraph

Frank, Adam. "Scientists Found Ripples in Space and Time. And You Have to Buy Groceries." *Atlantic*, June 29, 2023. www.theatlantic.com/science/archive/2023/06/universe-gravitational-waves-nanograv-discovery/674570.

CONNECTION: Listening to Animals

Adams, Tim. "The Big Picture: Bonds of Friendship across Species Boundaries." *The Guardian*, February 26, 2023. www.theguardian.com.

da Vinci, Leonardo. *Paris Manuscript F*, fol. 96V.

Berger, John. "Why Look at Animals?" In *About Looking*. New York City: Pantheon Books, 1980.

Kolbert, Elizabeth. "Can We Talk to Whales?" *New Yorker*. September 4, 2023.

Krause, Bernie. *The Great Animal Orchestra: Finding the Origins of Music in the World's Wild Places*. New York: Little, Brown, 2012.

Mustill, Tom. *How to Speak Whale: A Voyage into the Future of Animal Communication*. New York: Grand Central Publishing, 2022.

Popova, Maria. "Why Look at Animals: John Berger on What Our Relationship with Our Fellow Beings Reveals about Us." *The Marginalian*, April 1, 2014. www.themarginalian.org.

Shah, Sonia. "The Animals Are Talking. What Does It Mean?" *New York Times Magazine*, September 20, 2023. www.nytimes.com/2023/09/20/magazine/animal-communication.html.

Fire and Flood, Forest to Sea

Burns, Jes. "Tsunami Debris Continues Delivering Invasive Species to the West Coast." Oregon Public Broadcasting, September 29, 2017. www.opb.org.

City of Cannon Beach. "Sneaker Waves, City of Cannon Beach, by Marcella-Ogalata-Day." August 27, 2020. www.youtube.com/watch?v=NAG3tZQaF9M.

"Civilization Lost . . . and Found." *Washington Post*, June 24, 1979. www.washingtonpost.com.

Gua Gua La (Barbara Smith). *Renewal: The Prophecy of Manu*. Penticton, BC: Theylus Press, 1986.

Keller, S. J. "Yellowstone Flooding: Why Is It Happening Now?" *National Geographic*, June 16, 2022. www.nationalgeographic.com.

Pacific Coastal and Marine Science Center. "Native American Legends of Tsunamis in the Pacific Northwest." Presented by Jim Bergeron. Oregon Sea Grant, USGS, 1995. www.usgs.gov.

Peterson, Brenda, and Linda Hogan. *Sightings: The Gray Whale's Mysterious Journey*, Washington, DC: National Geographic Books, 1997.

Salahlieh, Nouran. "Storm Lashes Alaskan Shore, Bringing Severe Coastal Flooding and Prompting Evacuations." CNN, September 18, 2022. www.cnn.com.

Tzu, Lao. *Tao Te Ching*. Translated by Ursula K. Le Guin. Boulder, CO: Shambala, 1997.

"Understanding Tsunami Hazards in the State of Washington: How Vulnerable Is the Makah Reservation to Tsunamis?" 2012/2013. Washington Emergency Management Division, Washington Military Department. https://mil.wa.gov/asset/5ba420a6b230c.

Zhong, Raymond. "The Coming California Megastorm." *New York Times*, August 12, 2022. www.newyorktimes.com.

Girls in Woods, Women on Waves

Centers for Disease Control and Prevention. "Youth Risk Behavior Survey: Data Summary and Trends Report, 2011–2021." National Center for HIV, Viral Hepatitis, STD, and TB Prevention. www.cdc.gov/healthyyouth/data/yrbs/pdf/YRBS_Data-Summary-Trends_Report2023_508.pdf.

Egan, Tim. "Everyone Is Always on Nature's Side; People Just Can't Agree on What's Natural and What's Not." *New York Times*, December 19, 1998. www.newyorktimes.com.

Kodiak National Wildlife Refuge. "The Kodiak Gray Whale Project." YouTube, November 29, 2011. www.youtube.com/watch?v=hF7zb2OmA-s.

Morena, Sabrina. "Teen Girls Bear Worst of Mental Health Crisis." *Axios*, February 14, 2023. www.axios.com.

Peterson, Brenda. "Friendly Gray Whales Baja, Mexico, San Ignacio Lagoon." YouTube, July 22, 2015. www.youtube.com/watch?v=BJ-26K6p9eI.

Sassi, Janet. "10 Trees Not to Miss in Manhattan's Inwood Hill Park." Untapped New York, October 27, 2021. https://untappedcities.com.

Wolfe, Daniel. "Gray Whales Are Dying along the Pacific Coast: The Warming Arctic May Be to Blame." CNN, March 16, 2022. www.cnn.com.

Beluga Baby

ABC News. "Beluga Whale Sounds Like a Human." Current Biology. www.youtube.com/watch?v=HDDgJPKuSf0.

Defenders of Wildlife. "Defending Cook Inlet Belugas: Bringing Our Beloved Sea Canaries Back from the Brink of Extinction." December 8, 2021, https://storymaps.arcgis.com/stories/9760c6e5b99f46e1ab95f63b88e418ff.

Frohoff, Toni. "Shedd Aquarium Shamed as #10 Worst." In Defense of Animals, July 22, 2016. www.idausa.org.

McIntyre, Joanna. *Mind in the Waters: A Book to Celebrate the Consciousness of Whales and Dolphins*. New York: Charles Scribner's Sons, 1975.

NOAA Fisheries. "Species in the Spotlight: Cook Inlet Beluga Whale." February 14, 2018. https://videos.fisheries.noaa.gov/detail/videos/alaska.

——. "New Abundance Estimate for Endangered Cook Inlet Beluga Whales," June 15, 2023. www.fisheries.noaa.gov.

Nollman, Jim. *The Beluga Café: My Strange Adventures with Art, Music, and Whales in the Far North*. San Francisco: Sierra Club Books, 2002.

——. 2021. "Beluga Tells a Joke." From *Music for Swimming and Flying*, Other Minds Records. www.youtube.com/watch?v=ZvX0Cm_U_n0.

Peterson, Brenda. "Beluga Baby: An Afterlife with Animals." In *Edge Walking on the Western Rim: Twelve Northwest Writers*. Edited by Mayumi Tsutakawa. Seattle: Sasquatch Books, 1994.

Scripps Institution of Oceanography. "Beluga Whale, White Whale: Beluga Whale Sounds (*Delphinapterus leucas*)." Discovery of Sound in the Sea. https://dosits.org/galleries/audio-gallery/marine-mammals/toothed-whales/beluga-whale-white-whale.

Shedd Aquarium. "Meet the Belugas." November 2, 2019, www.sheddaquarium.org/stories/meet-the-belugas.

——. "Shedd Aquarium Welcomes Healthy Beluga Whale Calf." July 4, 2018. www.sheddaquarium.org.

Sutphen, John. "Body State Communication Among Cetaceans." From *Mind in the Waters* by Joan McIntyre. New York: Charles Scribner, 1974.

"Webinar: Cook Inlet Belugapalooza: Research for Recovery," March 18, 2021. www.youtube.com/watch?v=zTh5zaM6s9M.

Listening to the Sea Breathing

Explore. "OrcaLab Main Cams." www.explore.org/livecams.

OrcaLab. Northern Resident orcas—British Columbia. https://orcalab.org.

Winter, Lisa. "Grandmother Orcas Help Young Whales Survive and Thrive: Study." *Scientist*, December 11, 2019. www.the-scientist.com.

Wolf Music

Bekoff, Marc, and Jessica Pierce. "The Ethical Dog." *Scientific American*, March 1, 2010. www.scientificamerican.com.

Berendt, Joachim-Ernst. *The World Is Sound: Nada Brahma: Music and the Landscape of Consciousness*. Rochester, VT: Destiny Books, 1991.

Fort, Tom. "Wild Justice by Marc Bekoff and Jessica Pierce." Book review. *The Telegraph*, May 24, 2009. www.telegraph.co.uk.

Griffiths, Sarah. "Wolves Have Accents Too! Canines Can Be Identified Using 21 Different Types of Howling 'Dialects" *Daily Mail*, February 8, 2016, www.dailymail.co.uk.

Grimaud, Hélène. *Wild Harmonies: A Life of Music and Wolves*. Translated by Ellen Hinsey. New York: Riverhead Books, 2006.

———. "Wolf Moonlight Sonata." www.youtube.com/watch?v=fwf1Db8hbJQ.

Harrington, Fred H. "What's in a Howl?" Wild Wolves. PBS NOVA. www.pbs.org/wgbh /nova.

Holleman, Marybeth, and Gordon Haber. *Among Wolves: Gordon Haber's Insights into Alaska's Most Misunderstood Animal*. Fairbanks: University of Alaska Press, 2013.

Meeker, Joseph W. *The Comedy of Survival: Literary Ecology and a Play Ethic*. 3rd ed. Tucson: University of Arizona Press, 1997.

Moss, Doug, and Roddy Scheer. "Do Animals Like Music?" Earthtalk, July 31, 2018. https://earthtalk.org.

Neoclassic TV. Rachmaninoff Concerto #2, Hélène Grimaud pianist. www.youtube.com/watch?v=Uyz0kuw4dv8.

Peterson, Brenda. "The Sacredness of Chores." In *Nature and Other Mothers: Personal Stories of Women and the Body of Earth*. New York: HarperCollins, 1995.

———. Interview with Hélène Grimaud, 2016, from recordings and notes.

Peterson, Brenda, and Sarah Jane Freymann. *Your Life Is a Book: How to Craft and Publish Your Memoir*. Seattle: Sasquatch Books, 2014. See also an excerpt in *Utne Reader*. www.utne.com.

Rodgers, Christy. "At Play in the Comedy of Survival." *CounterPunch*, April 10, 2015. www.counterpunch.org.

Root-Gutteridge, Holly. "The Songs of the Wolves." Aeon Media, May 26, 2016. https://aeon.co.

Sound Tracks Quick Hits. "Hélène Grimaud interviewed by Alexis Bloom." www.youtube.com/watch?v=N_dw9-Bt_sM.

Swearingen, Marshall. "MSU Researcher Helps Untangle the Language of Wolf Howls." *Montana State University News*, Montana State University, March 10, 2016.

Whitehead, Hal, and Luke Rendell. "Culture in the Ocean?" Introduction in *The Cultural Lives of Whales and Dolphins*. Chicago: University of Chicago Press, 2014.

"Why Wolves Howl?" www.britannica.com.

"Why Wolves Howl," National Park Service. www.nps.gov.

Wolf Conservation Center. Alawa and Zephyr. http://nywolf.org/ambassador-wolves /alawa.

Singing with Animals

CBC News. "Orca That Carried Dead Calf for 2 Weeks Gives Birth Again." www.youtube.com/watch?v=2H9FrgagdXg.

Gaskill, Melissa. "Scientists Race to Figure Out Why Grey Whale Deaths Are Spiking." *Scuba Diving*, June 13, 2022. www.scubadiving.com.

Gregg, Justin. "What Does Animal Grief Tell Us about How They Understand Death?" In *If Nietzsche Were a Narwhal*. New York: Little, Brown, 2022. Reprinted in *Lit Hub*, August 10, 2022. lithub.com.

Gumbs, Alexis Pauline. *Undrowned: Black Feminist Lessons from Marine Mammals*. Chico, CA: AK Press, 2020.

Howard Hughes Medical Institute. "Warbling Whales Speak a Language All Their Own." ScienceDaily, March 24, 2006. www.sciencedaily.com.

Marine Mammal Center, Sausalito, CA. www.marinemammalcenter.org /featured-news.

Morell, Virginia. "Humpback Whale Songs Undergo a 'Cultural Revolution' Every Few Years." *Science*. November 20, 2018. https://www.science.org/content/article /humpback-whale-songs-undergo-cultural-revolution-every-few-years.

Pappas, Stephanie. "Mama Dolphins Sing Their Name to Babies in the Womb." *Live Science*, August 9, 2016. www.livescience.com.[new entry]

Suzuki, Ryuji, et al. "Information Entropy of Humpback Whale Songs." *Journal of the Acoustical Society of America* 119 (2006): 1849{en}1866.

Suzuki, Ryuji, et al. "Information Entropy of Humpback Whale Songs." *Journal of the Acoustical Society of America* 119 (2006): 1849–1866.

Birdsong Blues

Aleixandre, Vicente. "The Old Man and the Sun." In *A Longing for the Light: Selected Poems of Vicente Aleixandre*. Edited by Lewis Hyde. Port Townsend, WA: Copper Canyon Press, 1979.

Audubon. "Audubon's Priority Birds 2021." www.audubon.org.

Berendt, Joachim-Ernst. *The World Is Sound: Nada Brahma: Music and the Landscape of Consciousness*. Rochester, VT: Destiny Books, 1991.

#BringBirdsBack. "3 Billion Birds Gone." www.3billionbirds.org.

Bronwyn Edwards Musical Catalyst. "'3 Billion Birds' Performed by the Fauntleroy Virtual Choir." www.youtube.com/watch?v=Qtl_sE4odlk.

GrrlScientist. "Listening to Birdsongs Can Calm Your Frayed Nerves." *Forbes*, October 19, 2022. www.forbes.com.

Hall, Sophia Alexandra. "1,000 Musicians Just Played the Sound of Our Future at COP26—And It Doesn't Sound Good." Classic FM, November 8, 2021. www.classicfm.com.

Haskell, David G. "The Voices of Birds and the Language of Belonging." *Emergence Magazine*, May 26, 2019. https://emergencemagazine.org.

Hempton, Gordon. "Earth Is a Solar Powered Jukebox." The Sound Tracker. www.soundtracker.com.

—— and John Grossmann. *One Square Inch of Silence: One Man's Quest to Preserve Quiet*. New York: Free Press, 2009.

Krause, Bernie. *Wild Soundscapes: Discovering the Voice of the Natural World*. New Haven: Yale University Press, 2016.

Kuczynski, Alex. "Can You Hear Me Now?" *New York Times*, April 7, 2010. www.nytimes.com.

Levertov, Denise. "Settling," poem from the collection *Evening Train*. New York: New Directions, 1992.

Marsh, Robert. "Final Journal: Natural History of the Schmitz Park to Alki Trail." June 5, 2012. www.inaturalist.org.

Mock, Jillian. "North America Has Lost More Than 1 in 4 Birds in Last 50 Years, New Study Says." *Audubon News*, September 19, 2019.

Olympic Peninsula. "Hoh Rain Forest—One Square Inch of Silence." https://olympicpeninsula.org.

Pannes, Volker. "Bird Song Opera." ShakeUp Music & Sound Design. https://vimeo.com/243312820.

Peterson, Brenda. "Bread on the Waters." *Sierra*, January/February 1992.

Tippett, Krista. "Gordon Hempton: Silence and the Presence of Everything." *On Being*, May 10, 2012 (updated December 30, 2021). https://onbeing.org.

United Nations: Act Now. "The [Uncertain] Four Seasons." https://the-uncertain-four-seasons.info/experience. To listen to recordings, visit the @theuncertain-fourseasons YouTube channel.

Wild Sanctuary, founded by Bernie Krause. www.wildsanctuary.com.

Yong, Ed. "How Animals Perceive the World." *Atlantic*, July/August, 2022. www.theatlantic.com.

Alliance: Learning from Animals

Yong, Ed. "How Animals Perceive the World." *Atlantic*, July/August, 2022. www.theatlantic.com.

Feral Children and the Big, Good Wolf

Chapman, Marina. *The Girl with No Name: The Incredible Story of a Child Raised by Monkeys*. New York: Perseus Books, 2013.

Cockroft, Lucy. "Russian 'Bird-Boy' Discovered in Aviary." *The Telegraph*. February 28, 2008. www.telegraph.co.uk/news/worldnews/1580159/Russian-bird-boy-discovered-in-aviary.html.

du Plessis, Susan. "Feral Children: The Story of Amala and Kamala." Edublox. October 14, 2022. www.edubloxtutor.com/amala-kamala.

Eiseley, Loren. *Collected Essays on Evolution, Nature, and the Cosmos*. Edited by William Cronon. New York: Library of America, 2016.

Gaertner, David. "The Red River Is Mother and Healer in Katherena Vermette's New Book of Poetry." May 29, 2019. https://rabble.ca.

Grandin, Temple. *Thinking in Pictures: And Other Reports from My Life with Autism*. New York: Vintage, 1992.

History Extra. "Raised by Wolves: The History of Feral Children." *History Extra*, BBC History magazine, June 22, 2022. www.historyextra.com.

Newton, Michael. *Savage Girls and Wild Boys: A History of Feral Children*. New York: Picador, 2002.

Oregon Wild. "Don't Stop Believing: The Journey of OR-7." *Oregon Wild*. www.oregonwild.org.

Peterson, Brenda. "The Big, Good Wolf: Real Lives of Alpha Males." *Huffington Post*, June 10, 2015,www.huffpost.com.

———. "Wolves in Our Back Yard." *Seattle Times*, May 15, 1997. https://archive .seattletimes.com.

Safina, Carl. "Tapping Your Inner Wolf." *New York Times*, June 5, 2015. www.nytimes.com.

Sparks, Kova Kay. "Wild Child, the Story of Feral Children." *The Learning Channel*. www.youtube.com/watch?v=1vjZq6TS668.

Vermette, Katherena, and Julie Flett. *The Girl and the Wolf*. Penticton, BC, Canada: Theytus Books, 2019.

Weiss, Amaroq. "Remembering OR-7, the Wolf Who Journeyed Back to California." Center for Biological Diversity, *Medium*, December 23, 2021. https://medium.com.

Weston, Jonah. *Wild Child: The Story of Feral Children*. Texas: Optomen Television, 2002.

Leopard and Silkie: A Friendship

EarthFix. "Seal Sitters: Share the Shore." January 9, 2013. https://vimeo.com /57053070.

Halverson, Matthew. "Robin Lindsey Loves Seals." *Seattle Met*, August 1, 2013. www.seattlemet.com.

Living on Earth. "Seal Sitters." Interview of Brenda Peterson by Bruce Gellerman, April 20, 2012. www.loe.org/shows/segments.html?programID=12 -P13-00016&segmentID=6.

Peterson, Brenda. "Seal Sitting by the Salish Sea." *Seattle P-I*, August 21, 2007. www.seattlepi.com.

Peterson, Brenda, and Robin Lindsey. *Leopard and Silkie: One Boy's Quest to Save Seal Pups*. New York: Macmillan/Christy Ottaviano Books, 2012.

———. "Seal Sitting: On Beach Patrol in Seattle." *Wildlife Conservation*, Sept./Oct. 2008, www.sealsitters.org.

Robin Lindsey, photographer. https://robinlindsey.photoshelter.com/index /G0000qGhEcFwrbks.

Seal Sitters. www.sealsitters.org.

Granny: The Grandmother Effect

Bittel, Jason. "Grandmother Orcas Help Their Grand-whales Survive." December 9, 2019, *Washington Post*. www.washingtonpost.com.

Breda, Isabella. "Southern Resident Orcas Are Visiting Us Less Often, Study Shows." *Seattle Times*, March 31, 2023. www.seattletimes.com.

Center for Whale Research. "Celebrating World Orca Day: July 14: Encounter #39." July 11, 2022. www.youtube.com/watch?v=GVfyWJI4NXU.

Cooke, Lucy. *Bitch: On the Female of the Species*. New York: Basic Books (Hachette), 2022.

Cougar Fund. "About the Cougar: Family Life." No date. www.cougarfund.org.

Croft, Jay. "Lolita the Killer Whale Set for Release into 'Home Waters' After 50 Years at Miami Seaquarium." *CNNWire*, March 31, 2023. https://abc7chicago.com.

Engelhaupt, Erika. "Lucy Cooke's New Book, 'Bitch,' Busts Myths about Female Animals" *Science News*, June 14, 2022. www.sciencenews.org.

Getten, Mary J. *Communicating with Orcas: The Whales' Perspective*. Newburyport, MA: Hampton Roads Publishing, 2006.

Gill, Victoria. "What Can Killer Whales Teach Us about the Menopause?" *BBC News*, San Juan Island, August 11, 2016. www.bbc.com.

———. "Orca Mothers Make 'Lifelong Sacrifice' for Sons." *BBC News*, February 9, 2023. www.bbc.com.

Glausiusz, Josie. "Bitch by Lucy Cooke Review—A Joyous Debunking of Gender Stereotypes in Nature." *Guardian*, March 11, 2022. www.theguardian.com.

Heimlich-Boran, Sara and James. *Killer Whales*. World Life Library edition. Beverly, MA: Voyageur Press, 1994.

Hogan, Linda, Deena Metzger, and Brenda Peterson, eds. "Life Among the Whales." In *Intimate Nature: The Bond Between Women and Animals*. New York: Ballantine, 1998.

KING 5 staff. "It's a Girl! Southern Resident J Pod Orca Calf Born Earlier This Year Is Female." KING 5, May 27, 2022. www.king5.com.

Langlois, Krista. "When Whales and Humans Talk." *Hakai*, April 3, 2018. https://hakaimagazine.com.

Morgan, Chris, and Lucy Soucek. "Eavesdropping on Orcas: Love, Grief, and Family." *The Wild*, KUOW, March 14, 2023. www.kuow.org.

Morton, Alexandra. *Not on My Watch: How a Renegade Whale Biologist Took on Governments and Industry to Save Wild Salmon*. Toronto: Penguin Random House Canada (Vintage Canada), 2021.

NOAA Office of Response and Restoration. "More than Two Decades Later, Have Killer Whales Recovered from the Exxon Valdez Oil Spill?" March 23, 2012 (updated November 2020). https://response.restoration.noaa.gov.

Peterson, Brenda. *Sister Stories: Taking the Journey Together*. New York: Viking/Penguin, 1996.

———. "Other Teachers than Terror: Sisterhoods among Animals." *About Place Journal* 5, no. 3 (May 2019). https://aboutplacejournal.org.

———. "Wild Dolphins Encounter with Jane Goodall, Brenda Peterson, Pierce Brosnan." www.youtube.com/watch?v=fnXqOF0uamk.

———. *Wild Orca: The Oldest, Wisest Whale in the World*. New York: Henry Holt and Company, 2018.

Robertson, Linda, "Before She Died, Lolita's Former Vets and Trainers Raised Issues about Her Seaquarium Care," *Miami Herald*, August 25, 2023, www.miamiherald.com/news/local/community/miami-dade/article278408624.html

Saulitis, Eva. *Into Great Silence: A Memoir of Discovery and Loss among Vanishing Orcas*. Boston: Beacon Press, 2013.

Shields, Monika Wieland. "K40 Raggedy." Orca Salmon Alliance, June 16, 2021. www.orcamonth.com.

Welsh, Craig. "World's Oldest Known Orca Presumed Dead." *National Geographic*, January 3, 2017. www.nationalgeographic.com.

Wolf Eyes

Ancient Geographic. "26,000-Year-Old Ancestors of Native Americans Hunted in the Arctic." www.youtube.com/watch?v=VtSKT2kt9Ik.

Breski, Mati, and Daniel Dor. "Are Humans More Like Wolves or Dogs?" *Frontiers for Young Minds*, November 2021. doi:10.3389/frym.2021.751566.

Cooper, Anderson. "Studying the Genetics and Evolution of Dogs' Friendliness." *60 Minutes*, CBS News, November 27, 2022. www.cbsnews.com.

Derr, Mark. *How the Dog Became the Dog: From Wolves to Our Best Friends*. New York: Overlook Press, 2011.

Lamplugh, Rick. "A Brief History of Wolves and Humans, Part 1." September 11, 2021. http://ricklamplugh.blogspot.com.

Newsome, Thomas. "The Coevolution of Wolves and Humans." *Bioscience*, March 1, 2018. doi.org/10.1093/biosci/biy017.

Nield, David. "Wolves Really Can Become Attached to Humans Like Dogs Can." *ScienceAlert*, September 25, 2022. www.sciencealert.com.

Peterson, Brenda. "El Lobo Returns Home." *TMN: The Morning News*, April 25, 2017. https://themorningnews.org.

Shipman, Pat. *The Invaders: How Humans and Their Dogs Drove Neanderthals to Extinction*. Cambridge: Harvard University Press (Belknap Press), 2015.

The Elusive Beauty of Big Cats

American Museum of Natural History. "Ultra-Sensitive Whiskers Let Mountain Lions 'See' in the Dark." November 15, 2017. www.amnh.org.

Foreman, Laura Bowers. "The Secret Family Life of Cougars." *Wildlife Conservation Magazine*, April 2009.

Gray, Morgan. "Why Wildlife Corridors? Wildlife Corridors Keep Our Landscape Healthy." Pepperwood Field Notes, February 12, 2019. www.pepperwoodpreserve.org.

Panthera. "Nature's Brokers: Scientists Show Pumas Maintain Relationships with Nearly 500 Living Species, Holding America's Ecosystems Together." January 18, 2022. https://panthera.org.

Peterson, Brenda. Unpublished interviews with Laura Foreman and Dana Kennedy Silberstein, March 2023, from notes and emails.

Stiffler, Lisa. "Native American Tribes, Wild Cat Conservation Groups Use Tech to Help Study and Save Cougars." *Geek Wire*, February 21, 2022. www.geekwire.com.

Washington Nature Mapping Project. "Project Cat (Cougars and Teaching)." http://naturemappingfoundation.org.

Wearn, Anna. "Preparing for the Future: How Wildlife Corridors Help Increase Climate Resilience." Center for Large Landscape Conservation, January 28, 2021. https://largelandscapes.org.

Wilder, Charly. "The Return of the Jaguar." *New York Times*, November 8, 2022. www.nytimes.com.

Yong, Ed. *An Immense World: How Animal Senses Reveal the Hidden Realms Around Us*. New York: Random House, 2022.

Great Blue: A Spiritual Life with Animals

Carolan, Trevor. "Compassion and Forgiveness: An Interview with His Holiness the Dali Lama." *The Bloomsbury Review*, September/October 2001.

Elder, John, and Hertha D. Wong, eds. *Family of Earth and Sky: Indigenous Tales of Nature from around the World*. Boston, MA: Beacon Press, 1994.

Hinton, Ladson, and Peter Zokowsky. "A Return to the Animal Soul." *Psychological Perspectives*, 1993, published January 17, 2008. www.tandfonline.com.

Huanchu Daoren. *Back to Beginnings: Reflections on the Tao*. Translated by Thomas Cleary and Zicheng Hong. Boston and London: Shambala Publications, 1990.

Keen, Andrew. "Can Our Capacity for Empathy Actually Save Us from Ourselves?" Literary Hub. https://lithub.com.

Naumann, Robert. "*Arda Herodias*, Great Blue Heron." Animal Diversity Web, University of Michigan Museum of Zoology, no date. https://animaldiversity.org.

Peterson, Brenda. *Singing to the Sound: Visions of Nature, Animals, and Spirit*. Troutdale, OR: NewSage Press, 2000.

Storynory. "The Grateful Crane." www.storynory.com.

Wikipedia. "Tsuru no Ongaseshi." https://en.wikipedia.org.

Yong, Ed. "How Animals Perceive the World." *Atlantic*, July/August 2022. www.theatlantic.com.

Adaptation: A Change Is Going to Come

Hearne, Vicki. *Animal Happiness*. New York: Harper Perennial, 1994.

Meeker, Joseph W. *The Comedy of Survival: Literary Ecology and a Play Ethic*. 3rd ed. Tucson: University of Arizona Press, 1997.

Peterson, Brenda. "Animals as Brothers and Sisters." In *On Nature's Terms: Contemporary Voices*. Edited by Thomas J. Lyon and Peter Stone. College Station: Texas A&M University Press, 1992.

Wendle, John. "Animals Rule Chernobyl Three Decades After Nuclear Disaster."
     National Geographic, April 18, 2016. www.nationalgeographic.com.

The Secret City Life of Racoons
Bradford, Alina. "Facts about Raccoons." *Live Science*, October 30, 2015.
     www.livescience.com.
Forterra. "The Secret City Life of Raccoons." *Ampersand: People and Place*. January 3,
     2021.
PBS Nature. "Raccoon Nation: Raccoon Facts." February 7, 2012.
     www.pbs.org/wnet/nature.
Wilson, Ben. "Let the Postpandemic City Grow Wild." *New York Times*, May 9, 2023, and
     May 14, 2023. www.nytimes.com.

Humpback Hip-Hop: Speaking in Song
Bakker, Karen. *The Sounds of Life: How Digital Technology Is Bringing Us Closer to the
     Worlds of Animals and Plants*. Princeton: Princeton UP, 2022.Center for Biological
     Diversity. "Biden Administration Protects Endangered Pacific Humpback Whale
     Habitat." April 20, 2021. https://biologicaldiversity.org.
"Does Military Sonar Kill Wildlife?" *Scientific American* June 10, 2009. www.scientific
     american.com/article/does-military-sonar-kill/.
Ellis, Lucy. "The Impacts of Noise Pollution in the Ocean." *Earth.org*, February 22,
     2022. https://earth.org.
Fischer, Tobias, and Lara Cory. *Animal Music: Sound and Song in the Natural World*.
     Cambridge: Strange Attractor Press, 2015.
Good News Network. "Zero Humpbacks Off Seattle Coast 25 Years Ago—Now 500
     Return with Record Number of Calves." November 20, 2021. www.goodnews
     network.org.
"How Technology Is Mapping the Unheard Conversations of the Natural World."
     Interview with Karen Bakker. NPR/KUOW, September 22, 2022. www.kuow.org.
Jourdain, Robert. *Music, the Brain, and Ecstasy: How Music Captures Our Imagination*.
     New York: HarperCollins Publishers (William Morrow), 1997.
Kennedy, Deirdre. "Brenda Peterson on Protecting Whales and Dolphins." NPR inter-
     view, *Animals Aloud*. KQED, San Francisco. https://on.soundcloud.com/h8KJj.
McLellan, Joseph. "It's a Whale of a Song," *Washington Post*, December 26, 1978.
Mustill, Tom. *How to Speak Whale: A Voyage into the Future of Animal Communication*.
     Boston, MA: Grand Central Publishing, 2022.
"Navy Training Blasts Marine Mammals with Harmful Sonar." EarthJustice. Press
     release. January 26, 2012. earthjustice.org/press/2012/navy-training
     -blasts-marine-mammals-with-harmful-sonar.
New Dimensions Radio. "The Soul of a Dolphin with Brenda Peterson." Interview by
     Justine Willis Toms. August 1, 2003. https://programs.newdimensions.org.

Peterson, Brenda. "War Games in a Whale Nursery: Scientists Worry Sonar Testing Will Destroy Fragile Habitat." *Seattle Times*, February 15, 1998. https://archive .seattletimes.com.

———. "Killing with Sound: What Happens When the Whales Stop Singing?" *Huffington Post*, February 22, 2013. www.huffpost.com/entry/why-is-the-key -source-of_b_809719

Phair, Vonna, "Record-Breaking Year for Whale Sightings in the Salish Sea." *Seattle Times*, January 12, 2023. www.seattletimes.com/seattle-news/environment/ record-breaking-year-for-whale-sightings-in-salish-sea.

Rothenberg, David. *Thousand-Mile Song: Whale Music in a Sea of Sound*. New York: Basic Books, 2008.

Sacks, Oliver. *Musicophilia: Tales of Music and the Brain*. New York: Alfred A. Knopf, 2007.

Schulkin, Jay, and Greta B. Raglan. "The Evolution of Music and Human Social Capability." *Frontiers in Neuroscience*, September 17, 2014. www.frontiersin.org/ journals/neuroscience.

Weilgart, Linda. "When Sound Is Dangerous." *Christian Science Monitor*, October 28, 1999. www.csmonitor.com.

Yong, Ed. *An Immense World: How Animal Senses Reveal the Hidden Realms Around Us*, New York: Random House, 2022.

Zhuang, Yan. "The Whales Gathered in a Heart Shape. Experts Feared What Would Come Next," *New York Times*, July 26, 2023.

Scent of Snow

"ABoVE: Animals on the Move." University of Montana Wildlife Biology. April 26, 2018. www.youtube.com/watch?v=e2gC1lCay1o.

Baker, Robin R., ed. "Caribou." In *Fantastic Journeys*. San Francisco: Fog City Press, 1991. https://archive.org/details/fantasticjourney00drrr.

Currin, Grayson Haver. "The Poignant Music of Melting Ice: Have a Listen." *New York Times*, March 16, 2023. www.nytimes.com.

"Declining Caribou Population Victim of Ecological Chain Reaction." *Science Daily*, March 18, 2021. www.sciencedaily.com/releases/2021/03/210318091644.htm.

"Former Yukon MLA Darius Elias Has Died." *CBC News*, February 18, 2021. www.cbc.ca.

Giilck, Tim. "Tributes Pour in for Former MLA Elias." *Whitehorse Daily Star*, February 19, 2021. www.whitehorsestar.com.

Joly, Kyle, and David R. Klein "Complexity of Caribou Population Dynamics in a Changing Climate." National Park Service. www.nps.gov/articles/aps-v10-i1-c7.htm.

NASA Earth Observatory. "Caribou on the Move." 1995–2017. https://earthobservatory.nasa.gov.

Peterson, Brenda. *Wolf Nation: The Life, Death, and Return of Wild American Wolves*. Philadelphia: Da Capo Press, 2017.

Publisher's Weekly. "Wings Moist from the Other World." Review of *Wings Moist from the Other World* by Peggy Shumaker, Pitt Poetry Series, Pittsburgh: University of Pittsburgh Press, 1994. www.publishersweekly.com/978-0-8229-3774-6.

Shumaker, Peggy. *Wings Moist from the Other World (Pitt Poetry Series).* Pittsburgh, PA: University of Pittsburgh Press, 1994.

———. "The Story of Light." *Underground Rivers: Poems.* www.poetryfoundation.org.

Tekiela, Stan. "Reindeer, The Domesticated Caribou." *Drummer*, December 3, 2021. www.thedrummer.com.

Wright, Charles. *Caribou: Poems.* New York: Farrar, Straus, and Giroux, 2014.

When We Stayed Home

Anthes, Emily. "Wild Mammals Roamed When Covid Kept Humans Home." *New York Times*, June 8, 2023. www.nytimes.com/2023/06/08/science/anthropause -pandemic-animals.html.

Einhorn, Catrin, and Lauren Leatherby. "Animals Are Running Out of Places to Live." *New York Times*, December 9, 2022. www.nytimes.com.

Kirsch, Adam. "The People Cheering for Humanity's End." *Atlantic*, December 1, 2022. www.theatlantic.com.

Macdonald, Helen. "Animals Are Rewilding Our Cities. On YouTube, at Least." *New York Times Magazine*, April 15, 2020. www.nytimes.com.

Meyer, Robinson. "Human Extinction Isn't That Unlikely." *Atlantic*, April 29, 2016. www.theatlantic.com.

Milne, Stefan. "Is Seattle Wildlife Actually Behaving Differently While We Quarantine?" *Seattle Met*, May 12, 2020. www.seattlemet.com.

Peterson, Brenda. "When We Stayed Home." Illustrated by Brittany Nicole Smith. *Medium*, April 14, 2020. https://bsp808.medium.com/when-we-stayed-home -47032a6a2757.

Rott, Nathan. "A UN Biodiversity Convention Aims to Slow Humanity's 'War with Nature.'" NPR, December 7, 2022. www.npr.org.

Smith, Daniel B. "Is There an Ecological Unconsciousness?" *New York Times Magazine*, January 27, 2010. www.nytimes.com.

Sommer, Lauren. "Whales Get a Break as Pandemic Creates Quieter Oceans." NPR, July 20, 2020. www.npr.org.

Spears, Dean. "All of the Predictions Agree on One Thing: Humanity Peaks Soon." *New York Times*, www.nytimes.com/interactive/2023/09/18/opinion/human -population-global-growth.html.

Weisman, Alan. *The World Without Us.* New York: St. Martin's Press, 2007.

World Health Organization. "The True Death Toll of Covid-19." WHO, 2020. www.who.int.

Apprenticeship to Animal Play

National Geographic. "Animals at Play." December 1994. https://nationalgeographic
    backissues.com.
The On Being Project. "Animals at Play." http://vimeo.com/282517.
Meeker, Joseph. *The Comedy of Survival: Literary Ecology and a Play Ethic*. 3rd edition.
    Tucson: University of Arizona Press, 1997.
Peterson, Brenda. "What We Learn from Animals: How to Play." *Huffington Post*,
    January 21, 2011. www.huffpost.com/entry/why-is-the-key-source-of_b_809719.
———. "Apprenticeship to Animal Play." In *Intimate Nature: The Bond Between Women
    and Animals*. Edited by Linda Hogan, Deena Metzger, and Brenda Peterson. New
    York: Ballantine, 1998.
Robinson, Joe. "The Key to Happiness: A Taboo for Adults?" *Huffington Post*, January
    18, 2011. www.huffingtonpost.com.

Bringing Back Bears

Ad Council. "Story of Smokey." https://smokeybear.com.
Cabanatuan, Michael. "On Smokey Bear's Birthday, a Burned Bear Cub Is Rescued from
    Antelope Fire." *San Francisco Chronicle*, August 12, 2021. www.sfchronicle.com.
Cappiello, Vin. "GOAL Explains Position on Grizzly Delisting." *Cody Enterprise*, June 29,
    2016 (updated July 1, 2016). www.codyenterprise.com.
Cecco, Leland. "Great Bear Sea: Vast New Marine Zone a 'Mindset Shift' for
    Conservation." *The Guardian*, February 7, 2023. www.theguardian.com.
Chadwick, Douglas. *Four-Fifths a Grizzly: A New Perspective on Nature that Just Might
    Save Us All*. Ventura, CA: Patagonia Books, 2021.
Explore.org. Bear Cam, Alaska Brooks Falls, Katmai National Park. https://explore.org
    /livecams.
Houghton, Katheryn. *Hungry Horse News* (no headline), August 17, 2016.
    https://hungryhorsenews.com.
Landers, Rich. "Poll: Majority Favors Restoring Grizzly Bears in North Cascades."
    Spokesman-Review, June 6, 2016. www.spokesman.com.
Molseed, Megan. "National Park Service, Fish and Wildlife Investigating Bringing
    Grizzly Bears Back to Pacific Northwest." *Outsider*, November 12, 2022.
    https://outsider.com.
Murray, David. "Tribes Gather in Glacier to Oppose Grizzly Delisting." *Great Falls
    Tribune*, August 16, 2016. www.greatfallstribune.com.
Peterson, Brenda. *Build Me an Ark: A Life with Animals*. New York: W.W. Norton, 2001.
———. Interview with David Bearshield, GOAL, in Yellowstone, from notes. Summer
    2016.
Rice, Bonnie. "Big Win for Great Yellowstone Grizzlies." Sierra Club, July 14, 2020.
    www.sierraclub.org.

Schmitt, Kristen A. "Grizzlies Could Return to Washington." *GoHunt*, March 29, 2023.
    www.gohunt.com.

Sottile, Zoe. "Colorado Wildlife Camera Accidentally Captures Hundreds of Adorable
    'Bear Selfies.'" *CNN*, January 28, 2023. www.cnn.com.

Thompson, Luke. "Plans to Bring Grizzly Bears Back to North Cascades Move
    Forward." *Seattle Times*, March 22, 2023. www.seattletimes.com.

"Three Bears Rescued from Dixie, Antelope Fires in 2021." *Redding.com*, January 2,
    2022. www.redding.com.

"Tribal Leaders to Gather in Glacier Park for Grizzly Bear Ceremony." *Flathead Beacon*,
    August 9, 2016. https://flatheadbeacon.com.

US Fish and Wildlife Service. Responsive Management Survey, conducted for the
    Association of Fish and Wildlife Agencies, 2019. www.fishwildlife.org/application
    /files/7715/5733/7920/NSSF_2019_Attitudes_Survey_Report.pdf.

US Forest Service. "The Story of Smokey Bear." August 4, 2014. www.fs.usda.gov.

US Forest Service, Klamath National Forest. "Bear Cub Found on Smokey Bear's
    'Birthday' on the Antelope Fire." Yubanet.com, August 12, 2021.
    https://yubanet.com.

Woolston, Chris. "Why Amazing Discoveries About Bear Hibernation May Help
    Improve Human Health." *Smithsonian Magazine*, April 15, 2022.
    www.smithsonianmag.com.

Yoder, Kate. "Study: A Third of the West's Burned Forests Can Be Traced to Fossil Fuel
    Companies." *Grist*, May 16, 2023. https://grist.org.

Super Pod

Abhang, Priyanka A., Bharti W. Gawali, and Suresh C. Mehrotra. "Technical Aspects
    of Brain Rhythms and Speech Parameters." In *Introduction to EEG- and Speech-
    Based Emotion Recognition*, 2016. www.sciencedirect.com.

Ackerman, Diane. *Deep Play*. New York: Vintage Books, 1999.

Herzing, Denise. "Wild Dolphins: The Bahamas." www.explore.org/livecams.

Peterson, Brenda. *The Drowning World: An Aquantis Series Novel*. Seattle, WA:
    Delphinius Publishing, 2012.

Peterson, Brenda. "Wild Dolphins Encounter with Jane Goodall, Brenda Peterson,
    Pierce Brosnan." www.youtube.com/watch?v=fnXqOF0uamk.

Summer Tree Institute. "Whale/Dolphin Ocean Discoveries." https://summertree.org.

Weyer, Pat. "Sacred Vessels and the 'Vesica Piscis': The Cosmic Story of the Human-
    Dolphin Relationship." American Cetacean Society. www.acspugetsound.org.

Wild Dolphin Project. www.wilddolphinproject.org.

Yuri Makino

About the Author

Brenda Peterson is the author of more than twenty books for adults and children, including the memoir *I Want to Be Left Behind*, selected as a "Top Ten Best Nonfiction" book by the *Christian Science Monitor* and an Indie Next "Great Read," by Independent Booksellers. One of her most recent nature books, *Wolf Nation: The Life, Death, and Return of Wild American Wolves*, was selected by *Forbes* magazine as a "Top Ten Best Conservation Book of the Year." Her memoir, *Build Me an Ark: A Life with Animals* was chosen as a "Best Spiritual Book." Her animal books for children include *Leopard and Silkie*, *Lobos*, *Wild Orca*, *Catastrophe by the Sea*, and the illustrated art book *Crane Maiden*.

Peterson's writing has appeared in the *New York Times*, *Christian Science Monitor*, *Seattle Times*, *Tikkun*, *Huffington Post*, *The Morning News*, *Utne Reader*, *Orion*, and *O, the Oprah Magazine*. Her novel *Duck and Cover* was a *New York Times* Notable Book of the Year and her most recent novel, a mystery, is *Stiletto*. A regular contributor to her local NPR stations, Peterson lives in Seattle on the shores of the Salish Sea. Learn more at www.brendapetersonbooks.com.

MOUNTAINEERS BOOKS, including its two imprints, Skipstone and Braided River, is a leading publisher of quality outdoor recreation, sustainability, and conservation titles. As a 501(c)(3) nonprofit, we are committed to supporting the environmental and educational goals of our organization by providing expert information on human-powered adventure, sustainable practices at home and on the trail, and preservation of wilderness.

Our publications are made possible through the generosity of donors, and through sales of 700 titles on outdoor recreation, sustainable lifestyle, and conservation. To donate, purchase books, or learn more, visit us online:

MOUNTAINEERS BOOKS
1001 SW Klickitat Way, Suite 201 • Seattle, WA 98134
800-553-4453 • mbooks@mountaineersbooks.org
www.mountaineersbooks.org

An independent nonprofit publisher since 1960

YOU MAY ALSO LIKE

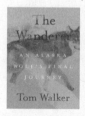    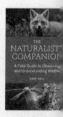